SEQUOIAH
SPEEDS

MEMOIR OF A
FAMILY AFLOAT

To Heidy,
May all your time
spent on boats make
special memories for you.
Bon Voyage! HELEN S. WARREN

Helen M Warren

FOR
MY FAMILY
ON LAND AND SEA

TABLE OF CONTENTS

FOREWORD

WARNING: Sailing is a chronic disease, often unrecognizable in its early stages due to the gradual onset. It is quite addictive and should be approached with extreme caution as, once contracted, it is incurable. Some severe cases have been successfully put into temporary remission after large overdoses, but it requires the patient's complete cooperation and self discipline, and relapses are inevitable.

This sailing disease is a state of being, a certain mindset, much more than a sport, as I had once assumed before experiencing it myself. Sailing is a paradox, or perhaps many. For me sailing generates contradictory feelings, emotionally and physically: power and insignificance, exhilaration and despondency, joy and melancholy, total relaxation and utter exhaustion, excitement and ennui, vitality and lethargy. I came on sailing unaware, love coloring the landscape and confusing the senses; and I contracted the disease at first exposure, rather against my will.

Now here is a curious thing about sailing, and probably the reason the victim doesn't realize he has the disease. There is a symptom similar to amnesia... similar but not quite the same. Although the memory of a bad experience remains, the reason for the fear or dislike is forgotten. Sailing, to the uninitiated, sounds romantic and evokes images of blazing sunsets, beautiful music, and contented people leisurely sipping drinks on the afterdeck in idyllic anchorages...just like the movies. But the real thing usually involves occasional terror and discomfort. After a period of time has passed, a frightening incident may seem inconsequential, silly, or even funny. Then other afflicted souls who, consciously or not, want to share the disease they have come to love, return after a day's sail describing glorious sunsets and exhilarating reaches over shimmering water.

"It was just perfect," they exclaim. "You should go out with us tomorrow."

It's all too much to resist, and before he knows it the reluctant sailor is on board again believing he's having fun... until the next crisis, which, with sailing, is never long in coming. And he is caught again. After several years I came to believe that I loved sailing too. Having realized I was married to an addict, perhaps it was partially the old "if you can't beat 'em, join 'em" adage coming into its own. At any rate, I did... join 'em, that is!

At the moment I haven't been sailing for six months and I'm trying hard to stay in remission, but the sky is blue, the leaves on the oak trees outside my open window are rustling in the southwest breeze, and I can smell the salt air. Maybe just a short sail in the Sunfish?

Charleston, SC 1990

CHAPTER ONE

ONE LITTLE BOAT LEADS TO ANOTHER

A pitch black, howling maelstrom of wind and water snatched at us as we tried to round the notorious Ile d'Ouessant off the coast of Brittany. Sequoiah bucked through the erratic waves of the October gale. The night lay close around us. The sky and sea were one. It was bitterly cold in the wind, and the waves breaking over the decks were icy. Although I had been at the helm for only an hour, my hands felt locked to the wheel of the heaving yacht as I fought to hold her on course. My strength was diminishing, and hot tears mingled with the salt and freezing rain on my face.

"What are we doing here...what ARE we doing here?" I screamed to the furious vast emptiness around me.

* * *

What were we doing there, indeed? I suppose it all started when I met Johnny Warren. At that time he was trying to build a boat, and his all consuming dream was to sail around the world, so I was forewarned even if I didn't recognize the danger signs at the time. Knowing nothing about boats and the sea and the passions they can arouse, I was oblivious to the subtle, ongoing chain of events that would lead me to cross

1

an ocean aboard a thirty nine foot yacht with only my family on board.

The first time we went sailing together should have taught me something, but Johnny was tall and handsome and we were teenagers in love. It was windy as the three of us left the Carolina Yacht Club dock in the little 13 foot Penguin sailing dinghy, my German Shepherd dog being the unlucky third that afternoon. Charleston harbor was full of whitecaps and we flew down the Ashley River. As we turned near the Coast Guard station to go back, I noticed an unfamiliar red flag whipping briskly at the top of the staff there. Johnny didn't tell me it was the gale warning flag until we were safely home many hours later, and by then I probably could have guessed its significance. Our return to the Yacht Club was a wild and desperate trip into increasingly larger winds and waves, and the first of many times that I would look over the side of a boat and ask myself why I was there. The Penguin was wooden and old and, whenever the waves weren't coming in over the sides, they were leaking in through the bottom. Since we had no sponges or buckets along, I learned first time out why it is best not to sail barefoot. The dog was seasick and, if I hadn't been so scared and so busy bailing with my shoes, I probably would have joined her. That day was also the first of many times that I told Johnny Warren I would never go sailing again.

Eventually Johnny and I married and as the years marched by, so came boats and children, boats more frequently than children, and each boat always a little bigger than the one before. In fact we have had twice as many boats as children but, unlike the children, we usually managed to dispose of each boat before the next arrived.

Our first purchase was a Lightning, 19 feet long, 20 years old, open and wooden, and jointly owned with our friends, Dave Norton and Jack Bryan. She was also a sloop, which, as

I later learned, indicated that she had only one mast. Every time we went out on the Lightning something broke. Twice it was the mast and, since bad things usually happen in threes, we vowed to avoid wooden masts in the future. Once when Johnny and Jack had taken some friends for a sail, a tiny fish jumped across the boat, followed swiftly by a 10 pound Spanish mackerel that struck Jack in the chest and fell into the boat. After the initial surprise, they duly thanked Poseidon and brought home dinner.

By 1971 we had two daughters, Weesie and Caroline, and our first sailboat spent much of her time in the backyard. The Lightning was the favorite neighborhood play toy, one day a pirate ship, one day a castle. Eventually she was sold at the Junior League Whale of a Sale, and the future owner asked, "Does she leak?"

"Lately she has been the neighborhood swimming pool, so she can probably hold water out as well as in," came my glib reply. We never saw her again, but I'm just sure she didn't sink.

Our next boat was a foot longer, new, fiberglass and, according to the flashy color brochure provided by the dealer, had a cabin that slept five. Now we were a family of five, a son, John, completing the brood, all three children too young for school. And I can tell you that the brochure was right. An O'Day 20 *will* sleep five if most are midgets, nobody is prone to claustrophobia, and all are on the most intimate terms. It took me a while to appreciate that boat, but I learned some important lessons from her.

Fortunately, the first time we sailed her we left the midgets at home. Johnny had his hands full with just me along. This boat was more tender than her predecessor. Every time we changed direction I had the sensation of going over backwards in a rocking chair - and I didn't hesitate to let the captain know just how I felt! He cheerfully agreed to take me home, but before we got there a wayward gust of wind caught us. I was crouched on the high side (that's the windward side in nautical terms) and Johnny told me to free the leeward jib sheet. In plain language I knew that meant I was supposed to leave my relatively secure position and go over to the low side where the water was just beginning to pour over the railing to untie a rope that would probably jerk itself out of my hand and then try frantically to beat me. I didn't relish the prospect and decided not to try it, because, in my ignorance, I was convinced my extra weight would be the final straw that would turn us over completely. To Johnny's dismay I dove for the cabin, swearing he'd never see me on a boat again, and left him to get us home in one piece. Before the week was out we were speaking again and soon I was aboard once more, eventually getting brave enough to handle the jib sheets.

Our first family overnight trip was not a roaring success. Whatever made us think that sleeping aboard a twenty foot boat with three young children would be FUN? First of all, it was August and most people of sound mind move to the cool of the mountains for the month. Not us. That Saturday it took us seven hours to load the boat and sail up the Intracoastal Waterway to Capers Island. By the time we arrived and had the anchor down, it was raining, two sets of diapers were wet, and three children were crying. The rain settled in for the evening and the mosquitoes began to arrive. It was ninety degrees in the cabin and I had brought corn on the cob for dinner. Somehow the ingredients for the rest of the meal had been left at home. Peanut butter and jelly sandwiches served with corn on the cob would be less than desirable in the best of circumstances, but eaten in the cramped quarters of what had become an ideal sauna, surrounded by howling infants and hungry mosquitoes, they were perfectly revolting. I could see that we needed better planning and more equipment if we were going to do this again. Screens, and most of all a tent, were what I dreamed about that awful night!

We did get a tent, a big tent, a twelve foot square tent with standing headroom, a Coleman special. The next time we set out for the weekend we were PREPARED. We had sleeping bags and pillows and flashlights and lanterns and games and charcoal and a grill and chairs and bug spray and enough food for an army. Johnny made a thousand trips down the dock loading the boat while I made sure nobody fell overboard. By the time we were ready to leave it was too late to sail all the way to Capers Island before dark. Since there was no wind, we motored to the back of Morris Island which is right in Charleston harbor. No one goes there much except for crabbers as it is only a few feet deep in most places, so we had it all to ourselves. We beached the boat to disgorge its unbelievable cargo, and spent what was left of the afternoon trying to erect the Big Top. There was a splendid sunset and we all went swimming before collecting wood for a bonfire. We needn't have bothered. The clouds gathered and rain began to fall. Our "clear with a ten knot breeze" forecast was wrong, but we weren't worried. We had our new tent. We set up the grill inside and cooked a feast fit for kings...well, maybe some kings eat like that. We sang songs and read stories while the rain outside pelted down even harder. We found that we had to shout at each other to be heard above the pounding on the canvas roof. At last the children were tucked into their sleeping bags, but for a long time the noisy torrent kept them awake. By the time all three were finally sung to Never Never Land, the wind came. Soon it was obvious that our tent was not meant for sand. The rushing wind lifted the stakes and collapsed one side of our beach house. Our older daughter, Weesie, came screaming out from under the soggy canvas absolutely terrified, just as the rest of the tent fell around us. I gathered the frightened children, feeling afraid myself as the only light came from the streaks of lightning outside in the storm. We decided it would be best to retreat to the comparative comfort of the boat.

Johnny found a flashlight, waded out to the boat, and took down the mast. The mast was stepped on deck and designed to be easily lowered, but how he managed it alone in the dark and difficult conditions that night I don't know. Almost all our clothes were wet so I undressed everyone and put our last dry things into a plastic bag. We made quite a parade wading toward the boat in the pouring rain with lightning all around. Johnny was in the lead carrying Weesie and Caroline, and I followed with baby John, all of us wearing our birthday suits. We dried as best we could with the one remaining useable towel, and I put the three children to bed in the forward berth where they could not fall out. They gradually settled into uneasy sleep, but I don't think I ever did more than doze that night. Windy rain squalls complete with thunder and lightning, kept passing over, bouncing the little boat around in the shallow, choppy water. The cabin was terribly stuffy and we all tossed and turned. Once we were roused by Caroline crying out in her sleep, "Yes, I would like some air!"

The next day I was in favor of leaving that tent where it lay. Even though I was overruled, we never did use it again on the beach, and finally sold it to some adventurous friends who live inland.

Things do happen in threes, only for us it wasn't just wooden masts, it was any masts. The O'Day 20 had an aluminum mast of which we were very proud. One spring weekend Johnny and my brother-in-law, Bill Lynch, sailed the thirty miles from Charleston to Rockville to spend the night. Early the next morning they sailed out the North Edisto river under a clear starlit sky, homeward bound. Johnny noticed a shrimp boat approaching from astern, and tacked to move out of the channel. Unfortunately, the shrimp boat was moving fast, and as she came closer lowered her long fishing booms. Too late Johnny realized disaster was imminent. Unable to get out of the path of the oncoming ship under sail, he started the ineffective six horse power outboard. As the big shrimper passed, her port boom severed the mast of our little sailboat about four feet above the deck. Mast, rigging, and sails came crashing down, luckily missing the two men. Johnny tried to read the name of the shrimp boat on her stern as she sped past, but within moments of the accident all lights on board were extinguished, and she steamed down the channel, shrouded by the early morning darkness. Neither Johnny nor Bill were hurt, and after bringing the wreckage aboard they limped back to Rockville, tied to a friend's dock, and telephoned me to come pick them up in the car. It was two months before repairs were completed and we were able to sail again.

The longest offshore trip we made in the O'Day 20 was sixty miles, from Charleston to Georgetown, South Carolina. With no charts, and a draft of only eighteen inches, we hugged the coastline, picking out landmarks that we recognized. Many sights were new to me. As we approached Cape Romain we could see something leaping into the air.

"Johnny, look!" I said. "There must be some huge fish fighting up ahead."

Johnny had a hard time containing his laughter, but managed to keep a straight face while explaining that what I saw were breakers in the shoal water around the Cape. When we passed near them, I could see the turbulent white froth angrily exploding into the air, and was glad we weren't going any closer. I then pointed out what looked like a stick, perhaps some kind of marker. This time Johnny did laugh, and it wasn't until we were quite close that I could see it was the abandoned Cape Romain lighthouse. With no means of comparison in the ever-changing waterscape, it was hard to distinguish size and distance. I was already adding some more equipment to my mental list. Just a few simple things like binoculars and charts might be helpful.

Since our boat was so small we simply pulled up for the night on the beach at Bull's Island, about halfway to our destination, and pushed off again in the morning. The next day's sail into Georgetown was as beautiful as the first, and after a night in the marina there, we turned south for home. The rest of the trip was a most uncomfortable blur. We beat into a headwind the entire way. The seas were short and choppy. The mast made horrid creaking noises that I feared might herald another disaster, and seawater continually poured over the bow. We began to wish for a larger, drier boat. I have always believed that bigger is better, and in my mind's eye I saw an ocean liner.

In those days we went sailing three or four times a week, usually leaving the marina as soon as Johnny finished work, and we would have supper on board before heading home. On those evening trips we never went far. Except for leaving and entering the marina we didn't use the engine at all and sometimes not even then. Back then we were purists and it took a long time to go anywhere!

After two years we began to feel cramped in 20 feet. Those of us who had been crawling had learned to walk and the walkers were now running. We needed more space and wanted something that would be more comfortable offshore. We and our good friends, Charles and Francie Geer, decided to buy a Pearson 26. Charles, being a physician, had little leisure time, and we had little ready cash. A partnership was born. The Pearson 26 looked huge to us as a crane gently dropped her into the water for the first time. She was the second, and last, new boat we were to buy.

After launching, the first order of business seemed to be finding a name for this beauty. Following a celebration dinner enhanced by freely flowing wine and with champagne glasses in hand, we began tossing out names. Francie and I soon retired from the fray, laughing as the names came forth, each more preposterous than the one before it. With no agreement in sight, Charles brought out a book of old sailing ships and began reading aloud. "Ah, here's one - Victorious. Or how about Invincible? Perhaps Courageous?"

The noble names came rolling out. Finally came a shout, "Superbus. Yes, that's it! Super..bus." With six children between us at the time, it seemed the perfect pun of a name. I remember that night at the Geer's house so well, but the reason why the name was never painted on the stern of our sturdy little yacht eludes me.

We had a half interest in Superbus for a year, and during those twelve months she spent much more time with the sails up than in the marina. We took many trips offshore along the South Carolina coast, never venturing too far away from land. Whenever we passed through the jetties leaving Charleston harbor, one of us would say, "Let's sail to England!", and a conversation would usually ensue about the things we'd need to take with us, or how long the trip would be, and what we'd do once we got there. Then we'd all laugh comfortably, knowing that we were really going home to our safe, warm, routine lives. Johnny and I were insatiable sailors and we yearned for something still larger, something we could sail whenever we pleased. We were not very good at sharing. We wanted to go sailing every weekend and as much as possible in between. What we really wanted was an Endeavour 32, but it seemed an impossible dream at the time. Then our ever ready broker made us an offer we couldn't refuse. He had a run-down Pearson 30 for a very special price, one he knew we could afford. She was inhabited by the state's largest colony of cockroaches and she was, in general, a filthy mess. We spent weeks cleaning and repairing and refurbishing before we felt at home aboard SeaGullah.

SeaGullah is the name she came with, and is most appropriate for this part of the country, Gullah being the local language spoken by slaves in the eighteenth and nineteenth centuries, and still preserved today among their descendants. I wanted to rename this boat Leaky Lady because of a certain propensity she had for collecting water, but reason prevailed when Johnny pointed out that we might want to sell her someday. Even though she had not one dry locker, she was quite fast and fun to sail. We soon learned to wrap everything in double layers of plastic and bail regularly. SeaGullah was really an interim boat for us while we looked for that Endeavor 32 that we couldn't stop thinking about. We went to look at several, but they always had something we didn't like: a gasoline engine or electrolysis problems or worse. Finally we answered an ad in the local paper and it turned out to be our friends, Anne and Mike Adair who were getting ready to move aboard a new Morgan Out Island and needed to sell their three year old Endeavor. Snorkey was in Key Largo, and Anne and Mike asked us to join them for the three day sail home to see if she would suit us.

That was a trip I will never forget. It was the first time I had ever been at sea overnight other than on an ocean liner. I loved the night watches with the stars close overhead, and the hot days with the big colorful drifter pulling us homeward, and most of all I loved the Tiller Master automatic pilot that steered the entire trip. The only thing I didn't like was the rough weather we had for about twelve hours one night when the only possible place to sleep was on the cabin floor. By the time we reached Charleston the skies were blue again. We were sold and SeaTurtle (renamed for me since I look rather like a turtle) was ours within a week.

We immediately put SeaGullah on the market. When no one bought her right away we panicked and put both boats up for sale. Owning two boats was too expensive and we needed to sell one fast. It took six black months, but SeaGullah finally leaked away to torment a new family, and we breathed a sigh of relief.

SeaTurtle was ours for three and a half happy years. She was a wonderful family boat; a seaworthy, comfortable, centerboard sloop, quite roomy for her size. Aboard her we explored the coastal islands and waters of South Carolina, Georgia, and Florida, and spent some memorable summers in the Abacos in the Bahamas.

Capers Island was still our favorite weekend destination. Capers, located about fifteen miles north of Charleston on the Intracoastal Waterway, is a 2,000 acre barrier island of dense woods surrounded by beaches on three sides and salt marsh to the west with access only by boat. It is inhabited by alligators, snakes, raccoons, white tail deer, loggerhead turtles, and numerous species of birds. There was one house on the island for the South Carolina Wildlife and Marine Resources Department's caretaker who lived there part-time. Except for holidays and weekends it was usually quiet at Capers and often we had it all to ourselves.

The tide runs swiftly in Capers Inlet, and that is where we administered our Spring swimming tests each year. It started because the children hated wearing life jackets all the time. Annually each child was assigned a certain number of laps that had to be swum around the anchored boat. Besides demonstrating that they could swim competently, this exercise really made them aware of the incredible power of tidal currents. After successful completion of this test they were allowed, in settled weather, to sail without wearing a life jacket, although in the ocean all of us wear safety harnesses whenever we leave the cabin.

We celebrated many birthdays aboard, often inviting the children's friends for overnights or weekends. There were picnics, treasure hunts, and bonfires on the beach, and dances and sing-alongs aboard. We even had fireworks on occasions like Fourth of July and New Year. Several times we spent whole weeks at Capers during school holidays. Johnny would borrow his father's open fishing boat and commute to work via the Intracoastal Waterway. Every day he would bring the mail from home, groceries, or sometimes the children's friends to spend a night or two. The days were filled with dinghy sailing, rowing, races, crabbing, fishing, and island exploration. On rainy days there were reading, games, puppet shows, and music on board. Once after a long morning ashore, we went back aboard to find that 'Not Me' or 'I Dunno' had left the head intake valve open and the cabin floor was awash with salt water. The rest of that day was spent pumping and mopping. The carpet never quite recovered and had to be replaced. Another time, at Ossabaw Island in Georgia, there was a herd of cattle on the beach watching as we anchored. Later while swimming, the children started making mooing sounds and then became terrified as several of the bovines answered their calls and began swimming towards the boat. Fortunately they turned around before reaching us. The idea of visiting cows was a prospect we did not relish!

Things are always breaking on boats; at least I think it must be *all* boats. It's a constant occurrence on *our* boats! Many things break for no apparent reason. Others, however, get a little help. For instance, one of our children, who prefer to remain anonymous, had an early fascination with making things disappear down the toilet. At home she enjoyed flushing increasingly interesting objects like shoes, pocketbooks, and dresses. The plumber loved us! On board the boat she had less opportunity for this pastime as someone was always watching her, and if she disappeared into the head, one of us followed quickly. The logistics of the thing were different too, since the size of the pipes is dramatically smaller on a sailboat, not to mention the fact that our boat plumber was

Johnny, who did not find plumbing lucrative or even remotely intriguing. The time that a clothespin was successfully wedged into the head as we were docking at Sea Island late one summer afternoon, was not good and is probably best left to the imagination.

At Hilton Head one night we had a fire on board while tied up at the marina. I was fixing supper on our alcohol stove when some liquid alcohol inexplicably ran out of the lighted oven like a ball of fire and ignited the rug. I yelled for Johnny but, before we could do anything, the fire had melted the plastic head of the fire extinguisher located next to the stove. It discharged itself all over the cabin, making a white powdery mess while doing absolutely nothing to contain the fire. One of the selling points of alcohol stoves is that their flames can be put out easily with water, making them "so much safer" than kerosene or gas. Water, we found, only spread the fire, but Johnny was finally able to beat the fire out with a wet towel. Later, over a delicious dinner at Harbour Town, I was facetiously accused of setting that fire to escape the galley for the evening. Besides a good meal, some other things were gained by that fire. We had never liked alcohol for cooking; it doesn't burn hot enough. That particular incident crystallized our decision to have something different on our next boat. We began investigating other fuels and learned that efficiency and safety can be combined. We liked the idea of a gas stove.

We also learned to pay more attention to the type and location of our firefighting equipment. All fire extinguishers are not created equal. There are different types for various kinds of fires, so several kinds may be needed on a boat. Those with plastic fittings are cheaper initially, but cannot be refilled and kept at the correct pressure for long. Only those with metal fittings are acceptable, and they too must be inspected each year. Also they should be located near, but not in contact with obvious sources of fire, and there should always be more than one fire extinguisher.

Losing someone overboard has always been one of our critical concerns. When we first took our babies sailing I would wear a life jacket and attach the children, wearing harnesses, to me. As they grew, they wore life jackets until they could swim to our satisfaction in the currents. They took swimming lessons year round and, over time, advanced to the top of the Red Cross swimming proficiency levels, including the drown-proofing courses that they took at summer camp. In addition, we held man overboard drills at intervals using old life preservers as victims. This was always sobering. Even on relatively calm days it was incredible how quickly such a brightly colored object could get lost in the waves if you took your eyes off it for a minute. We knew it would be even easier to lose sight of a person floating helplessly in the moving water, particularly on a dark night in rough weather. If nothing else, these exercises forcefully reminded us that it was essential for each of us to take every precaution to remain aboard.

One hot and windless summer morning in the calm of the almost deserted harbor, we decided it would be fun to take turns actually going overboard to be rescued. Caroline, ready for a swim, donned her life jacket and dove in. Intent on our roles in the operation at hand, none of us noticed a little motor boat cruising down the channel. Caroline, enjoying her part, was floating on her back, arms and legs thrashing about, and singing at the top of her lungs. Her portrayal of a floundering swimmer must have been convincing from afar, for the men in the Whaler saw us and sped towards Caroline. She noticed them first and began to scream for help in earnest, afraid the oncoming boat didn't see her and that she would be run over.

When we saw the boat we panicked and started yelling too, as our fears were the same as Caroline's. My heart was in my throat watching our little girl swimming awkwardly toward us in the bulky Type I life jacket with the motor boat closing in. Johnny was on the bow waving them away, and they finally realized there was no emergency when they were near enough to see what Caroline was wearing. As they drew alongside, we explained what we were doing and thanked them for their concern. However, that was the end of all in-the-water practices. Nobody wanted to be the victim, and we went back to saving life jackets.

We were totally immersed in our enthusiasm for sailing and it became a fact of life for the children. Except for occasional afternoon or evening dinner cruises when we entertained friends, sailing for us was a family affair. It was a real passion. All our leisure time was spent on the water.

CHAPTER TWO

Sequoiah

During our years with SeaTurtle we thought more and more about long distance sailing and read any accounts of blue water cruising that we could get our hands on. We bought a copy of Ocean Passages for the World and began studying it. The purpose of this book is to aid in planning ocean voyages; it gives general information on weather, worldwide, and recommends preferred routes, giving distances and average times between ports. We also discovered pilot charts, colorful fact-filled sheets containing statistical data compiled over many years, and found these extremely useful. They show the times of year and location to expect certain wind direction and strength as well as wave heights, ice limits, surface currents, air temperature, barometric pressure, frequency of gales and cyclones, and more. It was fun to plan different trips, and soon we were dreaming the big dream of circumnavigation.

After a business trip to New York, Johnny arrived home burdened with dozens of charts for the continents and oceans of the world. We filled notebooks with dates it was safest to travel in each ocean and the length of time we estimated it should take us to make the passages, using one hundred miles as the standard for an average day. We had a map of the world tacked to a board with pins stuck all over it, and, on the walls, maps of the prevailing winds and ocean currents. All of this planning was usually done at night after the children were tucked into bed. We tried to give them a feeling of security and permanence even though that was what we were planning to interrupt if we were ever brave enough to give up our comfortable lifestyle and take one of these trips we kept talking about. We talked about it so much that our friends often said, "One day you'll really just take off and do it, won't you."

We thought maybe we would and then we frightened ourselves. It was one thing to make the decision to change our own lives, but we had three children to consider and we weren't sure how this kind of adventure would affect them. Family and friends thought us imprudent when we mentioned our dreams and, continually reminded of the risks involved, we began to see ourselves as foolish and rather reckless. Gradually we came to the conclusion that we needed to sell SeaTurtle and forget about boats and sailing altogether. Maybe we should try to live a more conventional lifestyle and take typical vacations to the mountains or Disney World like all our friends.

Finally, truly convinced that we should give up this all-consuming pastime, we put SeaTurtle up for sale. It didn't take long to sell her and we were boat-less for the first time in years. Initially we were elated. We were free. Now we didn't have a boat to maintain, no dockage fees, insurance, or taxes to pay. We kept telling ourselves how lucky we were. We'd had such fun with boats and now we were ready for something else. But what else was there? I think the problem was that we wanted adventure and were never quite satisfied with conventional routine. Suddenly life was strangely empty. We didn't know what to do with our weekends, and thought that, perhaps we might have been a bit hasty. Maybe a really small, wooden boat to work on and day-sail in the harbor would be just what we needed to keep sailing as a hobby, not a lifestyle.

We read the Boats for Sale ads in the newspaper and even went to look at an old 24 foot wooden sloop with classic lines and a tiny cabin. She was in deplorable condition and we fondly contemplated the hours we could spend lovingly restoring this little yacht to her former beauty. This was a joke because neither of us have the patience to restore anything that takes more than half an hour, but we daydreamed through the Christmas holidays and borrowed the Geer's boat, our old Superbus since renamed John Barleycorn, to take our now traditional New Year's Eve sail in Charleston harbor.

As time went by we tried not to think about boats too much, but it was in our blood and we couldn't seem to quit. It had been only a month since our great decision to give up sailing and concentrate on more practical things, but we had not known, or perhaps unconsciously we did know, how hopelessly we were addicted to the sea. It seemed that everywhere we looked something would remind us of boats and cruising. As Johnny walked to work along the Battery he would see a yacht leaving the harbor with the tide and would guess at her destination. Living as we do on a peninsula in a busy port city, not a day goes by when we are not aware of the marine activity around us. Often to console ourselves we would imagine how life really was aboard a passing yacht.

"Isn't that a pretty boat!" one of us would exclaim, pointing towards the channel.

"Um hmm," and after a long look, critical eyes shaded by a hand held close against the forehead, "She has nice lines. I like the way her stern angles out."

"And look at the size of that cockpit. Not perfect for offshore, but great for parties."

"Well, it may be pretty, but you know those people on board are probably tired after dragging anchor last night when that thunderstorm came through. The holding ground over there isn't the best."

"Yes and the head is probably stopped up," I'd say, warming to the game.

"But they can't fix it right now, because there is salt water coming in through the cabin sole. Somebody's searching for the leak, while someone else tries to figure out why the bilge pump won't work."

"Yes and when all that gets sorted out, and they finally get out to the ocean, the wind will be right on the nose," I'd finish with grim satisfaction.

Somehow it was easier to be shore-bound when we imagined constant catastrophe and discomfort aboard all the boats we saw. The longer we were without a boat, the more we talked about them, and the stronger our desire became to go sailing again... on a boat of our own.

Finally we called a broker and told him that we wanted a ketch between 38 and 45 feet; one that slept five and was sound enough to sail around the world. After looking through the multiple listings and the brokerage sections of all the yachting magazines, we narrowed our choices down to either a Cheoy Lee 47 or an Allied Mistress 39 built in the early 1970's. We really yearned for a custom built Cherubini 44, but money was a major barrier. Johnny had been writing to Mr. Cherubini every few years for plans with which to dream, and although no money trees had sprung up in the garden, prices in the boatyard had continued to rise. When an old Cheoy Lee 47 came through Charleston we went to see her, looking past the worn out engine, dilapidated interior, and dull gray teak, and made an offer, only to find that someone else had sent in a contract just hours earlier. That served only to fan the fire, and we became fairly desperate to find the perfect boat despite our recent resolve to rid ourselves of this madness.

We avidly read boating magazines and scoured the used boat ads. We knew we couldn't buy a new boat of the quality we needed, and experience had shown us that a proven yacht was probably better anyway. Whether new or used, any boat can hold surprises and a good survey prior to purchase is the best safeguard available. Of course a survey is only as reliable as the surveyor himself, all a matter of how knowledgeable he is and how thoroughly he does his job.

As the weeks went by we drove up and down the East coast looking at boats whose virtues, in our opinion, were always overestimated. We alternated between hopeful anticipation before seeing a yacht that sounded just right on paper, and bouts of despondency and pessimism when, once again, our hopes were dashed. It was an uneasy time; each day our outlook changed. We weren't absolutely sure what we wanted, and fate seemed to be steering us away from what we thought we wanted. It was a time of anxiety and disquiet. Johnny tried to immerse himself in his work at the office and, between children's dancing and riding lessons, soccer games, and my volunteer work, we doggedly persisted in browsing through the boating advertisements. The more we looked the more dispirited we became. We were wracked with indecision, and seeing so many boats that did not quite measure up to our requirements was wearying. We were ready to give up.

Then came the day in March when Peter Dodds, from Charleston Yacht Sales, called and asked us to fly up to Oriental, N.C. with him to see a boat that had just come on the market. She was one of the hard to find aft cockpit versions of the Wright-Allied Mistress 39 that so interested us. Already we had seen several of these boats in various states of disrepair and we weren't sure what we'd find, despite Peter's glowing secondhand report from another broker who had been aboard her.

It was clear and balmy when we met Peter at the airport next morning. We weren't wasting any time! Being a pilot, Peter had chartered a small, single engine plane, and he flew up the coast low enough for us to enjoy the scenery beneath as we glided noisily along in the cloudless sky. Up there we could see the curve of the earth as the Atlantic Ocean stretched eastward, looking immense. The drive from the Beaufort airstrip probably took less than an hour, but, tense with anticipation, it seemed much longer to me.

As we approached the yacht Sequoiah for the first time she looked shiny and well-tended. She was big compared to other boats we had owned and we liked her generous lines. At least Johnny did. I really preferred the look of some of the old wooden boats we'd seen with sleek clipper ship bow and long overhang at the stern. Sequoiah was built in 1975 of hand-laid fiberglass and had a no-nonsense, utilitarian look about her. She had a white hull with a wide blue band painted below the practical stainless steel rub rail. Her decks were molded non-skid of light tan, and the cockpit was large with a huge sail locker on each side. Being ketch rigged, the mizzen mast was inconveniently located in the middle of the cockpit with the compass attached to it at knee level. The steering wheel was right aft with easy access to the rack and pinion steering gear underneath the helmsman's seat. An Aries wind vane was mounted on the stern and looked, to my uninitiated eye, more like a sculpture student's failed attempt at modern art than a major piece of cruising equipment.

Inside she was huge. To us the main salon looked like a ballroom. Sitting on the steps leading down into the cabin, I could see a long navigation station to my left, with bookshelf, pilot berth, and settee in front of it. On my right was a U-shaped galley, another settee forward of that and a table with fold up leaves between the two settees. Despite the ugly brown paint on the walls and ceiling, it was quite light and airy with two long fixed ports, two opening ports, and a hatch above the table. Forward of the main salon there was a wall of drawers on the right and a tiny enclosed cubicle to the left which housed the head and shower. In the forward cabin was a seven foot V-berth with bookshelves running full length on both sides, a large hanging locker, and a basin which, at the time, I thought should have been in the head. The headroom throughout was 6'4", just Johnny's height, so he could actually stand upright, a luxury he had never enjoyed on our previous boats.

While Johnny was finding out about the workings of the engine and electrical and plumbing systems, I was checking out the stove, storage lockers, shower, and all the comforts of home. From my point of view Sequoiah had some drawbacks, but Johnny felt that she was the yacht we had been dreaming about. She was well made and sturdy, and with some cosmetic attention and personal touches could be quite attractive as well.

The owners came aboard and we made an offer on the spot, which had the immediate effect of making them wonder if they really wanted to part with her. They left to discuss it and came back in half an hour with an affirmative answer, ready to take us out for a sail. It was windy and rough out on Albermarle Sound, and although she didn't point up very close to the wind, Sequoiah handled the choppy water with ease. After sailing boats with a tiller I couldn't seem to steer with the wheel, and kept turning the opposite way from where I wanted to go until someone told me to drive it like a car. Now that was something I could understand! We had a good trial sail and returned to the marina excited about the prospect of owning her. That night in a little restaurant in Beaufort, N.C. we signed the necessary papers. Sequoiah would be ours as soon as a favorable survey could be completed.

Two weeks later I took the Greyhound to North Carolina, met the surveyor at the boat, and watched as he inspected her completely inside and out, afloat and ashore. When he found her sound and had only minor changes to recommend, the purchase was completed and I moved aboard. Johnny joined me, and a day later we made the four hour trip to Beaufort to pick up Harriet and John DuBose who were joining us for our maiden voyage on Sequoiah as we took her home to Charleston. We met them at the Beaufort airstrip in a ramshackle blue truck, courtesy of the marina. The gears didn't work well and we jolted and laughed our way back to the boat with duffel bags bouncing in the open bed of the pickup. At the Net House Restaurant that night we feasted on freshly caught shrimp and, as we listened to the wind howling up from the Southwest, decided to go down the Waterway instead of heading offshore.

By morning the wind had not abated, and because the tide was running, we had a hard time getting away from the dock. In the process Johnny lost his glasses overboard, and we incurred the ire of the people on the boat next to us who awoke to find John DuBose standing on their bow trying to fend Sequoiah off. Before lunchtime we lost the chart overboard. Somehow, amidst a rush of confusion, we managed to retrieve it with a stab of the boat hook, wet but still serviceable!

In four days we learned things about Sequoiah that only a certain intimacy could teach, and Johnny resumed his never-ending apprenticeship of on–the–job training as plumber, diesel mechanic, and electrical engineer. In our years with Sequoiah we would wear many hats, but Johnny would own most of them. Before we reached Charleston the RPM indicator had stopped working, the shower pump had gone haywire (it could only be coaxed to work if the bilge pump was on), the hot water heater switch was smoking, and the engine was intermittently making a knocking sound... a royal welcome back to the joys of boat ownership.

Once Sequoiah was in her new home at the Charleston City Marina we began some fast work to get her ready for our annual summer trek to the Bahamas, only two months away. While the children were in school I spent my mornings scraping and painting the interior of the boat, including the insides of lockers and cabinets. What a difference a little white paint made! Everything looked much brighter and even larger. Outside I cleaned and varnished the teak, then oiled the wood inside and polished the teak and holly floors. Johnny spent the weekends working on the engine, rewiring the electrical panel, checking out the rigging and sails, and installing an Autohelm automatic pilot. Never having sailed with a wind vane before, we weren't sure if it would really do the job. We liked the fact that an automatic pilot can steer even when there is no wind. Having both would be like having extra crew aboard. Crew that wouldn't whine or talk back!

Sequoiah had a propane stove that operated just like any household gas stove. The only thing about it that I didn't like was the lack of a lock on the oven door. Even though the stove was gimbaled, there was always the chance, in rough weather, of food flying out of the oven if things weren't perfectly balanced. A cook's belt was attached to the galley counters. It had heavy duty, easy to use with one hand, quick release snaps on each side. It was a wonderful aid. Even in the worst conditions there was no chance of falling onto the stove. That belt was one of my favorite boat gadgets, next to the automatic pilot, of course!

Despite the ongoing work, we managed to do a great deal of entertaining: sunset dinner parties with our friends and children's birthday parties. In those two months we sailed Sequoiah about one out of every three days. We sailed mostly in the harbor, taking her into the ocean only once during that time, something we would soon regret.

Finally school was out, and at dawn on June 7 we left for the Bahamas with our three children, along with Charles Geer, and his oldest son, Charlie, who is Caroline's age. Even before we were out of Charleston harbor our bad luck began; the mainsail fell to the deck. Fortunately, the water was fairly flat making the climb to the masthead bearable. At the top

Johnny found nothing broken. The shackle connected to the halyard, not being completely closed, had fallen open. With that fixed and a mental note made to rig extra halyards to the masthead to avoid climbing the mast someday in bad weather, we were on our way again.

We sailed well all day. By midnight the wind had died leaving uncomfortable swells in its wake and we resorted to the engine, but not for long. In an hour the engine stopped of its own accord, and we were sailing again at barely two knots while Johnny tried to discover the problem. Off and on for the next eighteen hours he lay coiled around the engine, repair book close at hand, replacing a blocked fuel filter and bleeding the system. At last the engine started again, but the problem remained. The engine would run for only an hour or so before the fuel filters got clogged up again and Johnny would have to repeat the horrible process. As he grew more proficient at the task it took less time to complete, but the results were always the same: short-lived.

The seas were confused and the wind occasional, so we mostly wallowed in the ocean swells with a sickly motion. On the fourth day out, somewhere off the coast of Florida, we gave up and set a course for home, unwilling to risk taking this boat that we knew so little about into the shallows of the Bahamas without an engine. When the wind began to head us, we turned into St. Simon's Island, Georgia and tied up at the Golden Isles Marina.

The children were so glad to reach land that they leaped to the dock as soon as we came alongside. After a few unsteady steps they all fell down! It took some concentration to keep their balance. After rolling constantly for four days their equilibrium was disturbed by the solid ground. We spent a day at St. Simon's, Johnny and Charles and a local mechanic working on the engine, the children and I swimming at a hotel and visiting Fort Frederica. We left late the next afternoon, after a brief but violent thunderstorm, motoring up the ICW to Hilton Head, one eye on the oil pressure gauge, and the other on the channel.

On the way up the ICW, twelve year old Weesie wrote a poem in her notebook that summed up her feelings about this aborted trip:

> On Sunday morning we set sail,
> We hoped for good weather, not for a gale.
> Our luck was not good,
> It was terribly bad.
> My, oh my, we were sooo sad.
> We crossed the Gulf Stream,
> Not once... but again!
> We changed our courses, we lost our way,
> And all we could see was water, day by day.
> The engine kept stopping
> And we were all sopping,
> 'Cause storms just kept coming our way.
> The Bahamas? All Wrong!
> The Trip? Too long.
> So we settled for a stay on land.
> The place we arrived was called St. Simons.
> It was very clean and sparkled like diamonds.
> Boy, we were glad to take a few showers,
> Because we had dreamed of it for Hours and Hours.
> After our stay (just one day)
> We started for Hilton Head.

The weather outside was hot, humid and rainy; and inside, disappointment fueled discontent. Charles and Charlie left us in Hilton Head and the Warren family headed for home in discord on June 15. All of us were out of sorts. The children squabbled continuously, Johnny was morose, speaking only when spoken to, and I fanned the flames with ill-tempered, random remarks.

It was a typical June day, hot and cloudless, the air heavy with excessive humidity. Within three hours, out in the ocean, the engine stopped working again and we had a repeat performance of the trip south, improving nobody's mood. There was very little wind. The wind vane refused to steer and, without power, the Autohelm was inoperable. Bribery became the main motivational force to keep someone at the wheel, and my secret stores of novelties and candy were seriously depleted in the bargaining that ensued. We had almost no steerageway for two days and nights and we sweltered in the still heat. Mutiny was at hand.

We reached Charleston wearing every sail in the wardrobe, and with hordes of huge black flies swarming around us making life miserable. Fortunately we caught the tide going into Charleston harbor. Adding insult to injury, however, the wind moved around to the west, and we tacked tediously across the harbor and up the Ashley River, arriving at the marina at four in the morning. As we quietly ghosted round the last turn in the dark and Johnny told the girls to drop the mainsail, I shouted from my stand on the foredeck, "There's a boat in our slip!"

"John, take the wheel," growled Johnny, standing and peering ahead into the darkness. Frantic, I was leaping around on the bow.

"What do you want me to do? Shall I drop the anchor? Hurry up and tell me!" I screamed as we glided closer and closer to the line of docks and boats.

Johnny gave a cool look around and spotted an empty slip further down the dock, ran back to the wheel, and turned toward it. We had just enough momentum, with the help of the tide, to carry us to the empty space. When Sequoiah was securely tied, we dropped in exhaustion, frustrated and angry, but home safe.

Our first call was to a diesel mechanic who listened to our tale of woe, nodded wisely, then proceeded to spend lots of his time and our money doing <u>something</u> down in that dark hole where the engine lived. None of his efforts were successful, but there was no way to tell until the engine failed again, always offshore in rough water. We took numerous short trips that summer, all inevitably ending with no engine if we ventured into the ocean. When we stayed in the relatively calm waters of the harbor and the ICW we had no trouble, but if we went out into the ocean for more than an hour or two and used the engine, it always stopped.

Finally, our third mechanic discovered the problem. The entire bottom of both the fuel tanks was covered in sludge, residue from years of dirty fuel. The tanks were pumped dry, the sludge removed painstakingly by hand, and the tanks steam cleaned. It was a miraculous cure. A friend from Annapolis, Juan Casasco, one of the offshore sailing coaches at the U.S. Naval Academy, later told us that this is a regular procedure every season on all the yachts at the Academy, and one that can surely save many headaches!

With our major problem on Sequoiah resolved, we began to enjoy frequent trips offshore on weekends, and started planning for our next trip to the Bahamas.

CHAPTER THREE

OUR BAHAMIAN LOVE AFFAIR

Our first affection for the Bahamas began when Johnny and I had been married only a year. We had flown to Nassau and spent what amounted to a second honeymoon, staying at the British Colonial Hotel, a large, pink landmark on the waterfront. We did all the touristy things, taking carriage rides and renting a motorbike to see the island. It was very crowded, but the tropical flavor of the place and the pristine beaches and blue water entranced us. Our most enjoyable day was spent with a native boy on a small chartered sailboat tacking around Nassau harbor. As we daydreamed, watching the isolated rain showers that dotted the otherwise blue sky, Johnny had said, "Someday we'll sail here on our own boat."

Although Johnny had long since given up his idea of building a boat, he still thought about boats constantly. I had no conception of his dreams. At the time it was an idle fantasy completely removed from real life.

Through the years, as we became more addicted to sailing, we longed to leave the coast and venture past the horizon, out to `blue water'. What IS blue water, anyway? The first few times I heard the term I had no idea what it referred to and, when I asked, I was told it just means ocean sailing. After we had sailed up and down the coast a bit, I began to notice that the water changes color the farther you go and the deeper it is. Close to shore the tidal flow churns up the bottom and carries dirt and minerals from rivers and streams making the sea look brown or dark green, and opaque, almost thick. Out past the tide's influence there is a line where the dark color meets a lighter, translucent green. Even farther from land, as the bottom deepens, the green turns into a deep blue, a magnificent color without equal. Depending on the light, it can look like rich, blue-black velvet or a silvery, royal blue satin.

After cruising the nearby coastal waters for a number of years, Johnny finally convinced me that it would be fun, and not certain suicide, to go farther from home. As my bravery increased, we took many trips to the Bahamas aboard SeaTurtle and Sequoiah, always leaving as soon as possible after the children were out of school. Officially the Atlantic hurricane season begins June 1, so summer is the off season for tourists visiting the islands. Since our aim was to get away from civilization it was the perfect time for us. Of course there are drawbacks. It is hot and humid then, and the mosquitoes and "no-see-ems" thrive in this environment. However, Charleston has identical problems; we were used to the climate and, with wind scoops on the hatches, we were usually comfortable if there was even a hint of a breeze. For the times when there was no wind we had cabin fans to keep the air moving, and screens for the ports and hatches. Long ago we discovered Avon Skin So Soft, bath oil that is marvelous protection against insects, and I found that wiping it full strength on the screens kept the 'no see ems' from squeezing through. Through trial and error, mostly the latter, we were learning some useful tricks.

Johnny worked for a large law firm where each partner was entitled to three weeks of vacation every year. Though most didn't take it all at once, Johnny did. He found that he was able to relax after he'd been away from the office about a week and could then fully enjoy the next two. Since the Bahamas are so close to home - Marsh Harbor in the Abacos is only 450 miles (or about four days) from Charleston - it seemed the perfect destination for a three week holiday.

Our friends, Anne and Mike Adair, from whom we had bought SeaTurtle, had been diving and sailing in that area for many years. Professional photographers, they showed us their slides, intriguing us with underwater pictures of the multi-hued corals and brilliant fishes that abound in Bahamian waters. Some other friends, John and Charlotte McCrady, captivated us with stories of their family visits to the Abacos, and the friendly islanders they had grown to love. Both couples looked at charts with us, answered our endless questions, and gave us helpful ideas for planning our first Bahamian cruise.

The Commonwealth of the Bahamas became an independent nation in 1973 after 300 years as a British colony. The name comes from the Spanish word, bajamar, meaning shallow water. Aptly named, the 700 mile island chain is situated on a sand bank that rises out of the ocean depths. There are nearly 700 islands in the Bahamas and less than 30 are inhabited, so the cruising and exploring possibilities for us were endless.

Our first boat trips to the Bahamas were made aboard SeaTurtle, our Endeavor 32, and in her we explored the Abacos. She was the first boat we'd owned that we felt was comfortable and safe enough to cross the Gulf Stream. For this first trip we started planning months in advance. There was no refrigeration on board so I tried keeping food in a cooler at home to see how long things would last. I made detailed menu plans so that we wouldn't have to buy anything for the three weeks we would be travelling. We had great fun poring over charts and reading through Cruising Guide to the Bahamas marking all the best anchorages and snorkeling spots recommended by friends.

Since I was nervous about the passage across, we decided to move the boat to Florida. That way we would have only an overnight sail to West End, our intended Bahamian landfall. It sounded simple enough, but Johnny was extremely busy at the office and had only one free weekend, which was not long enough to take the boat as far south as we wanted. We looked into having her delivered, but that was too expensive, so Johnny suggested that I deliver her myself. Everyone laughed, but Johnny wasn't joking. To him it was a simple solution to both our problems: time and money. He would take SeaTurtle offshore as far south as possible one weekend. I would find a crew to take her to Boca Raton via the Intracoastal Waterway. Our friend, Scott Morrison, was managing the Boca Raton Hotel and Club at that time and had often told us what wonderful facilities they had for yachts, so Johnny and the children planned to meet me there when school was out.

It wasn't easy to find a crew. Remember this was quite a few years ago and "ladies" didn't do this sort of thing. Most of my closer friends didn't even like sailing, so I asked several college age girls with sailing experience. Their parents prudently refused to let them take such a foolhardy trip with a captain who had never been out of Charleston harbor without her husband aboard. My mother, who is always ready for any adventure, volunteered eagerly and signed up for a Coast Guard Auxiliary sailing course so she would have some idea of what we were doing. Johnny's sister-in-law, Ellen Warren didn't need much arm-twisting either. She had two tiny boys at home and jumped at the chance for a much-needed break. She didn't know a sheet from a halyard either so I kept looking for someone who knew something about sailing. Through volunteer work and church, I knew Jody Millis, who had her own boat and did some racing. Jody thought my plan sounded like a lark and came along to complete our crew. During the month before leaving we sailed together several times, concentrating on docking maneuvers which happen to be my personal boating nightmare.

Johnny, his brother, and three friends sailed out of Charleston the end of May with a strong East southeast wind that sped them in two days to St. Augustine, where I drove to meet them with my distaff crew. We traded the car for the boat and moved aboard. The next five days were mostly sunny without much wind and we motored fifty or sixty miles a day stopping at marinas every night. I think I lost ten pounds that week from worry! As long as we were in open water and moving, everything was okay. It was when we were in close quarters that scared me. At night I couldn't sleep, wondering if I could get the boat away from the dock in the morning without crunching another yacht. All day long I would feel the apprehension mount as we got closer to the next marina.

With only a 3 1/2 foot draft we still managed to touch bottom twice in the narrow Florida canals, but fortunately never went hard aground. At Vero Beach we tied up at my cousins' dock and spent a night at their house, a pleasant change of pace. By the time we neared Boca Raton we felt like professional boat handlers and I was beginning to relax a little. I called ahead, and as we approached the marina at the Boca Raton Hotel, the dock master and a helper, both dressed in white uniforms complete with shoulder boards, were on the concrete pier to meet us. With a following wind, an incoming tide and the engine in reverse, we went flying into the dock. The bow anchor was knocked out of place with a sickly crunching noise, but fortunately, with the expert help from ashore, catastrophe was averted and the only thing hurt was my pride.

The Boca Raton Hotel is understated elegance at its best, and we spent our last day together enjoying the hotel's facilities, all of which are available to yachtsmen staying at the marina. When I asked where the nearest phone booth was located, a telephone was brought aboard, and when we needed ice, a truckload arrived at the dock! Scott had made sure that we were well taken care of at the marina, and he entertained us royally at dinner that night.

The next morning I waved goodbye to Mother, Ellen, and Jody at the train station and spent the day cleaning the boat, doing errands, and waiting for Johnny and the children to arrive. In addition to our own three, my nephew, Dale Lynch, just eight months older than Weesie, was with them. Johnny had his hands full. Their trip down to Florida was a real trial. The train, which should have left Charleston at 5:00 AM, never arrived, having been derailed somewhere. Amtrak put the would-be passengers on buses, drove them to Savannah, Georgia, and loaded them onto another train which, plagued by delays, took until midnight to get to West Palm Beach where I met the tired and grumpy group.

After a good night's sleep, humor was restored and we spent two fun days looking at boats, swimming, and enjoying Boca Raton. On our last night we went to the Morrison's house for a visit. By 2200 hours we were back aboard, ready to leave for West End. Because it shifts often, the Boca Raton Inlet is a bit tricky, but easily navigated if you know how to run it. Johnny had talked to some local fishermen as well as the hotel's dock personnel. They had given him specific instructions and encouraged us to try it. We also had gone down by car one afternoon and watched boats going in and out, and Johnny felt confident that he could maneuver through it successfully. We left on the outgoing tide as the last of the sun was sinking behind us.

As usual, in spite of the beauty of the moment, I was filled with apprehension and an innate fear of the unknown that always strikes me at times like these. I had forgotten to tell Johnny that the flag halyard was fouled and he had to rig up a special line to raise the radar reflector. Then I noticed that the pipe to the bilge pump through-hull was broken and leaking, and Johnny had to fix that, too.

"Johnny, let's go back and spend another night at the marina," I wailed. "Everything's breaking and we're just not ready to do this." I was afraid.

"Go put the children to bed. And stop worrying. Everything will be just fine," he answered. "The weather's perfect, and in the morning we'll be in the Bahamas!"

"Or at the bottom of the sea!" came John's six year old prophecy. The children instinctively felt the tension that my fear had created. I was terribly ashamed. Pulling myself together, I laughed, pretending a gaiety I didn't feel, and managed to get everyone tucked into bed.

Johnny stood watch most of the night. I think he was afraid to leave me alone too long as he knew how I was feeling. At dawn we still hadn't picked up any lights. Then Johnny realized that we had overcompensated for the Gulf Stream's current, and we were down below West End. Instead of sailing directly east when leaving central Florida for the Bahamas, it is necessary to steer a more southerly course to make up for the strong sideways drift caused by the fast, north-flowing Gulf Stream. We turned up the coast, marveling at the magnificent color of the water, constantly changing as we continued into the shallows of the bank, and we arrived at West End before noon. We'd made it! My fears were for naught.

It is simply amazing what political barriers can do. We had travelled only 84 miles overnight, and yet we were worlds away from the society we had left behind the day before. There was an odd mixture of British colonialism, African laissez-faire, and plastic America, set in an atmosphere of decay, the semi-tropical heat adding to the general ennui of the place, everything moving as slowly as molasses in January. The damp smell of overgrown vegetation and the voices of unfamiliar birds pervaded our senses. It was wonderful...love at first sight.

Our first experience dealing with foreign customs officials was quite easy once we figured out what we were supposed to do. Ignorance is not bliss in these situations. The Yachtsman's Guide read, "A quarantine (yellow) flag must be flown and no contact may be made with the shore other than tying up until the vessel has been granted practique."

After waiting an hour tied up at the marina, Johnny ventured ashore to find the Customs officer, and a dockhand told him, "Don't worry. No problem. I will go fetch him here." This was accompanied by a meaningfully outstretched palm, and it was made clear that five dollars would be correct. The man, grinning widely, ambled a short distance to a small shack and disappeared inside. Shortly, a Customs officer appeared, and we never learned whether he had been summoned by our overpaid acquaintance or had simply arrived on his own. He welcomed us to the Bahamas, looked over our papers, glanced around the boat while filling out forms, and then wished us good sailing as he waved goodbye. It was quite simple and pleasant. On subsequent trips, if a Customs official was not around when we arrived, Johnny would take our passports and ship's papers to the Customs office himself, saving time and money.

Since we usually had only a three week vacation, we moved around quite a bit, exploring as much territory as possible. At each island we always anchored out, stopping at docks only long enough to take on more fuel and water. Anchoring is free and, being away from shore, there was usually a breeze and fewer mosquitoes; and it was always cooler and quieter than being at a dock.

At six and twelve, John and Dale were quite a team, often leaving a trail of destruction in their wake. They loved helping to run the boat so we tried to put their energy to productive use. John, with the help of a large winch could just manage to raise the mainsail while Dale pulled up the anchor. This could be tricky if the wind was strong or there were many other boats in the harbor, but with practice they became quite proficient at sailing us off the anchor. They, and the girls, too, would help Johnny scrub the waterline of the hull and the bottoms of the dinghies, and they all had regular housekeeping jobs as well, the main one being cleanup after meals. None of them liked this and often loudly wished for paper plates or maybe a 12 volt dishwashing machine. Even though most of them didn't like the local Bahamian food, they were always glad when we went out to eat. Their favorite place was the Green Turtle Club where they had struck up a friendship with some of the locals. They particularly loved the cook, Viola, who entertained by beating pans and singing.

One night at the Man O War dock as we were on our way to the Dock N Dine restaurant, John ran along the edge of the seawall watching Johnny and Dale take the dinghy around to tie it up. He lost his balance and fell, tearing all the skin off one foot as it dragged down the wall. Luckily, Dale managed to catch him in mid–air so no more damage was done. The day before, John had bought a glass bottom bucket, the type used by Bahamian spongers; and in the next several days while his foot healed, it really came in handy. Unable to get the foot wet, he would float along in the dinghy over submerged reefs and watch the fish through his glass. That bucket was useful, too, when diving for conch and for locating things lost overboard.

These summer trips to the Bahamas were similar in many ways, yet always different too, depending on who was with us, the people we met, and which islands we visited. For several years we visited the Abacos, the northeastern most islands. Although charter boat companies and hotels attracted a growing number of tourists, we found the islands and their inhabitants friendly and basically unspoiled. We would

Helen, Weesie, Dale, John, Johnny and
Caroline at Guana Cay, Abaco, Bahamas

swim and snorkel in the mornings, moving the boat to a good
spot or sometimes taking trips in the dinghy. After lunch we
always had a nap or reading hour when everyone was quiet.
The afternoons were for fishing, hiking, exploring, sailing,
swimming; the days passed too swiftly each summer and we
always wished for more time.

Some of our experiences were scary and some rather funny.
One nasty night at Man O War, Johnny and I were awakened
not long after midnight to the sound of the wind scoop whipping madly in the hatch above us. A squall was approaching
and our anchor was dragging. Three children slept soundly
through it all, but Dale jumped up with us and, while Johnny
started the engine, he and I raised the anchor. I was frightened
as the wind swirled around us in sudden fury and when the
rain came, it was in huge, hard drops. The visibility was poor
and we could see only few feet. The harbor was extremely
crowded and we were afraid we would hit another boat. As

we weaved along Dale managed to grab a mooring buoy and we tied to it until morning.

The wind and rain howled around us the rest of the night, but the next day was beautiful and, after paying Mr. Albury for the unexpected use of his buoy, we motored out of the congested harbor, raised the mainsail, and found to our surprise that we couldn't shut off the engine. We had experienced motors that wouldn't start, but we were unprepared for this eventuality. After Johnny had tried the most logical methods and was totally perplexed, he called Mike Adair aboard Snorkey via VHF radio. Mike was an engineer with Lockheed for a number of years and, at that time, was much more at home in an engine room than Johnny who, when I first married him, thought that when a light bulb burned out, it was time to call the electrician.

"Snorkey, Snorkey. This is SeaTurtle," Johnny spoke into the radiotelephone.

After several calls, Mike's familiar voice came back over the radio, "Hello, SeaTurtle. This is Snorkey. Let's go to six-eight."

Johnny changed the channel and said, "Hi, Mike. We've got a little problem and hope you might be able to help."

"Sure glad to try, Johnny. What's the trouble?"

"Well, it's a little strange, but the engine won't shut off."

There was a short silence, and then slowly, with disbelief, "The engine won't turn off?"

"That's right. We motored out of Man O'War after lunch and when we'd raised the sails, I tried to turn off the motor; but it wouldn't stop. After we anchored here at Guana Cay, I tried closing the air intake with my hand and then with a book, but it still keeps running. I can hear air leaking in... must be just enough to keep it going."

After about an hour of entertaining anyone listening in on the radio, Johnny and Mike finally stopped the engine by turning the decompression levers clockwise. I still don't know what decompression levers look like, but I sure was glad they did their job.

During the afternoon I had tried to calculate how long the engine would run. We had just refueled that morning, and the prospect was most depressing. The welcome silence that accompanied success was a real relief. After thanking Mike for his help, we promised to meet them later in the week at Marsh Harbor.

We did see them later, but not before we had sunk one of the dinghies and managed to tie the anchor line around the propeller while Johnny was trying to teach us how to anchor Bahamian-style using two anchors. There was never a dull moment aboard our boats. Calamity seemed to go with us hand in hand.

Then there was the first summer we had teenagers aboard. Why is it that when middle age approaches one can't remember what the teen years were like? Once again Bahamas bound with Dale and Weesie just entering that incredible decade in their lives, we were reminded, almost constantly! It was an amazing month, and our log reads like a comedy of errors. Dale breathed and lived for fishing. Before we were even out of Charleston Harbor he was wearing a rod holster and had two hand lines trailing astern. On the trip to the islands he did manage to provide one dinner and a great deal of entertainment for the other children with barracuda constantly hitting his lines.

The highlight of the sail down was the night we saw a satellite, launched from Cape Canaveral, burst across the sky, brilliant in the glorious colors of the sunset. That same night a little bird, which we were unable to identify, came aboard at bedtime, perched on the lee cloth of Caroline's bunk, groomed himself and tucked his head under his wing for the night. At first light the next morning, when we could just see the faint outline of Abaco on the horizon, Dale shouted, "Land Ho!", and our winged passenger fluffed his feathers and preceded us to the islands. John made a notation in the log that reads, "Bird flew the coop."

After clearing customs in Marsh Harbor we began a fortnight of island hopping through the Abaco chain. Our days began early, often with a swim before breakfast. If we added it up, we would probably find that more hours were spent in the water than out. We were all fascinated by the submarine world below us.

Children add an extra dimension to cruising. Within five days we had lost two flippers, naturally not a pair, one mask, and a fishing rod. Another mask had fallen out of the dinghy, but Dale managed to find that one on the bottom ten feet below, and dove for it. We had three dinghies: two inflatable Avons and an eight foot Dyer Dhow, a fiberglass rowing/sailing boat. We looked like a circus as we pulled into new anchorages with our menagerie of little boats bouncing and bumping along behind.

John came back from one dinghy expedition with Dale and seemed to be moving strangely.

"John, what is the matter with you?" I asked.

"Dale didn't do it!" came his too quick reply.

"Didn't do what?" I asked suspiciously. Then, "Good Heavens! What happened to you?" I gasped as John turned around. I could see the bloody slashes starting at his left foot and, fairly evenly spaced, continuing up to his shoulder.

"I really didn't mean to, Aunt Helen," Dale's contrite voice wavered from the dinghy, his face appearing over the stern.

"It's just that... well, I had to turn fast a few times and, well, John...well, you see...he just fell out. I turned the engine off as fast as I could," he explained haltingly.

Apparently John had been standing in the bow of the twelve foot Avon holding onto the painter while Dale guided the craft in a jerky, zigzag course to see how long John could keep his balance, a waterborne form of King on the Mountain, I suppose. Fortunately, the little boat was powered by a small four horsepower outboard and, with Dale's fast reaction, the propellers had stopped turning by the time John's head reached them. The cuts were minor, but we wanted to avoid a repeat performance, so the boys were given the smaller ten foot Avon with oars only. It did have an ancient British Seagull two and a half horsepower motor which hadn't run in years, and they spent many, thankfully unsuccessful, hours trying to make it run. They still had the responsibility of keeping the engine on the larger dinghy topped up with gasoline and oil.

One Sunday at Man O War we went to an interesting service at the Gospel Chapel where the unfavorable comparison of mankind to worms had disturbed John and made the older children giggle. Afterwards, trying to get back to the boat, the engine on the big dinghy broke. Johnny had to row all of us back across the harbor, hard work against strong wind and waves. Rain began and, closed up in the cabin we noticed a terrible odor of gasoline. On investigation, Johnny found that the boys had put a gas can in a sail locker...upside down. The top had not been completely closed and several gallons of gasoline had spilled into the bilge. The boys then tried to pump it out and, in the process, broke the bilge pump. Trying to redeem themselves, Dale and John went fishing for dinner while Johnny installed a replacement pump and bailed the gas out of the bilge. They caught a few bait fish, and also snagged a hole in the Avon. Johnny taught them how to make a patch. It was just one of those days!

During the next week, in between rain squalls, we snorkeled over magnificent coral reefs alive with schools of brilliantly painted fish of many varieties. We always wore T-shirts rain or shine, either to prevent sunburn or to keep warm. After an hour or two in the water it begins to feel chilly even in summer. Whenever rain came, we raced on deck with soap and shampoo to take advantage of the natural shower. Water is expensive in the Bahamas and is treated as a luxury item, not something to be taken for granted. We learned to conserve our fresh water and found we could get along with incredibly little compared to what we used at home.

The night of Johnny's birthday we planned to have supper at the Conch Inn to celebrate. I was wearing a new, white sundress as I stepped down the ladder into the dinghy, slipped on an open jug of motor oil left on the seat, and fell full length into the bottom of the dinghy. I came up yelling like a banshee, covered in blue oil. In fact, I was so angry that I told them to go on without me, and I stayed on board alone to clean up and change and vent my rage verbally away from all ears. Johnny was back within an hour to find me calmer and ready to join in the birthday fun. There is something about having children on board that tests the limits of Murphy's Law. We seemed to live a life the Three Stooges would have envied.

On a calm day, Bahamian water is like an aquarium and we could easily see the bottom twenty feet below the boat littered with starfish, an occasional ray settling into the white sand, and turtles paddling lazily along until they saw us and, zoom! they'd be gone in the blink of an eye. They can really move!

One summer on our way home from the Bahamas at the end of June we got into a large, fast-moving storm system that swiftly built up the waves and winds under beautiful sunny skies. The winds were from the northwest, right where we were headed, so we fell off and ran with it for a day. Twenty four hours can seem more like weeks when you're afraid. It was the first real storm I had experienced. Except for occasional rain squalls the sky remained blue, not at all how I had envisioned storms at sea. In fact, I think now that I prefer the black, cloudy ones, because then it is impossible to see those towering waves cresting above the mast, each in turn threatening to crush us, but only for an instant, before scooping us up and dropping us unceremoniously onto the next wave. The motion was erratic and, to avoid seasickness, I spent much of the time braced in a corner of the cockpit. The children, oblivious to the danger, kept me busy singing or playing Twenty Questions or reading to them. Once I paused while reading to John to stare up at the top of a breaking wave. He nudged my arm and said, "Come on Mother, please keep reading. You can look at the waves when we get through."

No fear there! We kept reading. Weesie was fascinated by our eerie surroundings. She aptly described the ocean that day as a "desert of blue, snow-topped mountains", and she enjoyed the thrill of our roller coaster ride.

With all necessities and a few luxuries aboard, and with the comfort of sleeping in one's own bed at night, sailing is travel in the manner of a snail, slowly, with time to enjoy the sights along the way; and all without ever leaving home. We loved it and tried to spend as much time as possible living on our boat. These Bahamian trips were the icing on the cake. Once home again we'd begin planning for the next summer.

CHAPTER FOUR

THE CAT'S OUT OF THE BAG

Short summer cruises to the Bahamas simply fueled our desire for more. After we'd had Sequoiah for a year we resolved to sell our house, take a shakedown sail to the Bahamas during the summer, make any necessary changes aboard, and leave for parts unknown after hurricane season was over in the Fall. We told our parents we were planning a circumnavigation and would be gone for five years, but still we weren't ready to tell our children or friends. Our house was put on the market and it sold within a month. We had been looking at country property off and on for years, somewhere to keep a boat and horses, so our friends weren't terribly surprised, and never suspected our true motives. On that June morning we were to leave for the Bahamas, we had cold feet. Johnny woke me early and said, "I've been lying here thinking. How would you feel about buying Daddy's house?"

"Yes, what a good idea," I agreed hastily. We were too entrenched in an easy lifestyle and couldn't quite let go. It needed no discussion. I had no questions. I was feeling afraid too.

Johnny dressed and walked the four blocks to his parents' house where he found them having their morning coffee. When Johnny told them why he had come, both he and Doe were amazed when Hertz replied that he would not only sell us the house, but he would close his office and retire from his busy medical practice within a month. The men in this family make decisions quickly!

That night we took the children to the Yacht Club and over an early dinner told them of our new plans. Afterwards we boarded Sequoiah and, under overcast skies, left for three weeks in the Bahamas, relieved in a way, knowing that for now cruising was still just a summer vacation. We could laugh easily when John said, "Let's sail to England!" as we left the harbor.

This was really a postponement of a dream for us. When we returned from the islands we moved out of our house, stored everything, and lived aboard Sequoiah for four months until Doe and Hertz had decided where they wanted to move. Life at the dock was fun during the summer when lots of vacationing friends were around, and the children were alternately away at camp and visiting friends. However, when school started we began to look forward to moving ashore again and having a little more space. Our German Shepherd dog and three active children were finding boat life somewhat confining.

A major bone of contention during those months was Johnny's starched shirts. With only one good-sized hanging locker, his suits and shirts for the office received top priority. Anyone who wrinkled a shirt was in big trouble... and it came at least once daily. Cruising clothes and office garb have very different care requirements!

Once September arrived, days became chaotic. Our mornings were hurried. All of us had to be up, washed, dressed, fed, and in the car by seven o'clock in order to have everyone at school on time since we had nearly an hour's drive to town. The afternoons were even wilder. All three children got out of school at different times, and every day presented a challenge with varying activities for each child, usually in opposite directions. At night with only one table on board we had study hall before and after dinner; then we all went to bed at the same time. There was no real privacy living in two small rooms. When we moved back to town to the large house where Johnny had grown up, we hardly knew what to do with all the space. For months we often found ourselves gathered in one room in the evenings reluctant to separate and go to bed. That winter when we read about the unusually violent El Nino winds causing havoc with the weather in the Pacific, Johnny and I congratulated ourselves on our cowardly behavior and were content to be safe and sound at home.

For the next two years we continued to sail as often as Johnny's work would allow, often taking offshore trips on long weekends and holidays, and, as usual, spending time in the Bahamas each summer. Once, at the city marina's transient dock, Johnny saw a Cherubini 44, the boat of his dreams, and wrote again to the company for a current brochure. It is a lovely yacht, designed along the lines of the old clipper ships like those for which Herreshoff became famous. With careful attention to detail, Cherubini has built a boat that is beautiful, fast, and comfortable, with each interior customized to the owner's specifications. Once again we were dissatisfied with what we had, and now longed for a new custom built Cherubini 44. There are some things in life that are always just out of practical reach and this looked like one of them, but dreaming had never been hindered by practicalities at our house.

By this time, Weesie was a junior at the Madeira School in Virginia so in October we combined a visit to her 'Parents Weekend' with a trip to the Annapolis Boat Show. At the show we met Mr. Cherubini and spent a long time looking at our dream boat and talking to the builder. The upshot of it was that we then went on up to New Jersey to the Cherubini boatyard, where we spent a wonderful morning watching the slow progress of three boats on their way to completion. We were impressed by the quality of workmanship, and left with a contract to sign and return, contingent on the sale of Sequoiah. This was really it. We would sell both our boat and our house to buy a Cherubini 44. We would wait and tell the children after the sales had been completed.

Our car broke down somewhere in New Jersey. While we waited to have a new transmission installed, Johnny went to a drugstore and bought notebook and pencils. We sat and made a list of all the reasons for and against taking a sailing trip. This is what we came up with:

PROS	CONS
Healthy now	Dangerous
Learning experience for all	Interrupt formal schooling
Second career still possible	Start over on return
Unrestricted travel	Use up savings
Might be too crowded later	Might need to sell house
Children can go with us now	
No responsibility for our parents	
Job change inevitable anyway	

Naturally the list in favor of going was longer, and the reasons for not going weren't very convincing anyway. The decision to go was a foregone conclusion. Driving home we continued to make lists of equipment we would need and jobs to be done. Just putting things on paper always made us feel like we were progressing towards our goal.

We spent the winter trying to sell Sequoiah, but not many people were buying that time of year and we had no luck. However we had worked ourselves into such a state that we regretfully wrote Mr. Cherubini, returning his blueprints, and modified our plans to a one year trip around the Atlantic aboard Sequoiah. For the first time we had managed to hone our plans down to something actually manageable.

* * *

Valentine's Day, 1985 dawned cold and gray, the day we had decided to announce our plans to our family and friends. Our children knew we had been talking about trans–oceanic voyages for years, and at least one of them hoped it always would be only a dream. All three thought we had been behaving strangely since our trip to the Annapolis Boat Show months earlier, but they had convinced themselves that it was just the old "getting ready to buy a bigger boat" syndrome surfacing again, since Sequoiah had been listed with a broker all winter. Their instincts were correct, for if Sequoiah had sold we would probably be in a rented apartment somewhere waiting for a new Cherubini 44 to be built.

Since Sequoiah was still very much ours, Johnny and I woke up that February morning saying to each other, "OK, are we REALLY going to do this?"

"Once we tell everyone, there's no turning back."

"Yes, let's go sailing! We'll tell the children first."

As the family sat down to breakfast, Johnny announced, "We've decided to sail to England!"

This was met with, "Oh, sure," from John, shoveling an overloaded spoonful of cereal into his mouth, and "Not again, you're not serious are you?" from Caroline, who was uneasy.

"Yes, we really mean it. We're going to leave the first week in June, right after school is out, and we'll be gone about a year. It will be..."

Here everyone started shouting at once.

"Great!" yelled John, who was at the adventurous, and still uninhibited, age of eleven. "I didn't want to go to school next year anyway."

Caroline dramatically threw her fork down and began sobbing, "I'm not going, and you can count on that. I can't believe you're really going to do this to me. I can't leave all my friends!"

"We think you are going to love it."

"I can't believe you! This is so embarrassing!" wailed Caroline, who was fast approaching the incredibly egocentric age of fourteen.

"Can I take my skateboard?"

"This just can't be true! I'll move in with Anne. I knew you had something weird planned. No, I'm NOT going!"

"I am going to tell everyone at the office today and ..."

"They'll know you are crazy."

"We'll spend the summer in Europe," I interjected hopefully.

"Normal people fly."

"Hey! What about the dog? Can Gerta go too?"

After the mixed reviews at breakfast, Caroline shouting in rage and John with enthusiasm, we called Weesie, away at school. Her initial reaction was one of great excitement until she realized what a big decision she would have to make about her education. At sixteen, she had only one year left before college. She would have to decide whether to remain at school for her senior year, which would mean sailing with us during the summer and on school holidays; forget about school for a year and finish her last year of high school on our return; or take a correspondence course and the GED examination, and try to get into a college when we returned. Johnny and I had discussed this problem many times and thought Weesie should make the choice. She had plenty of time to think about it.

Johnny announced his resignation at the office to partners who were reluctant to have him leave, but made it very easy by letting him know that there would be a place for him when he returned. We called our family and friends who all tried to sound enthusiastic, although most agreed with Caroline, wondering if we were mentally unstable. We advertised our house for rent, and before we could even begin to worry about what to do with our nine year old dog, our dear friend, Eleanor Carter, called and said, "Heyward and I are really excited about your trip. We sat down with the children last night and came to a unanimous decision. You can't say no. We want Gerta to stay with us while you're gone." It seemed that everything was falling into place.

* * *

That was three and a half months before our planned departure. Nothing else was quite so simple. The remaining days and nights were filled beyond remembrance. Now that our travel plans were verbalized we had to make the dream a reality, and that meant making time for completely renovating Sequoiah and loading her with everything a family of five would need for a year. Our world was too full already. I could think of our life only in one day fragments. The whole was too overwhelming.

From then on, we never had enough time in the day to do half of what we hoped to accomplish. It had been an unusually busy year for all of us as Johnny was, in addition to his law practice, serving as the president of the board of the Charleston Symphony Orchestra. It was a time of change for that organization and he was constantly conducting business for them. I was teaching horseback riding several afternoons a week and was president of the Junior League of Charleston. The latter is always a time consuming job, but we were hosting a huge fundraising party to celebrate the opening of the new Charleston airport at the end of March which left me with little free time. My calendar for the first five months of 1985 was black with meetings, riding lessons and carpools, before we started working in earnest on the boat. After we took the plunge and threw ourselves into this new commitment, we rarely had time to sleep. In fact, Johnny and I hardly saw each other, mostly communicating by telephone at moments snatched from the day.

We had Lists...and we had a List of Lists. We assigned each list to one of us to complete. Johnny kept the List of Lists and kept tabs on who was doing what.

Sequoiah, being ten years old, needed innumerable things replaced or repaired before the kind of trip we had planned. Johnny did much of the work himself, such as removing and refitting all of the ports and hatches, installing an extra port and a vent in the galley, and installing the new cabin heater, head, electronics, and stove. We were lucky to have expert help from several local men. Tom Pierson was retired, but enjoyed doing cabinet work. He made a new salon table for us as well as building new mahogany lockers, drawers, and a navigation tabletop. He also built a mahogany box in the cockpit to house two extra propane tanks. Since it was to go behind the helmsman's seat, he designed the forward side of the box to match the angle of his kitchen chairs so that it would make a comfortable back rest for whoever was steering. We saw a lot of Tom in those last hectic months. In fact, he almost drove me crazy because he did everything at his own pace and wouldn't settle for less than perfection. He said he was retired and only worked for the fun of it, and it wasn't fun if he had to hurry. I think he found me too bossy, for one day he told Johnny that he might be the captain of the boat but "she's the Admiral!" He managed to finish everything in time for our departure date and we have always been glad he was such a perfectionist. His work is beautiful and we have enjoyed living with it.

Another friend, Walter Prause, and his son, did our rigging work. They replaced all of the standing rigging and we kept some of the old wire for spares. Walter also did a myriad of other small jobs around the boat, helping us tie up all sorts of loose ends.

During February and March we removed everything possible from the interior of the boat. We needed all the space we could get and also wanted to make an inventory of everything we had aboard. Caroline and John helped with the sanding of the teak, both inside and out. We managed in less than a month to make a giant mess aboard Sequoiah.

Disorder reigned equally at home. I had all the berth cushions spread out on the living room floor so I could measure them for the sheets that I was trying to custom fit. Charts covered the library rug, and in one corner lay a large duffel bag that was our emergency kit, to be taken along in the life raft if ever we were forced to abandon ship. As things were collected we added them to our lists and cross references. The United Parcel Service truck made almost daily stops at our front door delivering the innumerable supplies and spare parts that we were unable to find locally. The stacks of charts were catalogued gradually and folded to fit in the new drawers Tom had built under the chart table.

Sometimes when we looked through the charts, pilot books, and cruising guides, reading the unfamiliar, tantalizing names of foreign ports, my heart grew tight with mingling excitement and apprehension as the realization of what we had set in motion swept over me. With just a few words we had changed our lives. At other times I had a feeling of elation so intense that I thought my throat would close up and my heart would burst through my skin. It was a sensation too large to be contained within me, yet too intangible to be expressed through words.

Those last few months before departure were unbeliev-able. How we got through them I can hardly remember. I think the last week in March must have been one of the worst. I had Junior League meetings of one committee or another every morning. I was helping to decorate the airport for the grand opening party for 2500 people that Friday night. We had a party, concert, or meeting to attend every night that week. I was teaching riding lessons and Sunday school, help-ing with the Symphony Designer house and one of Historic Charleston Foundation's house tours; not to mention that Weesie was home for Spring break, Caroline and John were having a week of tests, since it was their last week of school before their Spring break, and every day new parts were arriv-ing for the boat.

On the morning of April 1, two months before our pro-jected departure, I arrived at the marina to find Sequoiah's companionway closed as usual, but the lock was gone. I went inside and found the place quite neat except... we'd been robbed! Someone had taken time to do it carefully. The entire navigation area was empty. Gone were the Loran, VHF radio, radio direction finder, clock, and barometer, all the wires care-fully unplugged or cleanly cut. Gone were binoculars, stereo, and tape deck. Gone were all the new fittings that had arrived the day before. Gone were a Polaroid camera, flashlights, and many other items that had been stacked on a berth waiting to be put away. It was a dark moment. The police took fin-gerprints and photographs and said they'd call us if anything turned up. Nothing did. We felt violated somehow, and had a feeling that this thief had been watching us for a while, probably knew our schedule, and had given himself plenty of time to methodically strip Sequoiah of valuables. That day we moved the boat to Town Creek Boatyard where she was sched-uled to have the main mast removed and all standing rigging replaced, and there she stayed for the next six weeks.

Fortunately, our insurance helped to replace some of the equipment lost in the robbery. That was the first and last claim we would make on Sequoiah. We talked to our insurance agent about coverage for our intended trip, not anticipating more difficulty than an exorbitant premium. After a few weeks the agent called back to give us the news that unless we had three qualified adults on board, there was no company that would insure us. We didn't bother to ask what "qualified" meant. This was a minor setback in our eyes; we were going on this trip. Columbus made it without insurance, and we would too.

Town Creek Boatyard is completely fenced except on the river side. It is located in a lonely part of town near the State Ports Authority docks. Johnny rose before dawn and worked there until midmorning when he left for his office. At five o'clock he was back in his blue jeans and working again until midnight. On weekends, between soccer games, horse shows, etc., the whole family could be found there sanding, painting, polishing, fixing. One Sunday afternoon, for some reason, I was on board Sequoiah alone in the deserted yard. I had music playing and my head was inside the locker that I was painting, when I heard voices. As I backed out of the locker and looked around, I saw an unfamiliar face peering at me upside down from the forward hatch. Our eyes locked for an instant and then he disappeared. By the time I reached the cockpit two young men were swiftly descending the twelve foot ladder propped against the hull.

"What do you think you're doing here?" I demanded in my sternest schoolmarm imitation.

"We was just lookin'," came the surly answer from a retreating figure. I was shaking as I watched them run down to the marsh and wade through the mud and rocks, making their hasty departure. Both were twice my size. I counted myself lucky that they were only "looking", and resolved to take Gerta for company if ever I went alone again.

There were days when I looked around hopelessly at the horrible mess: empty holes covered with plastic where the ports should be, partially completed cabinets, head floor torn up, wires, hoses, and wood shavings everywhere, and I despaired of ever finishing. I can remember crying and asking Johnny why we had ever thought of trying to do this.

Somehow, by May, most jobs were almost finished. The new Seafrost refrigerator freezer was installed, and the crane arrived to replace the mast. That was quite an operation: lifting the mast, lowering it gently into that tiny hole in the deck and dropping it through the cabin and onto its step on the keel. The new head arrived from England with a crack in the porcelain bowl. With only two weeks left, I was afraid the replacement wouldn't come in time, and I, for one, wasn't leaving without that vital piece of equipment! I think I was beginning to panic.

At last the bottom was painted, and the boat was ready to return to her proper element. When the lift softly set Sequoiah back in the water, she began to flood immediately and the cabin sole was underwater within seconds. We shouted to the lift operator and Sequoiah came up again. When she was pumped dry the water didn't seem to want to leave as quickly as it had entered. We discovered that a cockpit drain gasket was leaking and the intake seacock for the head was open. Sequoiah had been on the land too long! Seacock closed and gasket replaced, back in she went, and she floated this time.

The next week was spent loading Sequoiah until she sat low in the water, right up on her new, higher waterline. All of our new equipment, linens and towels, books, clothes, non-perishable foods and other necessities were brought aboard by the carload. I made two major trips to grocery and discount stores, entirely filling my big station wagon each time. When it was all aboard and stowed, there was still more unused space, so I did it again. Only this time everything didn't fit. Barbara Zimmerman came to my rescue. She spent hours moving cans and boxes and, with the art of a magician, she managed to find a place for everything. While she worked her magic, I catalogued each item, the amount and location, in my book of cross referenced lists.

When all was in order, Johnny and I took Sequoiah out for a three day sea trial, testing the new suit of Hood sails, the new Dickinson stove, and the new head that had finally arrived intact. We tried to light the new kerosene cabin heater for the first time, but I forgot to take the rubber stopper out of the chimney. This produced flames, black smoke and black language, fortunately with no lasting damage...one of the many times we felt we were taking three steps backward for each one taken in the right direction.

Unbelievably we were approaching the end of our lists. At least most were only a half page long now instead of many pages each! We were almost ready to go.

CHAPTER FIVE

DETAILS

So many diverse details go into the planning of a long cruise. Provisioning, preparing medical and emergency kits, making arrangements for our house and car, mail, and school were some of the things we had to work out before we left for a year of sailing.

According to Funk and Wagnall's New Practical Standard Dictionary, provision is defined as a transitive verb, "to provide with the means of meeting a future want; specifically, to furnish with a food supply". It is a word constantly in use among sailors, with its wonderful connotations conjuring up visions of lockers overflowing with good things, giving a sense of preparedness and well-being. When I consider provisions for a cruising yacht, I include in my definition, not only food and drink, but also household and personal items that make life aboard worth living.

The thought of provisioning the boat for more than two or three weeks seemed overwhelming when we first began sailing. In anticipation of our first cruise to the Bahamas, I started planning. For me this was half the fun. In an easily-carried notebook I kept lists of everything we used regularly at home. I paid close attention to what just sat on the shelves and what we actually used and enjoyed. I also did lots of experimenting. Before going sailing I had not used canned meats and vegetables. I was surprised at the great variety and disappointed by the taste. By spending extra time in the grocery store I discovered all sorts of things I never knew existed. Today there are, besides canned foods, specially packaged items that will last many times longer than fresh foods. Frequently I tried to incorporate into our regular meals, dishes that utilized ingredients with a long shelf life.

I well remember the first time I took home canned corned beef. There was a recipe on the side of the can that I prepared for dinner. As I recall, the whole chunk of meat was placed on a baking sheet, glazed, studded with cloves and heated until warm enough to eat. It was so simple and sounded quite palatable. I thought I had found a real mainstay meal that would impress everyone when we were offshore in nasty weather. Wrong! The entire family rebelled. Only Gerta, my loyal dog, was happy that night, and she never goes sailing. Since then I have tried it several other ways, but to this day my crew won't touch canned corned beef...if they recognize it! I learned quickly that a good sea cook must be a master of invention and disguise.

We tried recipes from cruising books and magazines, especially helpful as they usually include long-lasting ingredients. Also, substituting canned or freeze-dried foods for fresh ingredients in our favorite recipes made some interesting meals. For example, I added reconstituted freeze-dried beef cubes to a tomato sauce to serve on spaghetti noodles. I found that this beef was equally as good when combined with one of the packaged rice mixes such as Uncle Ben's Long Grain and Wild Rice, or Rice Florentine. Herbs, too, played a large part in my experimenting. Dried herbs keep well in airtight containers and can usually be found the world over. They add zest to any meal and provide much-needed variety on a long passage. I also paid attention to which cookbooks I was using most frequently. I love cookbooks, but, for lack of space, could choose only a few to travel with us. The Joy of Cooking, that wonderful basic book by Rombauer and Becker, was the mainstay of my galley. It has directions on how to prepare anything that is edible. I also took with me a copy of The Enlightened Gourmet, written by friends, that contains some wonderful, adaptable recipes, and naturally, Charleston Receipts, the Junior League of Charleston's book of regional favorites on which we grew up. A card file of my own recipes stayed on the galley counter, being used and added to constantly. I am always inventing new recipes. Some turn out to be quite good, and I have learned to write things down as I go so the best results can be repeated.

Johnny's father brought me some canned bacon and ham requiring no refrigeration that he found at the K-Mart stores. The bacon in particular was delicious and, following his lead, I discovered excellent prices on paper products and canned foods at large discount stores and warehouses in the area.

There are also many mail order companies that have good buys on foods and specialty items. Johnny enjoys barbequed meat, and was excited to find a magazine advertisement about Smithfield Ham Company's canned pork and beef with barbeque sauce. We sent for samples to try, and they proved to be palatable substitutes for fresh barbeque when extra sauce was added. It has become a popular staple aboard Sequoiah and one that is quick and easy as well.

We learned the hard way to try new products before buying in quantity. This saves money and great unpleasantness later! One of our most disappointing mistakes, for the children in particular, was when we were leaving England hurriedly in October. We had lingered far too long enjoying the unusually pleasant Indian summer, and were racing with time to beat the first of the winter gales. The day before departure Caroline and I dashed through the supermarket selecting a number of intriguing looking items including canned beef burgers.

"Oh, boy! We can have hamburgers for our Thousand Mile Party!" she exclaimed happily. We kept this find a secret for weeks, then served up the great surprise for a mid Atlantic feast. Imagine everyone's dismay when we bit into those tasteless, spongy rounds!

Another detail to be addressed was formal schooling for the children. We looked into several options and after some research and the concurrence of the local schools, decided on Calvert School in Baltimore, Maryland. Calvert School was founded in 1898 and, over the years, has developed courses for each level, kindergarten through eighth grade, that are demanding, yet not overwhelming. Each course is divided into daily lessons with review sessions built in, and tests required at regular intervals. Tests are administered by the home teachers, in this case Johnny and me, and then are sent to Calvert School to be graded by an assigned teacher. These courses are used by many people who, like us, are traveling, or people living in areas of this country or abroad where the educational offerings are either poor or non-existent. Two cardboard boxes arrived one day in May, holding John's and Caroline's school courses. Inside each was everything needed for the entire year including paper, pencils, rulers and books. After looking through all the materials we added a typewriter and lots more paper, pens, crayons and pencils, and stored all of it away in the locker we had set aside for school supplies. On the trip across the Atlantic the children would read selections from history and art books to prepare them for all they would see in Europe. In addition, they would write book reports and compositions each week and keep daily journals. I was, and I think the children, too, were actually looking forward to this different approach to education, so the eventual outcome had nothing to do with our initial outlook.

Medical emergencies at sea are high on the list of problems that must be considered while planning trans-oceanic passages. When Johnny and I first decided to take this trip a major concern was that only Caroline had had her appendix removed. To me that meant we would be taking along four time bombs with the potential to explode at any time, destroying not only the trip but possibly a life. We had heard horror stories of emergency operations at sea, and we wanted no part of that. Charles Geer, who, besides being a good friend, was also our family physician. He had reviewed our medical kit annually for years, and he spent much time and thought preparing us for this voyage. Together we discussed the pros and cons of elective surgery prior to departure. Charles was opposed to appendectomies en masse for us, mainly because he felt the chances of that problem developing were relatively small. We knew that during the longest offshore passage, from the Canaries to Barbados, probably we would be no more than fifteen sailing days away from land at any given point. Charles thought we could keep someone alive on antibiotics for that length of time. He was more concerned that we knew how to clean wounds, suture, and administer injections correctly. He made notes in our medical books and listed all medicines in our first aid kit and their uses.

Even knowing we had on board everything necessary to cope with most medical emergencies did not keep me from worrying about appendicitis, just as so many long distance sailors do. I have my own peculiar theory about disasters. The worst things in life are always unexpected, so I believe that if my worst fears are regularly kept in mind, they won't happen. Therefore, in spite of all reassurances, I worried about appendicitis for nine thousand miles. When we reached Barbados, I checked appendicitis off my current list with a big sigh of relief. After all, we were back on the right side of the ocean.

I thought we were home free. Little did I know that later I would come to regret this omission.

An emergency bag, for use in case we had to abandon ship, was, like the medicines we carried, another of the things we hoped never to use, but felt necessary to have along. Our six man Avon life raft was mounted on the foredeck. When we bought it, we tested it in the store, pulling the cord to activate the CO_2 cartridges that rapidly inflated it. The raft came with only a few supplies, and we added to those in addition to filling a duffel bag with everything we couldn't fit in the raft. It was hard to envision what we would want in the event of extreme disaster. We had read several accounts of survival written by people who had lived for months in their life rafts, and from their experiences we arrived at a list of those things we might need.

A nagging loose end was the question of our house. We had advertised it for rent, fully furnished, since we didn't want the added expense of moving and storing everything, but most of the calls we received were young couples hoping that maybe we might be persuaded to let them "house sit" rent free for a year, or families with their own furniture. Time was running out and our optimism was beginning to ebb when we heard that the Board of Roper Hospital was looking for a furnished place to house the hospital's new administrator and his family while their house was being renovated. This was the ideal solution, and we were able to walk out confidently leaving everything in place and forgetting it all for a year knowing it would be well maintained.

Since Johnny generally walked to work, we had only one car. We really didn't want to sell it, as it was just a year old. The Geers had been looking for a new car, and it worked out that they could use it, postponing a purchase.

The problem of mail and bill paying while we were away was solved by Johnny's secretary, Carol Speicher, who took over for us. We changed our address to a Post Office Box and Carol checked it, most convenient for her when she retired as a legal secretary and joined the Postal Service. Carol threw out the junk mail, opened all bills, and paid them with checks signed by Johnny's father, Hertz, who had Johnny's power of attorney. She collected all other mail of interest to us and forwarded it at intervals to prearranged places. This was a constant and boring job, but one of great importance to all cruisers, and we will always be grateful to Carol for taking it on.

There was, however, one aspect of mail that bothered me in particular. I like to write letters, but as June drew closer I had promised to write to so many friends that I couldn't even remember who I'd promised. Kitty Beard must have read my thoughts. She called one day and said she, being a sailor too, wanted to hear from us in detail but realized that we wouldn't be able to do that for everyone so she had a proposal. Her idea was that we should write one long letter at intervals and send it to her. Anyone who wanted to hear from us could send her their self-addressed stamped envelopes, and she would make as many copies as needed. This turned out to be a super idea. I wrote Kitty's address and her instructions on the same sheet with our tentative itinerary and our address, and gave copies to friends and family. During the year when I sat down to write, it was wonderful to know I would have to do it only once! Of course we all wrote postcards and individual letters to special friends. I tried to return a letter to everyone who wrote me, in addition to what I began to call the Big Letter that I sent about once a month.

There was another problem, however trivial it may seem, and that was the problem of farewell parties. So many people wanted to have them for us that we had to say no to all, or we would never have had time to get the boat ready for departure. There would have been a steady round of festivities for months! It meant so much to us to have our friends think of us in such a thoughtful way. The trouble was that we didn't want offend them and we did want to have a chance to say goodbye to everybody, so we gave a Bon Voyage party ourselves the week before we left. It was great fun. All the food was done by Walter Prause, that man of many talents. Besides his great knowledge about yachts and their upkeep, he has a catering business. The food he made for our party was outstanding, and we especially enjoyed the artistically carved watermelon sailboat loaded with fruit. A Bon Voyage party means you have to go somewhere...and pretty soon too! People might get tired of seeing you around and begin to say, "When are you leaving? We thought you'd already gone."

June 4th was our target date for leaving. Even with the Lists shorter, we could tell there was no chance that everything would be done by then. We realized we would have to leave without completing every task. Later, in talking to other sailors and would-be cruisers, I found that this was the norm. We have yet to meet anyone who claims to have finished all that needed to be done before casting off. Those who think perfection is the key requisite for leaving are still at the dock trying to attain the impossible.

Our last day at home was a whirlwind. Richard Morrison, John's alter ego, went with Johnny and John to top off the fuel tanks. Then, while Johnny spent the rest of the morning running errands, the children and I made a stop at the bank to get travelers checks. Johnny had been by earlier in the week to get most of them but we wanted everyone to have some. When I told the woman at the desk that we wanted mostly hundreds she said, "We don't have many of those left. A man came in a few days ago and practically bought us out, and our new supply hasn't arrived yet."

So we had to settle for fifties and twenties. A year's supply of travelers checks took an hour to sign with all of us writing as fast as we could! This turned out to be time well spent. In addition to our American Express and Master Cards, travelers checks gave us the assurance of ready cash. We found that they were accepted virtually everywhere we went. John was the only one to have any trouble cashing them. When we were in Nassau nearly a year later on our last leg home, he went to a bank with his passport for identification and signed his name very neatly on his check. The teller asked for more proof of his identity for she said, "Your signatures don't match." John was quite upset and I had to go back to the bank with him to explain that his handwriting had improved dramatically in the past year. The teller was young and obviously had no growing boys of her own.

From the bank we returned to the marina, and all five of us spent that final afternoon aboard Sequoiah. Eleanor and Barbara brought groceries down to the dock. It was wonderful having them do the last minute shopping! Mother and Barbara stowed all the fresh food. A large crowd of Caroline's friends came down to say goodbye and family and friends came and went with hugs, promises, and tears. We had hoped to leave about six that night, but I listened to the weather forecast of severe thunderstorms everywhere and complained until Johnny gave in to my cowardly insistence that we stay put for the night. We went out to dinner with Mother, had one last real shower at her house, and spent the night at the marina. To this day Johnny marvels that he agreed to this. However, he humored me, and we all enjoyed a good night's sleep.

CHAPTER SIX

"LET'S SAIL TO ENGLAND!"

Johnny woke us before daylight on June 5, and by the time we were dressed Mother and Hertz were on the dock, cameras in hand. It was an emotional moment as we took our dock lines aboard and glided silently away from our life ashore. Well, almost silently. There was much sniffing and unsuppressed sobbing from most of us on board as we waved our tearful goodbyes to family we wouldn't see for many months.

Dawn came slowly through banks of clouds as we raised the sails and coasted down the Ashley River past the Battery with its rows of stately old homes, and out through the harbor past the ruins of Castle Pinckney and historic Fort Sumter. Our moods matched the gray of the morning until, as we passed through the jetties, Johnny called out, "Let's sail to England!" which brought smiles all around and lifted our spirits.

"Why not!" we answered, and set our course for Bermuda. We were really on the way! The first leg towards our destination had begun.

The six hundred miles to Bermuda had always loomed before us as a major ocean voyage when viewed in the context of a summer vacation cruise, but as part of an 11,000 mile, year–long venture it was just a baby step in the right direction.

The boat was charged with tension. Each of us was feeling the magnitude of what we were attempting, not all of us willingly. I was filled with conflicting emotions that day. Part of me exulted in the sense of adventure that washed over me, and the excitement of challenging the unknown. Part of me was shocked by the reality of breaking with the accepted lifestyle expected of us. Looking back at the receding shoreline, it was hard to believe that we wouldn't see it again for a year. I was frightened, too, for we were so small on this wide expanse of moving water. On another level, beyond the physical, fear made me wonder how we would be changed by this deviation from all we held as normal. Would we gain some new strengths and insights; or would we return, our lives shattered by as yet unknown consequences of a crazy dream? My racing thoughts were in turmoil as Charleston disappeared into the western horizon.

That first day out was, fortunately, rather easy. Hot and cloudy with a steady south-east breeze, the automatic pilot doing the steering, we were able to spend our time finishing jobs left undone in the wild rush of the last few days before departure. We all pitched in, wrapping fruits and vegetables individually in tissue paper, replacing a loose wire to the log, whipping the ends of some lines, and replacing a faulty water pump, at the same time trying to accustom ourselves again to the constant motion of the sea.

We all took small doses of Antivert every six hours. On board we carried a number of other seasickness preventatives, including the popular scopolamine patches that can be worn behind the ear (they work without fail, but can have some unpleasant side effects) and elastic bracelets with buttons that are highly touted by acupressure advocates. (I actually paid money for these and, with adverse results, tried them on a day that wasn't particularly rough. Maybe I just needed to believe harder!) Over the years we have found that the prescription drug, Antivert, works best for us. Caroline and I are the only ones who have much problem with motion sickness, but whenever we start out on a trip we all take something for a day or two to avoid any illness. After about five or six days even Caroline and I are able to do without medicine, and only use it as needed if the weather gets rough. It takes time to become adjusted to continual movement.

Somehow a great lethargy overcomes me at sea. I always think that, with so much time to do as I please, I will be able to accomplish those things that bustling city life never leaves time for. Drawing, painting, playing the guitar, studying French, all these are available and enticing; but when I am free I lie on my bunk and sleep, read, or just think about those things I will do when I have more energy. The constant motion at sea affects me that way.

On a boat at sea everyone takes a turn at standing watch. As the days passed we fell into a kind of routine which, of course, could vary at any time due to weather changes, or the sighting of a ship too close, or just a school of dolphin frolicking nearby. We have tried many different methods and have found that we seem to do better when we have the same sleeping hours every day rather than rotating them.

Usually Johnny woke up at 6:00 AM and John and I went to bed where we generally stayed until lunch time. Weesie and Caroline woke up midmorning and had breakfast with Johnny. Caroline fixed lunch and John and I went on watch at noon until 3:00 PM. Everyone was up during that time so it was rather lively...game playing, heated discussions, deck showers, playing musical instruments (we had a guitar and three recorders aboard), and navigation instruction. At 3:00 Caroline and Weesie took watch for three hours while Johnny took a nap or read. John read, fished, or bothered the girls, and I read and cooked. Dinner was between six and seven and we all watched from 6:00 to 8:00 since everyone was up and alert. At 8:00 the children wrote in their journals and we all prepared for bed except the captain who kept watch until midnight. At that time Weesie and Caroline stood watch until 3:00 when John and I took over until dawn, and it all started again.

To stand watch is an old nautical term that must go back to early naval days when the ship's officers were required to stand at the wheel during their watch. However, in our case, perhaps I should say sitting watch or often it was lying down watch. With the modern conveniences of an automatic pilot as well as the Aries, a wind-propelled mechanical device, we rarely had to steer by hand at all. Every ten or fifteen minutes we would check the compass heading and scan the horizon for ships; and each hour the speed, mileage, course, wind and sea conditions, and barometric pressure were recorded in the deck log. Watch time, at night, was a quiet time. Learning the stars was a favorite pastime. Reading and listening to music or to the short-wave radio were also good ways to pass the hours on watch.

It took several days and numerous changes before we reached this routine that worked so well for everyone. Most of the other jobs on board were allocated considering skills and interests. I cooked dinner at night and the children took turns cleaning the galley my skills and interest, not theirs! I cleaned the head (skill, but no interest), while they swept the cabins and scrubbed the cockpit (again, great skill but a distinct lack of interest). Johnny and John did most of the sail changing and foredeck work with occasional help from the girls. Johnny, besides being the captain, also was the diesel mechanic, electrician, plumber, and chief navigator. While Johnny's interests did not always lie with each individual job, his interest in our overall safety was constant and his skills were always increasing.

Sequoiah's seagoing cleaning crew, Weesie and Caroline, at work

Meals were very good on that first leg. Conrad Zimmerman had smoked two turkey breasts for us and the first was so delicious I put the other in the freezer to save for later. Eleanor's trip to Leland Farms had been over productive. Farmers must eat huge helpings! When I had called to order fresh vegetables, I asked for enough snap beans and squash for two meals. We ate them for six days straight and still had a grocery bag full! The crew threatened mutiny if the cook found even one more interesting way to prepare either beans or squash. Caroline thought the fish might like them and offered to deliver the vegetables personally.

Our second night out of Charleston, we were sailing quietly at 4–5 knots under jib, main, and mizzen sails. From my seat near the wheel I could see John slumped over the book he'd been reading under the protection of the dodger, the soft, red glow of the compass light hazily illuminating his silhouette. It was a dark night but an even darker wall seemed to be closing in on us from behind. I blinked and rubbed my eyes. Was it fog, or a cloud? Or was it rain?

"John, John! Wake up and look at this," I called to the prostrate form.

"Huh? What's going on?" answered a sleepy voice from the corner as John came slowly awake. Then, "What in the world is that?!"

"I'm not sure...but it doesn't look good," I said, peering astern at the growing opacity.

As his eyes adjusted to the blackness surrounding us, John shouted, "We're gonna get it!"

The black wall had kept advancing and now, with it almost upon us, we could see that it held menacing clouds with wind churning the water before it as it came. We yelled to Johnny sleeping below, who dashed up on deck to help John drop the mainsail just as the first hefty gust slapped us. For the next hour we ran with the wind off our port quarter steering a snake's path through all points of the compass as the quick windy squall lashed at us from one direction and then another. It was a rainless windstorm, so when it was over we were able to reset the wind vane and curl up on our pillows to read again in dry comfort, or at least try. Somehow I always find squalls, no matter how brief, to be somewhat unsettling, and it takes me a while to unwind and relax again. Shel Silverstein's "WhatIfs" keep leaping into my mind.

We had celebrated Johnny's birthday at sea for over ten years, so the tradition continued as it occurred again our second day out. John, unable to find "Happy Birthday" in any of our music books, spent his spare time that afternoon trying to pick out the tune on the recorder by ear. He succeeded admirably, and after supper, as Caroline brought Aunt Betty's pound cake from its careful hiding place decorated with a full complement of 39 candles, he played and the rest of us sang "Happy Birthday Dear Daddy, Happy Birthday to You". I had a local watercolor artist do a painting of our house before we left, and we hung it in the main salon for a birthday surprise. During the year it brightened the cabin and served as a reminder of home.

Early on the morning of our sixth day at sea, we calculated that we were three miles south of Bermuda, and all of us were on deck taking turns peering through the binoculars anxiously hoping to catch our first view of this island nation. Bermuda has an area of just over twenty square miles, and many ships have been known to miss it altogether. It is nerve-wracking when you think you're close, but can't see the land. There is always that tiny nagging trace of doubt, lurking in the corner of the mind. Has the navigation of the past days been accurate? There was only one way to know, and we kept searching the horizon. When we were two miles off, by our reckoning, we finally saw a white line to the north that gradually grew into a long rooftop. Through the haze it was hard to tell where cloud ended and roof began. As we drew nearer, the landscape slowly came into focus, gently sloping green hills littered with white rooftops. Though the houses were painted every color of the rainbow, all had these whitewashed, terraced roofs designed especially to catch water. Bermuda has no rivers or natural springs so all fresh water is processed through desalinators or caught on rooftops in rain showers. Each house has its own 30-50 thousand gallon tank for water storage, with pipes leading straight into it from the roof. We were told, perhaps with tongue in cheek, that each tank is required by law to have a goldfish in it, to keep the tank clean and eat any mosquito larvae that might be laid on the water. It is certainly true that there were no gnats or mosquitoes evident in June. We had no use for our screens while we were there.

As we motored through the entrance into St. George's harbor, we were accompanied by four yachts from the U.S. Naval Academy. The girls were impressed by the handsome young men lining the decks dressed in blue and white. We discovered later that they had sailed from Charleston the same day that we had left, and this was the first we had seen of them. It's a big ocean and, relatively speaking, a small horizon from the deck of a sailboat.

After six long days at sea our entire crew was ready for a change of pace. Except for an eleven day trip to Tortola which I had made several years earlier aboard a friend's yacht, this was the longest passage for any of us, four-day trips to the Bahamas being our longest until now. As soon as Larry (the friendly and efficient Customs officer who came aboard to acknowledge officially our arrival in Bermuda) waved goodbye, Weesie and Caroline were disappearing into the village of St. George's, each carrying her own weight in dirty laundry. While they located the best ice cream in town (first things first!) and the laundromat, the rest of us moved Sequoiah from the Customs dock and anchored out in the harbor. Anchoring was easy as the holding ground is good at St. Georges. When John inflated the Avon, Johnny discovered to our dismay, the ancient four-horsepower outboard had quietly died in the bottom of a sail locker. After hours of trying to revive it he gave up and rowed to town against big winds and waves to collect the girls, vowing to change things on the morrow.

Bermuda was all we had thought it would be. The country was lovely with soft hills sloping down to the brilliant blues and greens of the water. Many plants were in bloom but my favorites were the bougainvillea which grow to tree size there, and the hibiscus, which the Bermudans use everywhere as hedges.

We remained anchored in St. George's harbor during our eight day stay, using taxi, bus, and motorbike to see everything beyond walking distance. The first few days were spent as regular tourists visiting forts, museums, an aquarium, and a dolphin show. We taxied to the capital city of Hamilton where we bought a new outboard. The children spent one night there at the Princess Hotel, mostly taking turns soaking in the bathtub, after they discovered that the swimming pool contained salt water. One day we met June Stanton, the sister of a Charleston friend, and her husband, both native Bermudans, for lunch at the Coral Beach Club. The meal was served on a high terrace with a spectacular view overlooking the outlying reefs. After a stroll around the club, eleven year old John announced seriously, "This is where I'm coming for my honeymoon." And a good choice it would be, too!

Lunch at the Coral Beach Club in Bermuda,
John's idea of a good honeymoon destination.

Early June was cool in Bermuda with the temperature in the mid eighties by day becoming pleasantly chilly at night, and we went swimming and snorkeling much less than we'd thought at first. Johnny and John did swim out to an offshore reef outside Tobacco Bay, where they briefly made the acquaintance of a large group of reef sharks and beat a hasty retreat!

The end of our week in Bermuda was spent doing minor repairs and finishing little jobs that we had not completed before leaving home. In the process of greasing the jib halyard winch, a bearing was dropped and, almost like watching a slow motion film, Johnny saw it roll across the cabin top, down along the deck, and over the side. He tried to note our exact position, donned his SCUBA gear and dove for it. Unfortunately we were in over forty feet of water and the wind was strong. We were blowing around too much and Johnny finally had to give up the search. We also managed to lose our big wrench overboard but, mercifully, I cannot remember how that happened!

On Sunday morning John and I went to the service at St. Peter's Church in St. George's which is located on the site of the oldest church in the Western hemisphere. We were surprised to be seated next to some sailing acquaintances from Charleston, Steve and Sue Herlong. Later they came aboard for a visit and we found that they were on a vacation cruise aboard Rise, their Tayana 37. They planned to wait another year before crossing the "big pond", so we promised to keep in touch and tell them about our adventures.

The day before we were to leave, the wind was gusting up to thirty four miles per hour in the harbor. The inflatable Avon with our new outboard on the stern had been carelessly tied in a hurry by `Not me' and had worked itself free. There were good sized waves and white caps everywhere and the dinghy was floating away fast. While the rest of us stood there stupidly trying to decide what to do, John, without a moment's hesitation, dove over the side and swam after it. My heart was in my throat as we watched him in the turbulent water. John managed to scramble aboard the little tender and start the engine just moments before it drifted into the old rusting hulk of a half sunken ship, and disaster was averted. Having grown up around the water, and with an agile mind and body, John was well on his way to being quite a seaman.

On Tuesday, June 18, we cleared customs and left Bermuda, heading east for the Azores, after taking showers and filling our tanks with fuel and water. The water in Bermuda tasted wonderful and cost five cents a gallon, something we didn't appreciate as much at the time as we would in retrospect. Many times later we remembered that delicious water when we had to fill our tanks with a liquid bearing the same name, but hardly recognizable as such. Those later times we were so glad we had splurged and bought our wonderful Sea Gull IV water purifier that filtered out bacteria, chemicals, salt, and other contaminants, as well as bad odors and taste. Quite compact, it was mounted under the galley sink and the cartridges were easy to change. Since water is my favorite drink, I counted that little contraption as one of the best additions to boat life.

The first few days out of Bermuda we had a good breeze behind us which made for an uncomfortable rolling motion. We all felt a bit queasy off and on, but none of us were really sick. With the following wind and waves throwing us around so erratically, neither wind vane nor Autohelm were able to hold the course, and we had the onerous chore of hand steering. We found steering a tedious, muscle building occupation, and one universally disliked aboard Sequoiah. Having portable tape players with earphones made the job more bearable. With a story or music to listen to, the time went by more quickly.

While in Bermuda we had met several boats bound for Ponta Delgada in the Azores for a Cruising Club of America rally, and they gave us their radio schedule for the crossing. We had only a receiver and could not talk on the net (Johnny said the females in the family would spend all their time talking if we had single sideband), but the passage was made more interesting by being able to listen to the others. Since most of them left Bermuda a day or so ahead of us, we actually were able to avoid some bad weather by listening to their experiences and noting their positions. The crew of one yacht had an unfortunate accident when they unknowingly pumped their fresh water supply overboard and had to rely on other liquids to keep them going for the last week of their voyage. They were rationing beer and juices, and the coffee made with the remaining water was at a premium. Another yacht was heard on the radio teasing them with reports of daily fresh water showers from their 500 gallon supply, kept topped up with a water maker, and ice cubes with their evening cocktails. A real cruelty joke!

Occasionally we would see a Shearwater or a Bermuda long tail our first week out, but as our distance from land increased the bird population seemed to diminish. We saw flotillas of Portuguese Man O War bobbing along with their pink and purple sails aloft. Several times porpoises joined us for awhile. One afternoon about fifty or sixty of them came leaping through the waves from behind us and raced on by. Wherever they were headed, they were in too big a hurry to stop and play. It was an unforgettable sight!

One morning the sun rose up very round and orange heralding stillness without a breath of breeze. For two days we motored through a calm. The water was so flat and of such clarity it seemed that if our eyes were more powerful they should be able to see the ocean floor miles below. The temperature during the day averaged 79 degrees which felt hot in the sunshine, but at night we were beginning to need long pants and windbreakers to ward off the chill.

Aboard Sequoiah we carry 100 gallons of diesel fuel. Since we burn one half gallon an hour when motoring at five knots we have about a one thousand mile range. (Sounds like one of those sixth grade word problems, doesn't it?) Our trip to the Azores would be over 1800 miles so we were reluctant to continue motoring, not knowing how long we would be becalmed. We wanted to save enough fuel to motor into the harbor at Horta if necessary. We put up the big drifter and staysail trying to trap the tiniest breath of air, but finally gave up, lowering them again, unable to bear the sound of their continual slamming. Instead, we put the ladder over the side, deciding to go for a swim. Suddenly, standing on the deck looking down into the bottomless depths, a strange apprehensiveness overcame us all, keeping us frozen there for minutes. What if Sequoiah drifted away? What if "Something" came and ate us? The "WhatIfs" were at it again. That endless deep blue below looked so clear and inviting, yet the immensity of it was somehow frightening. Johnny took the lead, diving from the bow and swimming back to the ladder.

"Come on in. The water's fine." he called enticingly, then threatened to throw us overboard when his encouragements brought no movement from the cabin top where we sat watching. One by one the children jumped in. When they got used to it, they relaxed and enjoyed themselves. At last I took a turn too, finding it a refreshing change from the hot stillness on deck. Nonetheless I couldn't help looking around nervously for hungry sharks, with the theme music from the film, "Jaws", pounding in my head. Our national shark phobia, fed by the media, had surfaced from within me. Although we didn't discuss it, I think there was a bit of it in all of us that day, a fluttering of unnamed fear just below consciousness. There was no current, and other than the grand scale of the surroundings, swimming out there, halfway across the Atlantic, was no different than swimming in a lake, yet the feel of it was worlds apart, quite unique.

As the still afternoon wore on we all wished for wind. Weesie and John tried whistling for it. Caroline and Johnny tried shouting, heads thrown back towards the sky, "We want wind! Give us a gale!" Superstition kept me quiet. Wind would be nice, but please not a gale!

Around midnight a light zephyr found us and teased a while before deserting us again. Several hours later during my watch, we got a strong dose of wind. It had been drizzling off and on all night with lightning in the background. Suddenly we felt the first gusts of a squall buffeting us, and the erratic motion woke Johnny, who ran up, attaching his lifeline as he came, in time to help John drop the main and secure it as the first needles of stinging rain hit us. I took the wheel and fought to hold her on course as the sudden onslaught of thirty-five knot winds swirled around us. John loosed the jib and mizzen sheets, only to pull them tight when the wind shifted again. The lightning was severe and illuminated the sky eerily for several seconds at a time. Once it struck the water close ahead of us and another time to port; I could smell the scent of burning sulphur in the air. The rain was a welcome supplement to the water in our tanks and, when the worst of the storm had passed, I put buckets under the booms and caught enough water to wash clothes. By dawn the fierce little squall had blown itself out and we were again steering our course, with sails filled by a steady and more subdued breeze.

The night's rain had exposed the location of a few new leaks that kept Johnny busy the next morning until, becalmed and motoring once again, we found exhaust smoke and diesel fumes wafting into the main cabin. Johnny spent a dreadful day in the engine room repairing the crack he found in the exhaust pipe.

Every other day we made bread, the job of kneading given to whoever felt like punching something...usually no lack of volunteers! Because of the ship's motion, standing in the galley was often awkward, so the bread was kneaded in a large wooden salad bowl. That way it was easy to sit down, and the bowl could be wedged comfortably between the knees if necessary. Often Weesie or Caroline made a cake or cookies which disappeared fast. The sea air made us all appreciate specialties from the galley.

After nine days we were halfway to the Azores. Aboard Sequoiah any excuse was good for a party, and reaching the halfway mark on this leg of our voyage was true cause for celebration. We dressed up fit to kill...coats, ties, and party dresses, and I think Weesie even wore shoes! After a special dinner we watched a movie, and voiced our hopes that the next nine hundred miles would go even faster. The nights and days kept getting cooler and the hours of daylight lengthened. Soon we were wearing long underwear under our jeans and sweaters on night watches and the girls wanted to know what happened to bathing suits!

One night we motored over a flat sea through an unearthly thick fog. There was a sensation of being wrapped loosely in cotton wool. A strange quiet reigned. It gave me a feeling of timelessness, almost weightless, as if we were floating silently through space, with no reference points. It was a lonely feeling of isolation in an eerie cloud.

Weesie and Caroline began to notice birds flying close to the boat at night, but never landing, and one day I saw a huge school of dorado that stayed around our bow for several hours flashing their iridescent colors as they leapt through the waves. We knew there was usually a large population of whales in this part of the North Atlantic and we kept hoping to see some. Johnny saw the first one and, naturally, the rest of us were sleeping! He described the magnificent creature and we were envious. The very next day we were having supper in the cockpit when John saw one blow and pointed it out to us. It was big and smelled bad. It must not have liked us as it disappeared quickly and we didn't see it again even though we watched for an hour or more.

School work got off to a slow start when we left Bermuda. John and Caroline looked over their Calvert School courses and Weesie began a calculus course from the University of Nebraska. Combined with the wind dead astern or none at all the first week, causing a most unpleasant motion, tempers flared at the slightest provocation and no one wanted to study. School was a marvelous source of contention right from the beginning. John had a book on sculpture as part of his art history course so we had both John and Caroline read that in its entirety, along with excerpts from several history books on board. These were assigned with our upcoming European travels in mind, and, though it greatly enhanced their appreciation of all the churches, castles, museums, and ruins we later saw, coercing them to do the work was traumatic.

Johnny held navigation classes daily. Taking the sights was fun, but Caroline and I both felt nauseated when we had to go below and search through books of numbers to look up apparent angles, etc. We liked the Satellite Navigator best, but it did give each of us a sense of security knowing that we could do celestial navigation if we ever were in a crisis situation.

Weesie and John taking sun sights.

One morning John found a squid on deck which I offered to cook for him. He thought it would make better bait than breakfast. Before putting it on a hook he cut off a piece to examine under his microscope, and made a sketch of what he saw. John was fascinated by all the things man cannot see and he kept a notebook of these microscope drawings. He was not discriminating. Anything that came to hand was worth investigation; this helped to keep him busy.

We saw only four ships after leaving Bermuda, and only one other sailboat. Paul Fay from Devon, England aboard the sailing yacht, Faizark, called us on VHF and he and Johnny had a nice chat. He, his wife, and son were making the same Atlantic circle as we, but they were on their last leg home. We talked to them for three days until we were out of range. They too were stopping at Horta and we looked forward to meeting them in person.

Though I was cooking most of the meals, Caroline and Weesie both spent time in the galley. Caroline made salads and pizza while Weesie delighted everyone's sweet tooth with cakes and cookies. Her motto became "Bake, Bathe, and Be There!"... her three main interests on this trip. Weesie, like her father and brother, was not troubled by seasickness and could spend hours happily in the galley stirring up goodies and telling us all about it. She was not a quiet cook and made constant conversation. Bathing had never before ranked quite so high on her list of concerns; it was just taken for granted at home that teenage girls would shower constantly and wash hair daily. Now for weeks at a time water was rationed and even in port used conservatively as in most places it was an expensive commodity and often had to be ferried aboard in jugs. With 150 gallons of water in our tanks we had thirty gallons per person for each passage. We estimated that this leg from Bermuda to the Azores would take us 18 - 20 days. Since water would be used to rinse dishes, that left about a gallon per person per day for drinking and washing. Compared to the quantities of water we are accustomed to using at home, this sounds impossible. In actuality it was not hard to do. We turned off the pressure water system and used only the foot pumps at sea to reduce waste. For brushing teeth we'd use half a cup of water instead of running the tap as most people do at home. For washing hands and face several times a day, we used "Wet Ones", those pre-moistened squares, which were quite refreshing. Every other day we took complete saltwater showers and rinsed, sharing the two gallons of fresh water in the Sun Shower. This wonderful invention is a plastic bag, black on one side to collect solar heat, with a shower head extending from the bottom. We filled it, left it on deck in the sun for a couple of hours, and then hung it from the mast for use. We never used our built-in shower in the head. It was too easy to waste water, too much trouble to clean and dry everything afterwards, and, besides, being on deck prevented the chance of seasickness overtaking us, which was an ever-present complication for Caroline and me. Weesie's third priority, Be There, was shared by all but the captain. Johnny really loved those long sea trips but the rest of us focused on the next port of call. We now had the ocean version of the children's highway cry, "How many more miles, Daddy? When are we gonna get there?"

Unfortunately they quickly discovered that the Sat Nav had all the answers just a fingertip away. By punching several buttons it would give the mileage to the next waypoint and the date and time of arrival based on the entered speed. Early on Johnny had to limit these inquiries to once a day for the children began punching in almost hourly, entering different speeds to see what the maximum and minimum days left at sea might be. This was a great preoccupation and there was much discussion about whose watch was fastest. Whenever we had to reduce sail there was usually at least one voice of protest questioning the need to do so. When we were close to a landfall we made bets as to the time we would catch the first glimpse of land, and all waking hours were spent scanning the horizon.

Early on the morning of July 4, Caroline gently shook me awake, whispering, "Mommy, come out and look."

As the cloud of sleep slowly cleared from my mind, I pulled myself up over the lee cloth of the pilot berth and, carefully in the darkness, felt my way past John's sleeping form on the bunk below me. The motion was lively and I had to hold tightly to railings and walls to stay on my feet. As I passed the navigation station bathed in the soft red of the night light, I glanced at the clock and realized it was too early for my watch. A sudden pang of anxiety ran through my body bringing me instantly wide awake. The girls must have some problem. I struggled quickly into my harness and jacket and shot up the steps into the cockpit.

"What's the matter...?" I began.

"We're almost there, and it's just like Christmas morning!" cried Caroline.

And it was. Across the wide expanse of heaving water, a vision of hundreds of twinkling white lights rose before us in the moonlight.

"It's the Azores, Mother," said Weesie. "Can you believe we're really here?! Caroline is right. It feels just like Christmas, when we're so excited and we run down the stairs to get our first look at the Christmas tree all lighted up with presents everywhere. And today the best present will be going ashore."

"Christmas and the Fourth of July rolled into one!"

The three of us sat hugging each other in excitement watching our "tree" turn into an island in the cold light of dawn. The full moon was slow to relinquish its reflected image, and hung about the mist enshrouded peak of volcanic Mt. Pico looming seven thousand feet above sea level on the nearby island of the same name. The wind had not abated during the night and we were still moving swiftly over the building waves as we made our steady approach to land.

Early morning view of Mt. Pico in the Azores.
It was a beautiful sight after sixteen days at sea.

CHAPTER SEVEN

ALL THE WAY ACROSS

Entering a foreign port is always tense and exciting, but when approaching on a small sailboat, there's plenty of time for reflection about the place and the people. From the time of first sighting land, it sometimes may be a whole day before the anchor is actually dropped in the harbor. This day was no exception. Weesie and Caroline had first sighted the lights of Faial, one of the nine islands in the Azorean chain, at two in the morning, and it wasn't until almost lunchtime that we were finally at rest in the harbor at Horta, Faial's main town.

The land looked inviting in the sixty-five degree sunshine. Faial is often called the Blue Island because of the hedges of hydrangeas bordering the neat patchwork of fields on the lush, green hillsides. We motored slowly into the harbor, circled once to feel the current and choose a spot, then put the anchor over, paying out plenty of chain. Using the engine we backed down on it once and found that it held firm. Anchoring there seemed much too easy. We had been warned of the poor holding ground with its rocky bottom, so we had not expected to just drop the anchor and have it hold so well on the first try. "What luck," we thought. John had the dinghy inflated in record time and Johnny went ashore to clear customs while the rest of us cleaned Sequoiah from stem to stern.

Since it was an American holiday we "dressed ship", putting up all our flags from the bow over the top of the masts and down to the stern. There were several other American yachts in the harbor also dressed for the occasion and we thought we did look rather fancy. A number of yachties from other countries came by to inquire about our celebration, and one man said, "Why, I'll drink to that! What kind of beer are you serving?" Long distance cruisers, we found, are usually quite friendly and thirsty.

Sequoiah with all flags flying for the Fourth of July in Horta harbor

Our stay at Horta was magical, a very special time for each of us. It is hard to say just why all of us fell in love with this place but, in talking it over, we think the main reason is the people we met, both natives and yachtsmen.

Two of the first people that most yachtsmen meet on arrival in Horta are Peter Azeveda and his son, Jose. They own the Cafe Sport located on the main street overlooking the harbor. Cafe Sport is a combination cafe, bar, shop, mail service, museum, bank, and central meeting spot. It is open from eight in the morning until midnight and, in the summer, is usually full of people of all ages and nationalities, mostly yachtsmen. Both Peter and Jose are multi-lingual and make it their business to welcome all strangers and help them feel at home. Jose gave us a warm welcome when we walked in that first day, and told Caroline that she had some mail, a real thrill for her. We changed dollars to Portuguese escudos there before going to the yacht club for lunch. The exchange rate while we were there was 174 escudos to the dollar, so the children felt rich when they were given a 1,000 escudo bill to spend however they liked.

Peter directed us to the local laundry close by where a family washed and ironed everything for about five dollars for each huge load. Near the laundry was the Balneario, the public baths. There was one building for men and one for women, with an attendant at each to collect the fee of 50 escudos which included a towel and a bath. Inside there were many separate rooms, each housing a spacious porcelain bathtub or shower. Everything was immaculately clean and the attendants, though they spoke only Portuguese, were friendly and smiled politely when we made weak attempts at conversation with our Berlitz phrases. The Balneario was wonderful after our weeks of deck showers and most of us went there every day. John was afraid too much washing might ruin him and thought a quick swim was all he needed. His visits to the bathhouse were usually by forced march only!

By nightfall we had walked the entire town of Horta and our sea legs were fairly exhausted by the sudden return to such activity. As the wind had continued to rise we decided to have a "Red, White, and Blue" dinner aboard and celebrated with the wine Tom and Dede Leland had sent with us for that very occasion.

Our second day in Horta was one of major frustrations. We wanted to move to the fuel dock and spent an hour trying to pull up the anchor. Naturally it wouldn't budge. Johnny had a cold and couldn't dive, so Jean Pierre, a Frenchman from the boat anchored next to us, dove and unhooked our anchor from a huge chain lying on the bottom. We arrived at the dock just as the attendant was leaving for lunch. We took on water and waited. When the man returned we learned, without the benefit of a common language, that we needed to obtain a paper from Cafe Sport which would have to be signed by the police before we could purchase fuel. With our mission finally accomplished by mid afternoon, we went back out and tried to anchor...for two hours! We would drop the anchor and pay out what, when later trying to pull it back in, seemed like miles of chain; then we would back down on it with the engine and it would drag across the rocky bottom repeatedly in the most infuriating manner. The only good feature of the whole day was that we provided some fine entertainment for occupants of the other yachts in the harbor.

The evening, however, made up for the day. All visiting yachtsmen were invited to the Clube Naval for a barbeque. Young boys from the Navy rowed to every yacht in the harbor to issue the invitations and encourage everyone to come. There was to be a weekend race from Faial to Sao Jorge, an island 22 miles away. As it was explained to us, the race was an excuse for many parties beginning with the barbeque in Horta,

John painting a picture of Sequoiah on the famous wall at
Horta, on the island of Faial, Azores

then bullfighting, sightseeing, and folk dancing in Velas after
the race to Sao Jorge. Following the return race to Horta there
was to be an awards dinner aboard a Portuguese warship. That
night we attended the barbeque where fresh sardines were being grilled over a large, outdoor stone fireplace, very interesting but lacking in taste appeal for American children! There
we met several delightful couples and ended up going out
for dinner afterwards, to a restaurant whose name none of us
could pronounce, with the crews from the yachts Island Dog,
Sea Cedilla, and Raggles. Ian Mackie, from Raggles, set the
tone for the evening by ordering steaks for everyone with an
animated pantomime of a charging bull pawing the ground,
snorting, and waving its horns. It was just as well that he was
good at mimicry, because his broad Scottish accent sounded as
foreign as Portuguese to our inexperienced ears.

By the next morning the wind had died away completely
and the race to Velas began as a floater on a glassy sea. We
had decided not to participate as we were tired of being at sea

for awhile and besides, we'd have to anchor again at the end of the race!

While in Horta we went out for supper every night except once when Ian and Grace Mackie, and Paul and Valerie Fay came aboard for a Charleston dinner of ham and red rice. That night another British couple who had just arrived, rowed over to ask about a good restaurant in town, and they ended up staying too. It was a grey and rainy night so all eleven of us squeezed into Sequoiah's main salon to eat and swap sea stories. It was fun to see the Fays in person, after meeting them through radio conversations at sea.

One reason for going out for a meal was that a large and well prepared dinner never cost more than three to five dollars a person including drinks and tips. Cooking on board couldn't have been much less expensive, but was lots less fun and definitely much more trouble. One night we were invited to have dinner aboard a fifty foot Canadian yacht. The Food Editor for the <u>Montreal Gazette</u> was cooking his way across the Atlantic on his friend's boat. We had met, naturally, at Cafe Sport when he sat down with us one night and introduced himself saying, "May I join you? I'm Geoffrey Crocker, Betty's nephew."

A talented gourmet cook, his food was as delightful as his humor and he prepared a feast for us. Before parting I gave him a copy of <u>Charleston Receipts</u>, the United States' oldest and, perhaps, best regional cookbook, and next day he asked if he needed permission from anyone to mention it in his column. I assured him that he could praise it as often as he liked and hoped he would send me copies of the articles. I'm still hoping to hear from him.

Anyone sailing aboard a small yacht one thousand miles non-stop across open ocean is eligible to become a member of the Ocean Cruising Club, an international organization begun in England by the late Sir Humphrey Barton. The

Cruising Club of America and the Ocean Cruising Club had planned joint rallies in Spain and the Azores and, as luck would have it, they were having a final party in Horta while we were there. Juan and Heidi Casasco, OCC members from Annapolis (yes, we met at Cafe Sport!) offered to sponsor us for membership and invited us to go with them to the party being held at the Hotel Santa Cruz, on the site of an old fort. At dinner we sat with Mary Barton, Sir Humphrey's widow, a remarkable lady in her sixties. On this trip she had sailed from England with her friends Tony and Jill Vasey aboard their yacht, Whistler. Diminutive Mary Barton looked the picture of a refined elderly lady, very prim and proper, but someone told us that just the week before she had climbed the 48 foot mast of a large sailboat in order to photograph a group of club boats rafted together! Looks can be deceiving! As party favors, all of the ladies were given scrimshaw medallions of the crossed burgees of the two clubs done by Peter, a fun memento to recall the occasion.

One of the real highlights of our stay in Horta was meeting Othan de Silviera. Other sailors had told us we should be sure to see his scrimshaw work, so we went one morning in time to reach his house by ten o'clock when he starts working. He lived about a half mile from the harbor up on a hill. We were met at the door by Othan's wife, Zita, who escorted us through a hall running the length of the house, out the back door and around to a tiny low roofed room under the house. Opening into this room from the hall above was a trap door which was used in inclement weather, and when Zita was not home. Othan would stick his head up through the trap door and shout to visitors at the front door to come on in. And he had MANY visitors. We spent several days there watching and talking, and his tiny workroom was constantly filled to overflowing. Othan's room was cluttered with whale teeth, books, items for sale, and one corner was filled with his ham radio equipment. He had stacks of scrapbooks crammed with pictures and letters from acquaintances all over the world including a variety of people such as William F. Buckley, Maureen O'Hara, the King of Spain, and us. Othan was an amazing individual. He was an excellent artist and his scrimshaw work was beautiful.

One day during our stay, a visiting American from St. Louis bought two pieces from him for $6,000 each. They were very old teeth that Othan had said were not for sale, but the ugly American so insistently made higher and higher offers that Othan, after talking it over with Zita, decided to sell them. This man and his crew were so obnoxious that the entire town was muttering invectives against all Americans by the time they left a few days later. For the first time in my life I was ashamed to be an American, and felt the need to apologize for the abominable behavior of our fellow countrymen.

Scrimshaw is a dying art, and whale ivory is becoming scarce. The Azores had recently joined the Common Market, and in 1985 no whales were killed there. Only fifty-five whales had been taken the previous year, and it was done the traditional way in open boats. There were quite a few of those boats in the harbor and, after seeing some whales, I can't imagine going whale hunting in such in such narrow, oar-propelled little craft.I took Othan a picture of Sequoiah and he made me a medallion from a slice of a whale's tooth, with a perfect replica of her on it. The detail was amazing on such a small piece, right down to the wind vane on the stern. He also drew a whaling scene on a tooth for me. Othan's art was lovely, but it was his captivating personality and simple philosophy that won our hearts. One day as we were leaving after a five hour visit, John said, "I think I've learned lots about how to live a life".

Othan showed John how to polish a tooth and do the scrimshaw, covering the area to be etched with India ink, and then drawing the picture with a sharp needle. On parting he gave John the tools to work with and told him to come back in a few days with the finished product. John had great fun trying and when he finished, he held up my medallion next to his work and wryly commented, "It just goes to show you what years of experience can do!"

It's hard to find words to describe the warmth and love and pure goodness that exuded from Othan. He told us that he felt his mission on earth was to be of service to others, and that is how he lived. There are innumerable stories about the kind things he has done, as often as not for complete strangers. In fact, while we were there an elderly Swedish single-hander came limping into port with no money, hardly any provisions, and with his boat in an appalling state of disrepair. When Othan heard about him, he told the man to make a list of what he needed. In a few days Othan had sent everything down to the docks for him, never expecting a thing in return. We loved meeting Othan and spent many happy hours in his shop, watching him work and listening to him talk. He told us that when he died he wanted to leave his scrimshaw collection to the museum at Mystic Seaport in Connecticut. About a year after our return home we received the sad news that Othan had died, and I have since wondered what happened to all his treasures.

John met several Portuguese boys on the waterfront and had fun playing with them, although most spoke no English. One boy named Jose Vargas spoke English fairly well and spent many days playing with John. There is a law on Faial that the local people may not go aboard visiting yachts without a pass from the police, and children must have the consent of their parents as well. Jose was able to get permission and spent an afternoon aboard Sequoiah just looking around and asking questions. The following Saturday John was invited to spend the day at Jose's house. Jose's mother, a large and cheerful woman driving an ancient, dusty Volkswagen, picked John up at the harbor. The Vargas family lived up in the hills at Castello Branco. John later told us that they had what might be described as a small farm with chickens, dogs, cats, and rabbits running around everywhere. They grew much of their own food. Jose's father worked for the government in some capacity that I didn't quite understand. The whole family, which included Jose's younger brother, Pedro, came to bring John home. They got police passes and Johnny took them out to see Sequoiah, all except Mrs. Vargas who explained, in graphic sign language, accompanied by verbal Portuguese, that she got seasick. She and I sat on the sea wall and smiled at each other, periodically attempting to communicate for about an hour until Johnny brought her sons and husband back. She then presented us with a souvenir dishtowel painted with a map of the Azores, and a special kind of rice pudding she had made for us. One interesting thing was that Jose was 15 years old and Pedro was 12. Both seemed so much younger than Americans of the same ages. We found this to be true of all the Azorean children we met.

We kept saying we'd stay just one more day before going on to the island of San Miguel, but our anchor stayed down and we let the enjoyable days slip by. Finally England began to beckon to us and we started to get the boat ready to sail. I made a trip to the local supermerkado which offered free delivery to the waterfront for yachts. I also went early to the open air market several times and to the bakery for bread and rolls. The market was fascinating. Farmers from around the island sold fruits and vegetables and eggs. The choice of fruits while we were there was limited, but the cherries, plums and melons were delicious. There were many vegetables to choose from including beautiful lettuces and green beans. One end of the market was nothing but tables piled high with fish of all shapes, sizes, and colors. At the other end was meat. Beef, goat, and other carcasses hung from huge hooks. There are good herds of cattle on the island now and beef is a growing export.

Traditionally the farmers grew corn and wheat on the land, but in the mid 1950's there was a volcanic eruption followed by an earthquake the next year. There was much damage on the island and life was hard. A huge exodus began and over 20,000 people emigrated to the United States, Canada, and Portugal. Because of this tremendous loss of manpower, the farmers began to keep beef cattle instead of growing grain which is more labor intensive. Today more and more young people leave the island rather than continuing with the customary work of their families there.

Anyway, the beef is quite good and inexpensive, as we found at the restaurants. However, I was reluctant to buy any since none of the market vendors spoke English, and I was having enough trouble making myself understood at the vegetable stalls. I met a man at the market one morning who was Azorean but had lived in Canada for thirty years. He helped me buy some beef for a soup and also a roast, instructing the meat man just where to slice the carcass for the cuts I required.

When the boat was ready for sea we went to the dock for more water and last minute goodbyes; there was no trouble freeing the anchor this time, thank goodness! I must have taken a whole roll of film as we slowly motored out of the harbor, perhaps trying to hold onto this magic place just a little longer.

About 11:00 AM on July 15 we motored away from Horta with heavy hearts. Each leave-taking yanks up the roots so quickly planted and thriving, and it is hard to set sail and face the open sea. At least it is for me. The call of the sea is always beckoning to Johnny and he is anxious to feel the roll of the decks under his feet as we point toward a new destination, no matter how much he has enjoyed a place. I, on the other hand, could easily have stayed on indefinitely in most of the countries we visited.

We knew from the latest weather reports, that the Azores High stretched for hundreds of miles and we headed out in a flat calm that lasted two days. We tried sailing during the day, usually making no more than two to three knots, and motored at night when the constant noise and more regular motion helped those who were trying to sleep. When the wind finally came it steadily increased so that, beginning with the light drifter and staysail, we kept reducing canvas one sail at a time until we were down to storm jib and double reefed main and mizzen.

The northwest wind on our beam made Sequoiah roll horribly, and at suppertime a quart of milk splattered the cabin. No use crying over spilt milk. That's what I was always told. Well, whoever coined that little witticism has never tried to clean up the spilt milk when, with every roll of the boat, it seeps into a new corner. At sea the weather affects all aspects of daily living. The barometer kept dropping and we sped across the waves at six and seven knots. Many days were gray and drizzly, but there was never enough rain to catch a bucketful.

Our first day out while floating along in the calm, Johnny had seen a whale blow very close to the boat. Several times we had large schools of dolphin around us, and once a huge pod of pilot whales (there must have been a hundred of them) came swimming towards us. Calm and stately, blowing softly at intervals, they surrounded us momentarily and then were past, continuing on their pre–determined course as if we were invisible. It was an awe-inspiring sight. Some of the porpoises we saw had gray backs and white undersides and looked quite different from those we see at home. For about half an hour one evening a small group of them played around the bow. One stayed in the same place lying on its side looking up at us with its intelligent eye, and coming up for air periodically, obviously as curious about us as we were about him. We could hear them talking with a high pitched whistling sound and wished we could understand. One night we played Beethoven's Fifth Symphony for a group of them as loudly as we could, but I don't think they enjoyed it as they left almost immediately! These enigmatic mammals hold an endless fascination for us, and their visits brightened many a day.

Weesie took up baking with a vengeance on this passage and we had confections from the galley nearly every day. Her desserts were delicious, but when she tried her hand at bread, it tasted salty and bitter. We made jokes and she tried again. Subsequently we found that we had some bad flour which was sabotaging her efforts, and her chef's reputation was saved.

The weather was becoming cold at night and even the days were chilly when we had wind. Several times we talked to ships on the radio, primarily discussing the weather and comparing forecasts, as most of the big container ships had weather fax machines aboard. Johnny took great pleasure one night in being able to give a container ship a position. Their Sat Nav was broken and they weren't sure of their proficiency with the sextant. Once, a cargo ship with a Philippine crew aboard altered course to pass close to us and they called us several times asking if we needed anything. The children begged Johnny to request some ice cream, but their pleas were ignored. The captain, himself a sailor, said he loved talking to small yachts at sea and hoped to go sailing himself someday. His parting words were, "God bless your family... We are brothers on the sea." Captains of large ships are often maligned by cruising sailors, accused of not keeping a proper watch on the high seas, but we have had some good experiences in that regard.

One chilly day we washed each other's hair in the galley sink and then I gave John a haircut. Before leaving home I had bought some haircutting scissors and a Trimcomb, a small plastic comb with a razor blade inside the teeth of the comb. The girls refused my offers to trim their golden locks, but Johnny and John let me experiment. Once or twice their heads may have looked slightly moth-eaten, and they may have worn hats more often than usual, but with practice I did improve. Like the girls, I, too, waited until we reached England to have a professional work on my hair.

At three o'clock one morning Weesie and Caroline woke me up to see some strange streaks of white in the water around the boat. I had seen this once before years ago on one of my first night watches alone. Then I had shined a flashlight on the streaks to have a better look and had been frightened when there was a huge splash as something leaped high out of the water right beside the boat. I had gone screaming below and wakened Johnny who said it was dolphins. This was the same. The streaks of light are caused by the animals speeding through the phosphorescence in the water and, once you know what it is, it looks really beautiful.

During the afternoon of our seventh day Johnny announced that we had covered a thousand miles. Of course, on Sequoiah, that called for celebration. Caroline baked a Thousand Mile Party pie, and after supper we watched a movie even though it wasn't Friday. To complete the festivities a school of dolphin came leaping by and a huge whale blew several times close to starboard.

There is a two hour time difference between the Azores and England and we had arguments about whose watch to lengthen. Johnny, the peacemaker, made the final decision, and twice we turned the clock forward an hour at supper stretching our evening time together, which everyone felt was a fair solution.

The weather we had on the eleven day passage from Horta to Salcombe, if graphed, would make the stock market look stable by comparison! Almost every day we would have a little sun, a little drizzle, sometimes light wind changing to a small gale and then petering out to dead calm. The closer we got to England the cooler the days became.

One gray and foggy day while we were grumpily drifting along at 2-3 knots on a flat ocean, we were inundated with bees. They kept coming around and were so slow and drowsy it was easy to kill them. We certainly didn't want them in the cabin! Later when the wind picked up again they disappeared.

The Sat Nav stopped working three days before we entered the English Channel, so every time the sun came out, no matter how briefly, we would try to get a sight. Fortunately Johnny had been taking excellent sextant sights all along, so was quite confident about his dead reckoning, without our fancy electronic gadget... at any rate, he didn't tell me if he was worried. He knew better! Each day he managed to get at least one good sight when we had a break in the clouds, and as we drew closer to land we were able to take bearings with the radio direction finder which homed in on land-based radio stations as well as radio beacons.

Several times on our last few days at sea, we heard the unmistakable sound of heavy gunfire. Naturally I was terrified, and annoyed everyone by repeatedly wondering out loud if we would be okay. Being shot at wasn't one of the things I had planned to worry about, and I didn't want to start now. Johnny pointed out sections on the chart not far from us marked as Navy target practice areas. I didn't like it a bit, but he assured me that we were well out of range and, happily, he was right.

Our last day at sea when we entered the English Channel was our worst. The night before, we had been hand steering due to lack of wind and steerageway. However, by early morning we were making five to six knots with just the main and mizzen. When the jib was raised we fairly flew. We sailed faster and faster all day. Around noon we reefed down, and still our speed increased. Under the prevailing conditions reefing the sails was tricky business. Trying to turn the boat into the wind to take pressure off the sails, while watching the steep seas to make sure we didn't get knocked down by one hitting us broadside, took my breath away. With jib, reefed mizzen, and double reefed main, we were surfing sometimes at eight knots over ten foot waves, and some occasionally larger. Fortunately they were behind us as the wind was from the west and southwest. All day Johnny constantly took bearings with the radio direction finder and, luckily, managed to confirm our latitude with a noon sight in between squalls, or what the British weather broadcasters so whimsically call "thundery showers". Johnny and Weesie stayed in the cockpit all afternoon and on until midnight, hand steering and taking bearings. Weesie was exhilarated. The wild weather that filled me with fear and nausea thrilled her, and she was on a high of excitement all day. The motion of the boat was so erratic that the rest of us stayed in our bunks most of the day reading and looking out the ports at the incredible undulating scene outside. It was the only day of the whole trip that was so rough, cooking was impossible. Granola bars, fruits, crackers, and cheese were about all anyone wanted anyway. At suppertime I was able to heat some soup on the one burner gimbaled emergency cooker that featured a clamp to hold the pot over the flame. I had to use the pressure cooker since it was the only pot with a lid that screwed on securely, otherwise the soup would have ended up on the ceiling. The only way to eat it was to sit on the floor wedged into a corner and drink out of a captain's mug, the kind with a wide base and a narrow opening. Little rain showers passed over all afternoon and evening, and we continued to have huge following seas, some fifteen to twenty feet and with crests breaking above the stern as we were lifted and rolled and dropped. At one point Weesie shouted that we were surfing at ten knots. Sequoiah just wasn't meant to go that fast.

About 2030 Weesie called out, "Land Ho!" as the mist lifted momentarily and we passed the Lizard. A few minutes later Johnny was able to pick out the Lizard light. Shortly afterwards Johnny said, "Something's wrong. We're not moving!"

Johnny watching the enormous following seas, moments before cutting the line to our water-powered generator.

I couldn't believe my ears. It looked to me like we were flying, but he was really upset and I knew he meant it. Caroline, John, and I stood squeezed together on the companionway steps looking out through the half-opened hatchway at the chaotic scene. The boat tossed and rolled, the huge waves crested and broke above us, and the noise of wind, rigging, and crashing water was deafening. Suddenly Johnny realized why we were no longer making headway and shouted to John to grab a knife for him. With a daring thrust he sliced through the overly taut line holding the Ampair water-powered generator that we had been towing. The boat lurched forward and we were on our way once more. Johnny had cut the line right at the stern rail so that it couldn't snap back at him. The Ampair had been caught in a long-line fishing net and Johnny was the only one to notice that something was awry. It was lucky that he discovered the problem before the line popped on its own. We were sorry to lose the Ampair. It had generated untold hours of electricity for us and we decided we would try to order another one when we got to land.

By midnight the waves had reduced in size and become more regular. Though the wind was still blowing, the barometer, which had been steadily dropping for two days and had bottomed out at 1001 millibars, was starting to rise. Caroline and I came on watch to relieve Weesie and Johnny who had been at it all day and half the night. When we went out in the cockpit we could see the Land's End light off the stern and the Eddystone light off the bow. After eleven days on a lonely ocean it looked like a major highway out there. We were between land and the Channel's well-defined traffic separation zones. It was a thrilling ride. We could see the lights of Plymouth on the port side and a steady stream of ships out to starboard in the traffic zones. We were traveling easily under gradually lowering seas; the sky cleared and stars appeared overhead. At 0430 a thirty foot sailboat passed us with main and spinnaker up, and there we were with our reefs still in place. Johnny and John immediately went forward to remedy that! By 0830 we were off Bolt Head and two hours later we turned on the engine, raised our quarantine flag, lowered the sails for the last time, and motored in towards Salcombe. Our information told us that the Salcombe bar was dangerous in a strong onshore wind and particularly on an ebb tide. A lifeboat once was lost there in those conditions. It is also dangerous when a swell is running in until the tide is quite high. On the morning of July 27 conditions were ideal. We couldn't have timed it better if we had tried.

As we crossed the Salcombe bar we raised the Harbormaster on the radio and he said he was on his way out to meet us. In five minutes the Harbormaster's launch appeared with Marcella Dyson calling welcomes from the deck.

"Who is that lady who looks so excited to see us?" asked one of the children.

"That is Derek Dyson's wife, Marcella," I answered through happy tears. "We've told you all about them. I can't believe they're here to meet us!"

The Harbormaster drew alongside and Marcella came aboard Sequoiah to ride with us to our mooring. Once we had tied up, a Customs official appeared, and Marcella left to round up the rest of her family. The Customs officer was quite brief considering the distance we had come. We had heard that British Customs could be tough. The only difficulty seemed to be leaving Sequoiah in England while we traveled in Europe. This man told us it would be impossible to leave the boat for two months. We would have to take the boat or pay a sizeable tax. This was an unexpected obstacle and one we could not afford. The officer said he would discuss the matter with his chief over the weekend and we could meet with them on Monday.

As the Customs officer was leaving, Derek, Marcella, and Helen Dyson came alongside in their dory bearing three bottles of champagne, and there were greetings, hugs, and introductions all round, punctuated by the popping of corks.

I had met the Dysons twenty years previously when, at the age of nineteen, I spent a year in Warwickshire at a riding school. My father had written to Martin's Bank to arrange an account for me, and had been put in touch with Derek, then the manager of Martin's Stratford office. The two men struck up quite a correspondence by mail, and Daddy asked Derek to take good care of his little girl. When I arrived in England not only did Derek help me with the business end of things, but he and his family took me in and we became great friends. During that year, I stayed with them often and babysat with Paul and Helen, then two and four years old. In the intervening years we kept in touch through Christmas cards and occasional letters. Two summers before our voyage, Paul had come to stay with us, and both Johnny and Mother had visited the Dysons on separate trips to England. When Derek heard about our sailing trip he enthusiastically wrote and encouraged us to bypass Falmouth and Plymouth, the usual British landfalls for American yachts, and sail straight to Salcombe where they have a holiday flat and where their yacht is moored.

Salcombe was an old shipbuilding center centuries ago. It is located at the southernmost tip of England and was a jumping off point for American and British troops for the D-Day invasion of Normandy during World War II. Today Salcombe is a lovely resort village and is quite a sailing center with hundreds of yachts of all shapes and sizes dotting the harbor.

Having such a warm and welcoming reception after traveling 4,200 miles was an extraordinary pleasure and we were happy we had followed Derek's advice. When we had polished off the champagne we went ashore for a light lunch and real showers. That evening Paul, who was working in Salcombe for the summer, joined the rest of us for dinner in town. After the initial excitement of "Being There" we fell into our bunks that night and slept so soundly that not one of us was awakened by the strong gale which blew all night long with winds up to 45 knots. The Bag is the name given to the area of the harbor where we were moored, and it is well protected from the wind in all directions. In our part of the world it would be an excellent hurricane hole.

The next day, being Sunday, we attended the morning service at Trinity Church and then met the Dysons for a big dinner. Paul took the younger set out in the dory for the afternoon, and Johnny and I went for a long walk on the cliffs with Marcella and Derek up towards Bolt Head. Along the way we visited the National Trust property, Sharpitor, where some of the earliest British photographs can be found. The sun was out for a while and then came more rain and drizzle, what we assumed was typical English weather. On our way back down to Salcombe we stopped at an inn for a Devon cream tea. This is quite a specialty of the region. Along with hot tea (the real thing, not tea bags!) as only the British can do it, there were scones, piping hot, served with clotted cream and strawberry preserves. Devonshire clotted cream is known the world over as a delectable treat. I vaguely remembered that I had gained weight when I had lived in England before, and now I remembered why! After two months on the boat I was thin, but I knew suddenly that it wouldn't last. Johnny was hooked and proclaimed that afternoon tea must become a regular part of our day. By that night when Derek and Marcella left for Birmingham, we already felt at home in England and were looking forward to spending a month exploring this country, the birthplace of so many of our ancestors.

CHAPTER EIGHT

THE GRAND TOUR

Our first Monday in England was the major cleanup and clear out day. Weesie spent most of it at the laundromat. John and Johnny left right after breakfast to see the Harbormaster and Customs to arrange for leaving Sequoiah in Salcombe for the next two months while we were gone. We had always heard that British Customs officials were very fussy about guns. At Customs Johnny disclosed the fact that we had firearms on board, something that had been overlooked on Saturday in the confusion of arrival, not surprisingly, as Salcombe is not a usual point of entry for American yachts. The Customs officials, predictably, were horrified. Probably somewhat embarrassed by the omission, they sent a boat immediately to fetch the guns and ammunition in question. They would hold them at their headquarters in Plymouth under lock and key until Sequoiah left the country. Only Caroline and I were aboard when the Customs boat arrived and, being unfamiliar with the guns, it took us some time to locate the ammunition. All the while one of the men was muttering about how dangerous this was, and how terrible it must be in America where everyone carried firearms around with them.

Our next problem took a bit longer to settle. Apparently there is a law in Great Britain that requires the payment of a

Value Added Tax when importing a vessel. Because we would be leaving the country and the boat would stay, we were told that we fell in the category of importers. Since the VAT was computed as ten percent of the vessel's total value, it was well past our ability or inclination to pay it. Johnny argued in his best legalese, pointing out that Sequoiah was not for sale, that she would not be leaving Britain except to return to her country of origin, so therefore she could not be considered an import. After long discussion the officials were convinced that payment of the VAT was unnecessary. Resolving this in any other way would have meant a drastic change in plans. We were relieved.

Caroline and I worked all that day cleaning out lockers and taking inventory so that re-provisioning would be easier when we returned. Around noon, with the Harbormaster's help we moved farther up the Bag to our permanent summer mooring. It was over a mile to town so we were glad to have the use of Derek's dory, "BuzzB". During the afternoon we managed to make more of a mess than we'd started with. This job was taking longer than expected. All at once we heard shouting outside.

"Hello there, Charleston! Is anyone aboard?" called a British voice.

"Yes, we're here," I answered, climbing up to the cockpit.

Looking out I saw a dory holding an attractive English family who introduced themselves as John and Penny Russell and their son, Toby.

"Are you really from Charleston?" they asked.

"We sure are," I said.

"Well, perhaps you know our friends, the Middletons."

Middleton is an old Charleston name going back to the first colonial settlers. They fill two columns in the current telephone book and we know quite a few of them. It turned

114

out that we had mutual friends in Will and Beryl Middleton whom the Russells had visited in Charleston, and on that discovery they invited us to their summer cottage for drinks that evening.

At the appointed time we found our way to 24 Church Street and spent two delightful hours. The Russells' weekend houseguests arrived shortly after we did. The cottage was in the process of being renovated and, as there were no back steps, Weesie helped Penny hoist Ian and Joanna's suitcase to the second floor bedroom with a rope let down from an upstairs window! Everyone was intrigued by our living arrangements aboard, so we invited them to come by and have a look around Sequoiah the next day.

After leaving that jovial group we had dinner at one of the many restaurants in the village and then walked back to the town dock where we found Derek's dory high and dry. Somehow we had forgotten about the tremendous tide which could triple the six foot tides we were familiar with at home. It was a clear, balmy night so we sat on one of the benches along the waterfront and talked about our summer plans. After an hour or so the tide had risen enough for Johnny and John to push the dory the last several feet across the mud to the water. It took a lot of effort but we were tired of waiting, and in the end they successfully floated her. However, in the process, John's deck boots filled with cold water and it had a definite dampening effect on his humor as well. It was long after midnight when we climbed into our bunks. We had learned that lesson the hard way!

The next day we planned to leave for Plymouth and spent the morning completing final tasks. Packing was a challenge since we each had one suitcase which we would have to carry for the next two months; we tried to pack lightly. About mid-morning there came a knock on the hull. The Russells with their friends, Ian and Joanna, came aboard to have a look around. Joanna, in particular, was fascinated by our daily boat life. She looked in every locker and asked all sorts of outrageous questions until Ian loaded her into the dory again and they left us still laughing. They were such fun! John spent the rest of the morning cleaning fish with Toby Russell and then the two boys helped Johnny clean up Derek's dory before we left it on its mooring.

Roger Walker, a local man who looked after Derek's yacht, had been engaged to take care of Sequoiah while we were away, and he came by to meet us and go over the list of things that needed to be done in our absence. Johnny arranged to call him at intervals to check on the boat, and when Roger left us he took with him the sails that needed repair.

When our rental car arrived that afternoon we had an exciting ride to Plymouth. Johnny did very well driving on the tiny lanes in a right hand drive car for the first time, but it was scary because the roads were narrow and hedges grew tall on both sides, making it impossible to see approaching traffic.

That night there was a beautiful full moon and we walked through the Barbican and back along the waterfront past the Citadel. The main thing we remember about Plymouth, however, was the huge bathtub in our hotel. It is a long way from deck showers to seven foot tubs!

The next week was spent driving through Devon which we all loved. In between visiting museums and castles we did some hiking on the moors, seeing wild ponies, some as tiny as dogs, and hundreds of varieties of wildflowers. From the moors we wound our way down to the sea again and wandered through wonderful ancient villages clinging to the sides of sheer cliffs. Everywhere we went people apologized for the weather. It was one of the coldest, wettest summers ever in Britain we were told. We, however, could not have cared less. We were on terra firma and Mother Nature could do her worst. We felt safe after our last two months on the ocean. The day we went to Stonehenge changed our minds. It was pouring rain, freezing cold and very windy. Standing out in that gusty downpour uncomfortably looking at those stones, we unanimously decided to skip Avebury Circle (more stones), and made our way to the delightfully comfortable Randolph Hotel in Oxford. The sun did occasionally come out in the next month, but it was a rare treat and reason for celebration.

We reached Birmingham in time for a late tea with Marcella, on the same day that Mother arrived. The next week was sheer bliss. We were staying in the Dyson's cozy home in a village on the outskirts of the city. Johnny and Mother drove to Wales one day but the rest of our time there was spent driving around the Cotswolds and the surrounding areas on day trips. In Stratford, a new production of the Merry Wives of Windsor left even the youngest ready for more Shakespeare. John loved Warwick Castle, billed as the finest medieval example in England, and was particularly impressed with the dungeons and armory. He wrote an excellent essay on castles later that week. Marcella took Caroline and me to visit a needle museum in an old needle factory powered by a water mill. Needle making was a painstaking process and one I had no idea could be so complicated. In a nearby field was an archaeological dig in progress where Bordesley Abbey once stood. We made our way through a sheep-congested pasture and talked to the workers. For over fifteen years the Universities of London, Reading, and Rochester, N.Y. have been doing the work jointly. Two skeletons had been exposed in graves under the abbey floor so a few people were poring over them, but the constant rain had hampered the work and most of the students were washing shards and cataloging in tents. Derek was determined that we shouldn't miss anything or sit still for a second! We visited a crystal making company, art museum, and some National Trust properties, climbed to the top of cathedral towers, and had backyard picnics and fancy restaurant dinners. The days flew by, wrapped in a congenial aura of laughter and friendship.

Marcella is very talented with all kinds of needlework and encouraged Caroline to buy some yarn and needles to make herself a sweater. This was Caroline's first attempt at knitting, so Marcella worked with her every day while we were there and got her off to a good start. Wherever we went after that, Caroline attracted the attention of matronly women who usually ended up helping. That first sweater held the stitches of many, kind, and unknown hands by the time it was finished. It was a sleeveless cotton top so Caroline wore it often in the tropics and, in fact, wore it out!

All too soon we were boarding a train for London and a whirlwind of sightseeing. Caroline and John, having read John's art history book, were looking forward with great interest to seeing some of the things they had learned about. Our friend, Ethel Jane Bunting, had advised us that taking children on an extended trip like ours could only be successful if approached with commonsense. On her suggestion we made a rule that before going to any museum or art gallery, we would choose only three things to look at and talk about while we were there. Naturally there were many more things everyone wanted to see, and sometimes it was difficult to choose, so we devised a plan. After viewing our three selections together and learning about them, if anyone wanted to see something else we would split up and meet again in a given amount of time. Usually all of us wanted to stay and we would end up spending several more hours. Since we had decided not to start the Calvert School courses until we were back aboard the boat, the children were required to do a certain amount of reading and to write a composition each week on something that interested them. With all they were seeing and learning, this was not difficult and usually fun.

In London we wore ourselves out, getting up early, spending all day walking and looking, then going to the theater and staying up late every night. London is Mother's favorite large city and we all reveled in the beauty of its magnificent architectural treasures and its well-maintained parks, the quaint bookshops and variety of restaurants, and the vast array of theater, ballet, and musical offerings from which to choose. From the sublime to the ridiculous, we crammed into one week as much as was humanly possible.

One night we had a scare in the hotel. The girls and Mother were still out at a play when the rest of us came in. Johnny and I were having a drink in the lobby after putting John to bed when suddenly fire alarms sounded and firemen came running in the front door. All we could think about was John up on the third floor by himself. The elevators were inoperative and Johnny headed up the stairs only to meet John running down. He had heard and seen the fire trucks arrive and had stopped only to grab his room key before leaving. It seemed to be a false alarm. After things settled down John went back to bed. Several hours later more fire trucks arrived, only two this time. It took Johnny quite a while to calm John down. Even with Weesie and Caroline right in the room with him, he was scared. Johnny talked with the concierge and found that there was a problem with the fire detectors in the hotel basement, and there was no danger of fire. Even so, I don't think John slept very well that night!

Since there were six of us we often went in different directions according to our own interests. Caroline and Mother had lunch at the Hard Rock Cafe (Caroline's desire, her grandmother's indulgence!), Weesie and Johnny went to a disco at the Hippodrome for a late night of dancing; Weesie and I shopped for school clothes, and Johnny and John visited stamp shops and the Imperial War Museum. Some of us went to tour the Tower of London, some to the London zoo, and some went to Westminster Abbey. Other times we went en masse as on the afternoon we took a boat ride up the Thames to Greenwich to visit the National Maritime Museum. There we saw Chichester's Gypsy Moth IV as well as Cutty Sark, a famous clipper ship from the days of the wool trade, which holds the fastest record from India to England...under sail of course! Weesie and Caroline had fun standing with one foot in the Eastern hemisphere and one in the West. They were fascinated to be right at the spot where the lines of longitude begin.

Our week in London drew quickly to an end, with more goodbyes. The day we left for Cambridge, Mother left for Israel. We wouldn't see her again until spring. She stood on the sidewalk outside the hotel and waved farewell as we climbed into one of those huge black London cabs. The driver was quite chatty and when Johnny directed him to take us to Victoria Station he asked our destination.

"How much will it cost for all of you to take the train to Cambridge?" was the driver's next question. Johnny told him.

"I can get you there in less time for the same price," he said. And that's how we took a taxi from London to Cambridge. It was much more comfortable than the train, and hassle-free.

Visiting the university towns of Oxford and Cambridge, with their distinctive, yet decidedly different atmospheres of ancient traditions and serious intellectual pursuit, gave both Johnny and me the feeling that we would like to be students again. From Cambridge we moved north to the Lake District where we read Wordsworth's poetry and "wandered lonely as a cloud", discovered fell running, and gorged ourselves on Grasmere gingerbread, the recipe for which, we were told, is in a safe at the local bank.

Pushing ever northward we drove to Glasgow where we met once again our friends, Ian and Grace Mackie. Ian had been home only a week, having survived a harrowing sail from the Azores. He had been caught in a Force 10 storm in the Irish Sea. It was so terrible that Ian, seasoned skipper that he was, felt sure they had little chance of survival. He and his friend, Paul, dragged anchors, lines and buckets astern to slow the boat, but even under bare poles little Raggles was leaping and diving through that violently heaving white water. Still, in the worst situations Ian has an irrepressible sense of humor. He told Paul they'd better get busy and drink the case of beer they had aboard because it would be a real shame to go to Davy Jones' Locker with that good drink beside them and not in them! When they had finished that task they fell into a long, untroubled sleep. Ian said that on awakening he knew he had died and gone to hell. The storm was worse and continued for two more days.

Fortunately Raggles, being only 22 feet long, was like a cork, bouncing along the top of the water. When the storm blew itself out, Paul and Ian came to life again and managed to find their way home to the Clyde River without the benefit of charts. As their original plan had been to take Raggles to Bermuda, Ian had given us his East Atlantic charts to take home for him. So we were especially happy to see these friends alive and well!

After a day and a night in Glasgow, Ian and Grace took us to "East Glasgow" as they liked to call the capital and their rival city. The Edinburgh Music Festival was in full swing and the city was overflowing with tourists. Miraculously Grace had arranged a place for us to stay, right downtown within walking distance of everything we wanted to see. They had also managed to get tickets to a variety of events and we spent three packed and fascinating days there with them. While in Edinburgh we ran into two families that we knew from Charleston; sometimes the world seems so small.

Our time in Great Britain was ending and Ian and Grace sent us away with armloads of gifts. From Edinburgh we took the boat/train to Dover and over to Calais. While the girls sneaked away to smoke an illicit cigarette, their latest teenage venture, Johnny and I stood at the rail. Somehow the Channel wasn't nearly as forbidding from the high decks of the ferry. John explored the entire ship. He made friends with the girls at the duty free shop and came back with sample French perfumes for the girls and me.

The next month was spent in Europe. We arrived in Paris at midnight on August 27. It had been a long and tiring day but we were wide awake when we reached our hotel after a wild taxi ride. The taxis are allowed to carry only four passengers at a time, or so we were told. Somehow two of the children were whisked into one cab and all I could do was to keep repeating to our driver who spoke no english, "Follow that cab! Depechez!" straining my eyes to make sure that we didn't lose the children on our first night in France. From our hotel balcony, we could see the Arc de Triomphe close by on our left and in the distance to the right, the white dome of Sacre Coeur rising from Montmartre. Our days in Paris were our last with Weesie. On our final night together we toasted each other with champagne provided by the hotel and promised that we would gather again in Paris in twenty five years. We had fun trying to imagine what our lives would be like by then. On my birthday, the third of September, we put Weesie on a plane for Washington and school. Even Caroline and John were sad to see her go.

By the time we reached Switzerland, we were tired of museums, cathedrals, and old houses; it was a relief to take boat rides on lakes and trips up mountains. We fell in love with Rigi Kulm, looking down from 6,000 feet over steep meadows filled with cows wearing huge bells. We nearly stayed, but decided we would never forgive ourselves if we missed Austria and Italy. Besides, our few days in the clear mountain air revived us and gave us the energy we needed to go on.

None of us particularly loved Vienna, our enthusiasm dulled by the constant rain and cold that prevailed during our stay, and by the fact that we missed my Viennese friend, Marianne Durr, by several days. Marianne insists that we must return in the springtime, when we will see a completely different city, filled with flowers and music, neither of which were in evidence in that chill and wet September.

At any rate we were glad to go south to Italy where it was sunny and hot, the kind of weather we had missed all summer. Venice was wonderful with a special charm of its own. Having boats and canals instead of cars and streets was a pleasant change and we felt right at home there. Sunrise and sunset are phenomenal times of day in Venice as the quality of light seems almost to melt the buildings into the sky.

We spent a good bit of time on trains in Europe, and most of them were exceptionally good. Somehow the Italian trains were the only ones that ran late. The Italians seem to have that same laid back attitude toward time as can be found in the tropics, fine if you're not in a hurry.

Two days in Florence were not long enough to see more than a fraction of the treasures there, and we felt like we needed to rush to see it all. Besides the art books, we had read The Agony and The Ecstasy, Irving Stone's fictionalized biography of Michelangelo, and while walking through the Uffizi Gallerie, Pitti Palace, and the Duomo, we tried to imagine what it must have been like in earlier times. John was excited to see Cellini's Perseus and Medusa in the Loggia, larger than life and even more impressive than the photos in his sculpture book. The Medici chapel was as opulent and gloomy as the guide book so accurately described it. Michelangelo's David loomed impressively above us at the Gallerie dell Academie. We were awed by what we saw. Exhausted by our marathon of sightseeing in the incredible late summer heat, we went to see an American cowboy movie in Italian. Quite a contrast! At least it was dark and cool in the theater.

Our suitcases had swelled to enormous proportions during our travels on land, and we half carried, half dragged them to the station to wait for a train to Rome, two and a half hours away. We vowed to take a vacation in Rome and moved into an American hotel with a pool high on a hill on the outskirts of the city. We curtailed our activities, spending at least half of each day by the pool. In between swims, we made forays to the Coliseum, Roman Forum, the Vatican, the Pantheon, the Villa Borghese, and the San Sebastian catacombs. The children made sure to throw coins in the Trevi fountain to ensure their return to Rome.

During our travels through Europe Caroline and John did some writing each day and they both did quite a lot of reading, particularly in places where we didn't go out every night. It was fun to see their keen curiosity about the places we visited, and we hoped that their experiences would trigger an ongoing interest in the world community and a desire to travel later in life, perhaps prompting them to return to some of the same places for a more in-depth view. At times we got tired of so much family togetherness, but on the whole it was good. I was pleasantly surprised at the genuine friendship and mutual respect that was emerging between Caroline and John where there had been a wall of rivalry before. In retrospect, perhaps it shouldn't have been so astonishing considering how rarely they had any opportunity to talk to anyone near their own ages.

Leaving Italy was not easy. The French air controllers had gone on strike, allowing no traffic in French air space, and our flight to Spain had been cancelled. After much confusion and standing in lines, we booked another flight, and spent most of the day sitting in a plane on the runway waiting for permission to fly.

Madrid was large, busy and the dirtiest city I know. I kept wishing for one of those masks that I have seen Orientals wear over their mouths and noses. More than half of the population must smoke, and the rank air was thick with the stench of cigarettes and pollution. Even though everything smelled bad and our hotel was creepy, Madrid was the highlight of the summer because Heyward and Eleanor Carter met us there with their three children. It was so much fun to be with them. Unfortunately, each of their children in turn got sick. Someone was in bed the whole three days. I was worried that John or Caroline might get ill, too, for they hovered around the sickbed, but they remained healthy. One evening we left all of the children at the hotel while Heyward took us to some Tapas bars for drinks and hors d'oeurves. Clinton Carter overheard us discussing where we were going and told the other children that their parents were going to some topless bars. When we returned Caroline and John demanded to know why we would go to places like that. "How disgusting!" they concluded, and were relieved when we explained.

On September 21st, the Carters headed back to Charleston and we flew to London, completing one small circle, and continuing a larger one.

CHAPTER NINE

Sailing Again

After going through Customs at Heathrow Airport, almost as easy but not nearly as personal as our last encounter with British Customs, we had just enough time to take a cab into London for a final shopping spree at Harrod's. John had birthday money left over that was burning a hole in his pocket, and Caroline wanted another caramel sundae like the one she had enjoyed there with Granny earlier in the summer. The cab driver waited for us (by now we could hardly lift our travel-enriched suitcases and could never have carried them around the store); then he whisked us to the station in time to catch an express train to Birmingham.

It was wonderful to relax in a home again; no more hotels for a while! We stayed three days with the Dysons, resting and getting things together for the boat. Then we rented a tiny car, into which Johnny somehow managed to squeeze our grossly expanded luggage and our most recently acquired boat gear. Four hours later we arrived back in Salcombe. Leaving our suitcases at the Dyson's flat, we unloaded the contents of the car into Roger Walker's dory and hurried out to see Sequoiah. She looked well-tended with fresh varnish, sails repaired and reinforced, new lifelines, and some new rigging. Opening the ports and hatches to let in the warm Indian summer breeze, Caroline expressed what we all felt, "It's great to be home!"

Caroline and I spent the next few days taking an inventory of all the provisions on board, stowing everything we'd bought in Birmingham, and trying to make order from chaos. Johnny reinstalled the Sat Nav on which a faulty card had been replaced in London at no charge to us. John polished brightwork and scrubbed the waterline while Johnny and an electrician worked in the engine room trying to find the cause of a burnt wire they'd noticed, along with everything else they thought was wrong in there.

The engine room is the one area of Sequoiah that I have never ventured to explore. For me it holds an air of mystery about it and a dark feeling of misplaced power. When I look through the door to hand Johnny a tool or answer a question from that dark hole, I feel intimidated by the unfamiliarity of the huge machine enclosed there surrounded by its valves and twisting hoses. It seems alive and obstinate with a contrary will of its own dictating our fortunes. Our mastery of it is tenuous and luck seems to play a greater part than actual skill in keeping it in running order.

When the engine was running smoothly we motored to the fuel barge, a super British invention. This barge was permanently anchored in the estuary and it made filling our tanks so much easier than maneuvering to a dock in a crowded marina as is usual in most places. Here I learned that an Imperial gallon and a US gallon are not equal. The former is made up of litres and the latter of ounces. Our tanks held fewer gallons of the Imperial variety.

The water boat was another British innovation that we loved. When fresh water was needed on board, one had only to raise a bucket in the rigging and, sooner or later, the water boat would come alongside and pump water into the tanks. Again, it was so convenient and simple.

At five-thirty after a long day of boat work we piled into Roger's dory and headed for town. Almost there, we noticed two yachts flying American flags, a sight we hadn't seen before in Salcombe.

"Look at that one," I said, pointing to a Tayana 37 ahead of us.

"She's flying the Confederate flag and the Ocean Cruising Club's Flying Fish. I think it must be Escape."

Escape is owned by Allen and Elaine Jeter, two doctors from Charleston whom we had last seen six months earlier before they left home.

"No, can't be. They're in the Med by now, but let's go have a closer look," said Johnny as John turned the dory.

Then, "Yes, it is them," he added as we drew alongside. Finding nobody on board, we left a note and went on to town where I stopped in at the little grocery near the waterfront to pick up something for dinner. As I turned down the first aisle, there were Allen and Elaine. It was such fun to see them! Their plans had changed when they discovered that Elaine was pregnant. They decided to stay in England for the winter along with the couple aboard Hale Kai, the other American yacht we had seen.

After another busy day buying and stowing provisions, and working to complete more jobs on our endless list, we stopped for drinks aboard Escape and were back at the flat in time to greet Derek and Marcella and have dinner `en famille' when they arrived that night for a last weekend together. Caroline and John were watching television and heard on the news that Hurricane Gloria, packing winds up to 130 miles per hour was moving up the East coast of the United States. We wondered if any of our family were affected by it, but decided to wait and call them closer to our departure.

Johnny, John, and I worked aboard most of the next day and Caroline spent the day with Derek and Marcella surreptitiously enlisting another crew member. The three conspirators had begun by checking the local newspapers and then had driven to a farm near Start Point where they found just what we needed. He was only six weeks old, but quite lively and handsome too, with tiger stripes and leopard spots like T. S. Eliot's Gumbie Cat. He was a furry ball of charm, a typical English tabby cat. Caroline fell in love with him immediately, and she and Marcella bathed the kitten, and spent hours removing fleas. The grateful little thing reveled in the attention and purred contentedly while they worked on him.

Now, Johnny had never had a cat and, never knowing any personally, generally disliked them. Although we had often, on the passage over, wished aloud for a small animal to travel with us, Johnny was not aware that Caroline had taken the matter into her own hands. By late afternoon, Derek, with his hand-held VHF, having been forewarned of our departure from the boat, made sure the kitten was hidden. On our return to the flat everything appeared to be normal. We changed and prepared to go out for drinks and dinner with the Jeters and their friends. Caroline and John professed to be tired of restaurant food and said they would rather stay in and make their own pizza supper.

When we returned to the flat later that night Johnny was ready to reprimand the children for staying up past their bedtime, but Caroline interrupted him saying, "Daddy, please don't be mad. We stayed up because we have a present for you, and we're so excited we couldn't wait until tomorrow. Do you want to see it now?"

"I can hardly wait," he answered.

"Then close your eyes and hold out your hands," she said, running from the room.

She returned in a moment clutching her furry surprise, and deposited it carefully in Johnny's outstretched hands.

"Okay, now you can look," shouted John and Caroline in unison. Who could hate a kitten? Catherine Maxwell, named after the Dyson's yacht, sat there, a tiny ball of fuzz, in Johnny's open palms, blinking sleepily up at him. Johnny was bemused.

"Where did this come from?" he asked, trying unsuccessfully to sound severe, and Caroline detailed for him the events of her day.

"Don't blame me!" said Derek quickly, hoping I had been correct in guessing that this baby would capture Johnny's heart.

"Daddy, you know how much we all miss Gerta, and a dog might not be happy on a boat, but cats can keep their balance, and they keep themselves clean, and they don't eat much, and we won't let it bother you, and Daddy, don't you just love it?" Caroline enthused breathlessly, hoping she wouldn't have to part with her new pet.

Naturally, Johnny wasn't really excited about the prospect of a cat aboard, but he was willing to try it, since he thought it might make an interesting diversion for the children.

The weekend was busy. With Roger's help, Johnny put Sequoiah up on the quay. "Up on the quay" is a phrase we had heard before but, always having good boat yards available at home, we had never tried this procedure before. At high tide Sequoiah was secured to a wall near the town, weighted on one side so that she was leaning towards the wall, and then we waited for the eighteen foot tide to go out, leaving Sequoiah high and dry. Johnny had all afternoon to scrape the bottom, check the seacocks, and change the zinc on the engine shaft before the tide floated her again. Zinc, being the lowest metal, is used underwater to protect important metal parts of boats from electrolysis. The sacrificial zinc is eaten away first, and as long as the zinc is there, the bronze or steel is safe. Sequoiah was sitting low in the water, right down on her waterline. We were almost ready to go.

Leaving England was a wrenching experience for all of us. Being true anglophiles, we had felt right at home from the first glimpse of the country. Somehow this was like leaving home all over again; for, in addition to the usual concerns about weather, provisions, and last minute repairs, we all felt the terrible, emotional strain of leaving very special people.

The day that Derek and Marcella had to leave, we moved back aboard and helped them clean the flat. We had a farewell lunch aboard Sequoiah, all of us feeling rather restrained, not wanting to say goodbye. So we just said "au revoir" and Derek promised that we would see them in Charleston in two years. That night Roger Walker with his wife and children came aboard to have supper with us, and that was quite jolly. It was fun having other children aboard, and the kitten, which was beginning to learn his way around inside the boat, was a lively addition to the party. Catherine Maxwell, however, had turned out to be a male so we decided to call him Cat Maxwell, which very quickly was shortened to just Max. When the Walkers left we stayed up late putting things away and talking, starting to look forward to new adventures just over the horizon.

Early Monday morning I went into town to the greengrocers to select a variety of fresh fruits and vegetables that would last until we reached Madeira. At the butcher shop I stopped to pick up twenty packages of different meats that had been cut and flash frozen for me over the weekend. We spent the rest of the morning wrapping the fruits and vegetables and trying to find places for everything. By lunch time we were ready to go into Kingsbridge with Roger to buy some extra water jugs, run a few last errands, and take Cat Max to the veterinarian. We took our last "real" showers at the Salcombe

Yacht Club and Johnny collected our guns from Customs. Roger came by and stayed for tea. He had been wonderful to us, and had made our two months away from the boat worry free. We felt fortunate to have known him.

The first of October dawned clear and warm, and Johnny rose early to call the weather bureau in Plymouth. On receiving a forecast of SSW winds in the Channel at Force 3–4, and the promise of a three day window that should see us safely across the Bay of Biscay, we prepared to leave, dropping our mooring buoy at 0900. Twenty minutes later in rough and swirling water we crossed the Salcombe bar in intermittent sunshine. By the time we were actually out in the Channel, Caroline was throwing up and John was complaining of stomach aches and a general queasiness. I went below to get saltines to munch and a wet cloth for Caroline. Before I was outside again I was feeling shaky and a cold, clammy sweat had formed on my face and neck. By some terrible oversight we had forgotten to take any preventative medicine before leaving England. Johnny passed the pills around, but we threw them up again. Johnny alone was feeling fine. That first day he took all the watches and did all the cooking (which wasn't much since he was the only one able to even think of eating!). I can't remember ever being so miserable. During the day the children and I spent our time alternately leaning over the rail and trying to stay wedged in one spot in the cockpit so we wouldn't have to go below. What had begun as a lovely, clear, warm day in Salcombe had rapidly deteriorated. By noon we were wrapped in clouds and rain, four of us apathetically staring out at the wet grayness, Johnny working the boat alone. We remembered our furry new crew member down in the cabin when Max awoke and tumbled playfully out of his basket, crying loudly for lunch and staggering unsteadily around the moving room. After eating he curled up in Johnny's arms and promptly fell asleep again. I was envious of his easy adaptability, and wished I could escape to a dreamless unconsciousness.

Late afternoon brought patchy fog which gradually thickened to a cottony wall, effectively obscuring all vision. At 1900 we turned on the engine to cross the major shipping lanes of the English Channel as quickly as possible in the unpleasant conditions. Exhausted and empty, the children and I withdrew to our bunks, finally able to keep down our seasick medicine. During the night the breeze freshened. Over the radio we began to get gale warnings of Force 8 winds with the probability of a strong gale later. We were surrounded by traffic all night as we crossed the busiest shipping lanes in the world. Three different times we had to alter course to avoid collision. In between trips to the cockpit to help Johnny, I lay half awake, tossing and turning, with weird mind-wanderings, not quite dreams, tangling my thoughts. Johnny wearily went to bed at 0100 and I took watch until daylight, actively sick off and on all night. The sky was alternately clear and misty with a rising wind, and we raced along uncomfortably over lumpy seas. During my watch the radar reflector fell to the deck, the line holding it having chafed through in the rough weather.

Dawn arrived, shrouded in red, reminding me of the old adage, "Red sky at night, sailor's delight; red sky in morning, sailor take warning", and I felt a cold lump in the pit of my stomach, a foreboding feeling. Anxiously we listened to the morning weather reports forecasting storm force winds of 55 knots. I kept muttering ugly epithets for that stupid, lying weather forecaster back in England. He was a handy person to blame for our discomfort since I didn't know him and he wasn't on board. A large area of low pressure was moving in, remnants of Hurricane Gloria that had hit the Outer Banks of North Carolina and Long Island, New York the week before.

All day the wind rose, though the sky stayed fairly clear. We decided to go into France to take shelter from the approaching storm. Our major problem was that we had no detailed charts of the north coast of Brittany, only the Light List, which gives information about the location and signal of all lights in the area. Without a large scale chart we had no idea how far inland the lights actually were or how to navigate the entrance channels. After consulting the Light List and the inadequate charts available, we set a course for the town of L'Aberwrach. We made slow progress beating into the near gale. Early in the afternoon we saw ahead of us on the horizon a lovely old ketch with red sails, flying the Union Jack. Johnny called her on the radio. Talking to her captain, Nick Walker, he found that the yacht's name was Provident and she had on board a group of Englishmen bound for a holiday in France. She, too, was looking for shelter from the weather and was trying to make it to L'Aberwrach. Since Provident carried a complete set of charts for northern France, Captain Walker said they would lead us into port, an offer gratefully accepted. However, several hours later, it was apparent that we would never make it to L'Aberwrach before dark and we turned to run back along the coast to Morlaix. Providentially, Provident also changed plans and reached the entrance to Morlaix as we did. Without Provident we would never have found our way alone through that tortuous channel, winding inland for three or four miles with mountainous rocks on all sides. At dark we picked up a mooring in a protected bay surrounded by land on three sides, while Provident went on into the town.

With the cessation of motion the whole crew came, miraculously, to life again, and we ate a huge meal before going to bed. The barometer continued its steady fall. Although the area was well protected, we rolled and pitched all night as the wind continued to blow fiercely. All next day the wind howled around us. In the middle of the day the falling barometer hit a low of 997 millibars before beginning to rise slowly. There were gales all around, according to the weather reports, and we were glad to be tucked in that snug hole. We spent two nights in the deserted bay, then, as the weather failed to improve, we motored on up the river for five miles, went through a lock into the harbor of Morlaix, right in the center of town, and tied up to a floating dock at the marina there. On the way in, we passed Provident heading out. We waved, and thanked the men we had never met who had saved us.

We had an interesting experience with the French Customs officials. The first officer who came to clear us in was very friendly, but spoke no English. Since our French isn't the best, it took some time to fill out the immigration forms. First Johnny would talk while I looked in the dictionary, and then we'd reverse our roles. For the first and only time, Sequoiah was searched. The officer checked every locker and drawer on board, constantly asking questions about everything he saw. He seemed unusually concerned about our guns, which were still under seal from British customs. Everyone we had talked to said the French were quite relaxed about firearms. We were surprised by the once–over we were getting. Finally, the man left, telling Johnny to remain aboard. Later that afternoon he returned with a police officer and together they examined the guns, locked them in a closet, and sealed it. They explained that security was high because the French president would be in Morlaix on October 8, and they politely made it clear that the sooner we left, the better they would like it. They seemed to be suspicious of our reasons for being there.

Our stay in Morlaix was a delightful interlude. At the crack of dawn, Caroline would be off to the nearest boulangerie to fetch fresh croissants for breakfast. School work was done in the mornings and we went shopping and sightseeing in the afternoons. Morlaix is a lovely old city dating back to the thirteenth century. It was an important defense site for the Cote Du Nord for hundreds of years, and the ruins of an ancient castle stand in the mouth of the entrance channel, among all the other rocks we had passed on our way in.

We spent three nights at the dock at Morlaix. Finally, on October seventh with Johnny unable to stand the inaction any longer, we decided to leave. The weather had improved slightly, although the wind was still quite strong. As we were leaving the town, the lockmaster gave us a chart that the captain of Provident, thinking ahead, had left for us. While we waited in the lock for the water to reach river level, the friendly customs officer and his `superieur' came alongside and warned us to keep our firearms under their seal until we were twelve miles off the coast of France. They told us that their maritime police were patrolling the area heavily due to Mitterand's impending visit, and that we should expect to be boarded. Fortunately we never saw any of their Coast Guard ships and were spared the delay of another search.

Carefully we threaded our way out through the channel between the huge rocks. It was terribly windy, and all that day we beat into a strong breeze, slamming over large swells. Rain squalls came across us continually, one after another. We had taken preventive medicine well in advance this time so, although we didn't feel good, at least we weren't sick. The weather was dreadful. Waves kept washing over the decks and we discovered new leaks in the forward cabin. There were violent squalls all night. With the wind coming from dead ahead of us, we took down all but a reefed mizzen, left up for stability, and motored into the raging storm. Johnny stayed at the helm for six hours straight during the worst of it as he was the only one strong enough to hold the wheel. At intervals I would force myself from my bunk and, through a slightly opened hatchway, shout to Johnny to see if he was still okay or if he needed anything. Each time I guiltily felt relieved that he didn't want me to go out there into that fierce, raw weather. Conditions worsened all night and the wind screamed around us.

Rough weather at sea can cause all sorts of little disasters, just minor ones if you're lucky, and we were lucky that time. During that long night a can of okra got crushed in the bottom of a locker and leaked everywhere, and a gasoline can came loose on deck where it flopped around, fortunately doing no damage. There was a tremendous crash when 200 pounds of anchor chain broke the door between the chain locker and the forward cabin, and salt water flowed in. Towels were stuffed into the hawse pipes to slow the leak. Water was washing through the bilges and close under the floor boards of the cabins. We'd pump it out only to have it fill again. The worst part of a night like that is the knowledge that things may keep getting worse. Fear became a solid knot inside of me.

During the night we rounded the Ile d'Ouessant, or Ushant as the English call it, hugging the coast to stay out of the heavily used shipping lanes. Johnny was able to get a little sleep between 0200 and 0500 while I struggled with the wheel and my own misgivings. Down below in the cabin it was, comparatively speaking, peaceful and almost comfortable despite the erratic motion. Outside in the cockpit it was like another world. The high pitched shrieking of the wind in the rigging and the stabbing slash of rain were nerve wracking. It was bitterly cold in the wind, and the waves washing over everything were icy. It was a night of horror for me and one of the bleaker moments of the trip. Tears streamed down my face as I used all my strength to keep the boat on course, and my mind wandered back, trying to grasp the reasons we had chosen to do this. None of them seemed reasonable that night.

"What are we doing here?" I screamed in anger and fear, throwing my frustrations to the wind, my voice drowned by the roar of the elements.

We were really glad to have the proper clothes that our Scottish friend, Ian Mackie, had insisted were necessary for sailing in this area. Before leaving home we had purchased silk long underwear which Ian considered essential and, while visiting them in Scotland, he had insisted that we buy both silk and wool balaclavas, waterproof gloves, and the thickest wool socks you've ever seen. Armed with many layers of natural fibers, with our foul weather suits over it all, I can't say we were actually comfortable, but at least we were dry and warm enough.

By dawn the next morning the Autohelm was able to steer again, a relief to all of us, and we took turns pumping the bilges dry using a manual pump since the two electric ones had quit working. That day was sunny off and on with nasty clouds again by the middle of the afternoon. Johnny and I stayed in bed most of the day while John and Caroline worked the boat. By nightfall we were motor-sailing into Force 8 headwinds. On my watch in the wee hours of morning I had to wake Johnny and Caroline to pump out the bilges. Water was lapping at the bottom of the engine and I was having to hand-steer again. Even the manual pump was stopped up now and they had to use a portable hand pump to empty the bilge this time. The radar reflector fell again, fortunately landing once more on the deck and not in the sea.

After two days of nasty weather the skies cleared and the weather gradually improved as we crossed the Bay of Biscay in a growing high pressure. The nights held an ongoing display of brilliant stars. I would lie stretched out on a cockpit cushion watching the show for hours, the stars seeming so close that I felt I could reach up and touch them as they smoothly glided on their predetermined path across the sky. Once I saw a falling star so brilliant it looked like sharp lightning, leaving a streak in the sky for almost half a minute. One night I also saw a huge pool of phosphorescence in the water ahead of us about fifteen feet in diameter, making the water look silvery. As we got closer it slowly sank and gradually disappeared leaving me mystified. I wonder if it was a whale.

The twelfth of October was unforgettable. Everyone should have a day like that one, and it is even better if it is a shared experience as ours was. We had a Perfect Sailing Day. It was a sail to remember always. It was the sail of a lifetime. It was the kind of sailing that all sailors dream about, but very rarely experience. While I was sleeping, Johnny and the children raised the big drifter, the main, and the mizzen. The wind had come around behind us, and we were sailing a broad reach over a sea so flat the boat wasn't rolling at all. There was no sense of motion. I awoke around noon feeling disoriented. For the first time in days I felt still, but we were heeled over at a slight angle.

"What's happened? Are we aground? Where are we?" I called out, confused.

I was greeted with shouts of pleasure from the whole crew. It was a clear blue warm glorious day and everyone felt exhilarated. Sequoiah, absolutely still, was speeding across the sparkling blue of some of the most infamous water in the world like a dancer whose body glides effortlessly while her feet propel her along at great speed.

We all took sun showers outside and washed our hair. We made bread, watched a movie, and enjoyed the peaceful day. Max celebrated by galloping to the bow for the first time. I was still afraid that he might go overboard, but he was proving to be quite cautious and looked out at the constantly moving water with a healthy respect. We saw a school of Common dolphin flashing yellow on their sides. They came close and did some acrobatics, leaping clear of the water and even doing a few flips. Max didn't approve of them and stalked back to the cabin. Caroline wrote a note, sealed it in an empty wine bottle, and tossed it overboard, hoping that someday she'd hear from the lucky finder. She is still waiting!

Life aboard once again settled gradually into a pattern, but different now that school was in session. Johnny usually fixed breakfast around 8:00 when he woke up, and then spent the morning doing what I dubbed 'boat chores'. I slept all morning and John and Caroline did school work. Boat chores were Johnny's private domain and consisted of repairing everything that broke, from bilge pumps to tape players, and maintaining engine, sails, and lines in top condition. In general Johnny did most of the dirty work, but seemed to enjoy some of it. After a lunch fixed by Caroline or me, the children took watch all afternoon. When the weather was good, they would set the Aries or Autohelm and play games, read, go fishing, fight, or whatever else they felt like, just scanning the horizon every ten minutes for ships, and writing essential information in the deck log each hour. Caroline was still busy knitting her sweater, and John spent hours making battery operated machines with his Lego blocks, usually photographing each masterpiece with his Polaroid before dismantling it to build another. Johnny and I usually read in the afternoons. Sometimes I made bread or played the guitar and sang with the children. I usually prepared a big dinner that we ate about 6:00 so we could go to bed early. John and Caroline, generally with protestations and endless argument, cleaned the galley after dinner while Johnny took star sights at dusk when the weather was clear. Johnny stood watch until 1:00 AM and slept, on good nights, until 8:00 in the morning. I took the 'dog watch' from 1:00 to 6:00 that nobody else liked. It suited me perfectly as I enjoyed the feeling of owning the universe that darkness brings on the ocean, and now I had Max to keep me company. John and Caroline came on deck at 6:00 and took watch until Johnny had breakfast ready and another day began.

Max had grown by leaps and bounds in his first few weeks of our acquaintance. He was a constant source of amusement for all as he learned about his unlikely new home. Perhaps because he was so young, he adapted easily to life afloat. His ride in the dory to board Sequoiah that first time in England had terrified him, and he had clawed Caroline horribly. We had ended by wrapping him securely in a flannel shirt and covering his head so he couldn't see the world whizzing past him. Besides that trauma and two unhappy days in the rough weather leaving France, when he lay inert in his basket and wouldn't eat, he had been full of boundless energy and curiosity, and our only problem was in trying to avoid stepping on him when we lost our balance on the always moving boat. Max was a cautious cat and lived totally in the cabin for the first week aboard and then ventured only to the confines of the cockpit for another week. Only on very calm days did he dare to explore the far reaches of the open decks and bow. We kept track of his whereabouts continually because we were so afraid of losing him overboard. One night on my watch I looked around and couldn't find him. He wasn't in his basket, and I looked everywhere trying to be very quiet since everyone else was asleep. After about fifteen minutes of searching I'd begun to panic, thinking he'd gotten out into the dark cockpit and had gone over the side. Finally, at the risk of awakening the entire crew, I called him, and after a few minutes a very sleepy kitten poked his head out of John's sleeping bag, yawning questioningly. I was really relieved to see him!

As we moved steadily southward we gradually began to discard our layers of clothes. The day after our Perfect Sail, we put on shorts and bathing suits for the first time, although we still were wearing jeans and sweaters at night. When I heard the frost warnings on the British weather broadcasts, I was glad to be moving towards the Southerly latitudes.

The last few days before reaching land were frustrating. The steering system had gradually worked itself loose and we had to steer by hand constantly. Both the Autohelm and the wind vane were unable to handle the less responsive wheel, but there was nothing Johnny could do until we reached the calm water of an anchorage.

At 0200 on October 18th we sighted the light on Porto Santo Island and three hours later in the faint light of dawn, we could see the hills themselves. We were nearly out of fuel and tried to sail, but with little progress in the fading breeze. When the wind finally died, the thought of sitting becalmed for untold hours within sight of our destination was too depressing. With barely any fuel we turned on the engine and motored in, probably running on fumes, to anchor on the leeward side of Porto Santo. The holding was good on the sandy bottom and the clear water looked inviting.

CHAPTER TEN

EAST ATLANTIC ISLANDS

Johnny and I went to three separate places to clear customs and immigration: Bureau de Estranger, Maritime Police, and Guardia Civil. Simply locating these offices was difficult. Though no one spoke English and our attempts at Portuguese were unintelligible, we managed finally, through trial and error, and by walking the length of the town, to find them. We were given a six month visa and there was no fuss at all about having a cat aboard. We had been warned that many countries were quite strict about animals, but so far nobody cared about Max.

There were three other yachts anchored in the open bay when we arrived and several more came in over the weekend. As in most small ports in isolated places, yachties came by in their dinghies to compare travel notes and perhaps share a drink in the cockpit. Magne Hovland and his daughter, Hedvig, were the first among these, and they invited us to come aboard Svanhild after supper that night. Svanhild is a 75 foot Norwegian coastal cargo ship built in 1889. Nine families from Florø, Norway, had bought her jointly with their local museum. They had completely re-designed the interior as living accommodations using natural woods, and the result was a pleasing airy feeling. Their plan was to complete a circumnavigation in three years. All the families involved would sail part of the way in turn. The ship would then become part of the Florø museum. Only the captain and his family would actually be on board for the entire trip. At the time we met, there were thirteen adults on board, four children between the ages of three and five, and Hedvig, who was fourteen, just Caroline's age. Both girls were happy to meet someone their own age and sex. There seemed to be a dearth of teenage girls cruising the Atlantic.

Our weekend in Porto Santo was wonderfully relaxing. As usual the children spent their mornings doing schoolwork while Johnny and I read and worked on various projects around the boat. While I packed the sleeping bags and put our winter clothes away in the bottom of the forward lockers, Johnny cleaned and greased the rack and pinion steering system, hoping that would remedy our steering problems. In the afternoons we went ashore and enjoyed the beautiful sand beach and wandered through the little town. On his way to the New World, Christopher Columbus stopped in Porto Santo and ended up marrying the Governor's daughter. We were following in Columbus' wake. In the main square of the town, we saw his statue, the first of many we would see as we went along.

We were amazed by the numbers of tourists on the long stretch of beach. In talking with several German couples we met there, we found out that the island of Madeira has a rocky shoreline with no real sand beaches; therefore, tourist boats made the short trip over to Porto Santo daily, bringing loads of sun seekers. Because of this, restaurants were springing up along the beachfront and there were bath houses where, for 20 escudos, it was possible to have a cold, freshwater shower, a simple luxury that we took advantage of and enjoyed.

It was clear all weekend. The nights were still cool and John, bundled up in his sleeping bag, spent the nights in a hammock slung between the main mast and the forestay where he marveled at the stars as he rocked to sleep. He tried to induce Max to keep him company. However, most cats like their creature comforts and, being no exception, Max preferred to sleep on a real bed. His favorite place was next to Johnny.

We left Porto Santo under sail after being waked early by what sounded like the muffled rumble of a generator. It was only Max curled up on the berth between our heads purring his loudest. We had a fast sail under sunny skies to Madeira, thirty-five miles to the southwest. We slid down the coast of Madeira and had a few bad moments when we mistook a statue on a promontory for the light house on the west end of the island, and thought we had gone too far. However, when we rounded the point we could see the capital city of Funchal in the distance below gathering clouds. As we hurried toward Funchal hoping to beat the oncoming rain, a Portuguese fisherman passed and shouted in heavily accented English, "Welcome to Madeira!" We waved back feeling a warm glow, and I thought we should remember to do that more often at home when we see foreign yachts in our harbor.

There were only a few yachts anchored in Funchal's open roadstead, and those were rolling horribly. We passed them and went on, motoring slowly, into the walled yacht harbor. John, our bow lookout, shouted, "Dead dog off the port side!" as a bloated carcass drifted by, heralding the state of the marina's cleanliness. Because of the rough ocean swell running outside, the marina was terribly overcrowded. Yachts were rafted side-by-side up to twelve boats deep. There was trash floating in the water and black oil was thick along the walls. During our stay I saw numerous rats scurrying along the docks. I hoped Max would be a deterrent to any rodents eyeing Sequoiah. We tied up alongside four other boats, making quite a cosmopolitan group as we added our American flag to the lineup from Finland, Australia, Canada, and England.

Caroline and John remained aboard while Johnny and I, in the rain which had arrived just as we had, searched out the authorities, again located in three widely separated buildings. When we returned we took on fuel, and what a production that was! Four boats were rafted up to the fuel dock and we had to back Sequoiah to the wall between them and another raft of boats. The people on all the boats were helpful in fending us off and we managed to complete the task without injury to anyone. All of them had been anchored out and, unable to stand the violent rolling, had begged the harbormaster to let them stay at the fuel dock, the only available space at the time.

We had to move to another spot to take on fresh water. I hooked up our hose to what looked like a gigantic fire hose on the dock, and turned the handle one full turn. The hoses parted under the tremendous pressure that erupted and we had a geyser spraying everything for yards around until I could get the water turned off. There was so much pressure that just barely turning the faucet was enough to send a fast flow into the hose. With instructions from several onlookers, I tried again, managing to fill the tanks this time.

Caroline took nineteen days worth of dirty clothes and linens to a laundry at the Shopping Infante, a mall across the street from the marina, and found it would cost us 2,000 escudos, not nearly as much as we would pay when we reached the Caribbean Islands.

That night for supper I made some wonderful omelets, but met with much grumbling because I had put peas in them. They were such tender, fresh peas. How is it that if you like peas and you like omelets, you don't like peas in the omelets? I thought it was inspired and quite delicious, but no one else agreed. I had to promise not to repeat that innovation.

Madeira is a beautiful island thirty-four miles long and fourteen miles wide with a rocky shoreline and mountainous interior. Because the central mountains form a geographic barrier, with the highest, Pico Ruivo, reaching more than six thousand feet, the north side of the island gets about eighty inches of rain annually, while the south may be dry for months at a time. Most of the higher elevations of the interior are uncultivated and uninhabited, and there are countless roads and trails throughout, providing unlimited hiking opportunities with breathtaking views.

In 1419 the Portuguese explorer, Zarco, found the densely wooded island to be deserted and named it Ilha Da Madeira, island of timber. Prince Henry the Navigator began the colonization of this spectacular island just 600 miles from mainland Portugal. Forests were burned and sugar cane planted. Later grapes and bananas were added, and today the Madeira economy is still based on sugar, wine and bananas, with handicrafts, tourism and fishing following closely.

The people have used great ingenuity in harnessing their water power with a system of levadas, open, concrete, ditch-like channels to irrigate their land. In 1939 the Portuguese government combined hydroelectric power with the levada system to make the most effective use of the plentiful rain in the north.

We rented a car and spent two days driving through contrasting landscapes, from high stark mountains where we shivered in jackets, to lush green valleys and banana plantations where the heat and humidity reminded us of home in August. It was amazing to find such extremes in so compact an area. There were flowers everywhere, huge hydrangeas and hibiscus, and forests of eucalyptus trees. We drove along twisting narrow roads hovering on the edge of precipitous cliffs with nothing between us and the sea 500 feet below. Sometimes I had to close my eyes! In fact, I sat in the back seat just so I wouldn't upset the driver by gasping and clutching the seat. Caroline did quite well as the navigator and irritated her father only about half as often as I usually do under like circumstances, not to mention the fact that she and John couldn't poke each other across the seats!

At one point we thought the road had grown bumpier. Because the roads were so rough we didn't realize we had a flat tire until, near the village of Santana, some native men waving and pointing on the side of the road made us aware of it. We were in a peculiar little car without the luxury of an instruction manual and we couldn't even find the spare tire, much less figure out how the jack worked. The same two men came to our rescue and we spoke in nods and smiles and phrasebook sentences that made them giggle.

We took walks along a few of the levadas. There are 1300 miles of them! We walked through huge groves of bananas. It was the first time we had seen bananas growing at close range and it was fascinating to find that they grow upside down, the tips pointing up towards the sun. Because much of the country is so steep, all the farmland is terraced. Even the grapes for the famous Madeira wine are grown on sheer cliffs, where fences have been erected at the edge of the fields to keep the farmers from falling into the sea.

We had picnics high in the mountains and out on the flat, barren moors. One day, we saw a sheep roundup on the Paul de Sera. Several times we went up to Monte to visit the lovely old church there, and rode back down into Funchal on the carros do cesto, upholstered wicker toboggans mounted on runners, which are propelled down the steep street by gravity. Two `drivers', dressed in white pants and shirts, straw hats, and heavy, rubber-soled boots, hang onto the toboggan on its downward run to keep it from going too fast. It was an exciting ride.

Caroline and Hedvig managed to spend a good bit of time together, and we met two boys the same ages as Caroline and John. They were Chad and Eric Miller from Minnesota aboard the yacht, Solvejg. Though Madeira has no sand beaches, the three boys spent time at some of the rocky pools where the water is beautiful, and on the beaches of black stone which the rest of us found too uncomfortable. They discovered a movie theater within easy walking distance showing American films with Portuguese subtitles. The price was less than a dollar so the children attended frequently! One night Johnny and John went to see a bullfight. Caroline and I were afraid it would be too gory. We should have gone. It was mostly pageantry, and the bulls were not killed.

Madeira is not only famous for her wine, but also for the fine embroidery that keeps thousands of women employed, and the beautiful, handmade wicker furniture that we admired. It was all so reasonably priced that we did buy towels and a tablecloth, and even had some porch furniture shipped home to wait for us.

Most of the yachtsmen we met were, like us, bound for the Caribbean. We particularly hoped to see Svanhild and Solvejg again as they were the only yachts we had met with children of comparable ages aboard, and ours were much happier having a few friends of their own generation.

We loved the island of Madeira, but for a number of reasons we were ready to move on. The waterfront was much too lively and noisy for us and we were squeezed between the wall and two other yachts rafted alongside. People living on the other yachts had to cross our decks each time they went ashore or returned, which wasn't too bad except late at night and even then they tried to be quiet, removing their shoes before stepping aboard. The biggest problem was the constant stream of pedestrians on shore, tourists and townspeople.

They would stop and stare and, if the tide were high enough, try to peer into the ports. We finally tied a large sheet in the rigging on the side closest to land to provide a little privacy in the cockpit.

As a child of ten, living in London, I remember going to the zoo and being fascinated with the large monkeys. One orangutan would fill his mouth with water and when a good crowd had gathered around his cage watching his antics, he would spit on the nearest bystanders. His motives had puzzled me then, but during our stay in Madeira I began to understand!

I had a touch of flu our last day in Madeira. We had meant to leave that morning but a falling barometer and rising Southeast wind helped us decide to stay another twenty four hours, and I was glad we had. After looking unsuccessfully for pumpkins at the local market, I fell into my bunk and slept all day, waking at nightfall with chills and fever. Johnny and the children went out to a restaurant for dinner and managed to have fun on their last night in town.

Sunny skies greeted us the morning of October 30, and we left Funchal with a fifteen knot following breeze, bound for Teneriffe in the Canary Islands. Again I spent the day in bed and Caroline cooked the meals. Early on the morning of the thirty-first we had a couple of rain squalls before the day cleared. It was Halloween and John's entry in the log that morning showed his preoccupation with that holiday: "I am on my watch having a great time. The Aries is steering well. I don't know what I am going to be, so far."

By evening I had come to life again, and everyone dressed in costumes for dinner. We painted sugar cookies with orange frosting since we hadn't been able to find any real pumpkins. John, after great indecision all day, had become a fierce pirate complete with a black eye patch, and brandishing a beautifully handcrafted silver sword. Even Max, with Caroline's help, appeared in disguise. He was complacently wearing a cape and sporting a rather chic bow on his tail.

Early on the morning of our third day out Caroline spotted Mt. Teide on the island of Tenerife. The wind was light and fitful. We ran all day with both sail and engine, but by mid afternoon, realizing we couldn't make Tenerife before dark, turned off the engine, and fell off on a course for Gran Canaria. Perversely the wind began to increase. First we took down the big genoa, then the main, and then we reefed the mizzen. Even with just the jib and reefed mizzen we were approaching land too fast. Shortly before midnight we shook out the reef in the mizzen and hove-to about ten miles offshore. At 0400 I woke Johnny and we motored on to our destination, the recalcitrant wind having died once more.

Las Palmas, the main city on Gran Canaria with a population of 300,000, is on the main shipping route between Europe and South America. With her acres of oil bunkers, thousands of ships stop there each year to refuel. There was a constant stream of freighters and we were glad to be arriving in daylight. By 0900 we were anchored in Puerto de La Luz at Las Palmas. We'd heard from another yacht that the Customs officials would come out to the boat so we raised our yellow Q flag and Johnny and I stayed aboard, sending John and Caroline to town to find out about laundry and mail. Either the officials weren't very organized or just didn't care too much about who came into the country, but it took us four days of searching to find someone who would officially acknowledge that we were there! Only the boats staying in the marina were checked in at the harbor office and we were sent from one place to another with no results. Communication was difficult. Very few officials spoke English or French, and none of us spoke Spanish.

Pedro Abrante, who ran the Texaco fuel dock, was great fun and quite a help to us. He spoke only limited English, but his eyes and gestures were so expressive that he was delightful to talk to. Pedro told us how to clear into the country after our first frustrating attempts. He came aboard for coffee, showed us his scrapbooks, and regaled us with funny incidents involving the yachties he had met through his job. He had been especially impressed by a Japanese family who kept bowing to him while he helped fill their fuel tanks.

We spent eight days in Las Palmas. Both Solvejg and Svanhild had arrived before us, so the children had friends to play with after school. Johnny spent the better part of two days working on the engine and the steering system. I did some varnish work and John went aloft to make repairs and adjustments in the rigging. John loved riding up the masts in the bosun's chair, a little wooden seat that we attached to the main halyard, and it was certainly easier to haul him up since he weighed less than the rest of us.

I had always assumed that the Canary Islands got their name from the little yellow birds, but the Roman historian, Pliny the Elder, wrote that it came from the big dogs, canes in Latin, found there on an early expedition by the King of Mauritania in 40 BC. This explanation is just as likely, I suppose, though we saw neither dogs nor canaries!

There are at least ten inhabited islands in the archipelago ranging from low, flat desert complete with camels, to mountains above the clouds, the tallest being Mt. Teide which heralded our approach to the islands, reaching over 12,000 feet. Although the economy of the Canaries is still mostly based on agriculture, tourism is an ever-growing industry and new hotels and resort complexes are growing up all along the coasts. We were told that Tenerife had no beach until some developers hauled in thousands of tons of sand from the Sahara, and it is now a popular vacation spot for droves of winter-weary Europeans.

The Canary Islands average five days of rain in November, and we had only one of them during our two weeks there. With highs in the eighties and lows around seventy, it was really my kind of weather. At certain times of the year, when African dust storms rage over the Sahara Desert 500 miles to the east, clouds of sand are blown across the ocean causing a fine layer of yellow dust to settle on everything in the Canaries. Fortunately we were spared that phenomenon!

Because of the wealthy cosmopolitan community, and because the Canary Islands are duty-free, there was an abundance and variety of goods in the stores. There were two huge department stores. El Corte Ingles was our favorite. Part of a Spanish chain, it stocked everything from the latest French fashions to fine furniture from all over the world. Best of all, in the basement was a supermarket to rival any at home, with specialty items from the U.S., Britain, and several European countries. There we saw Oscar Meyer hot dogs and Breyers ice cream, things nearly unheard of outside the U.S. Also we found marshmallows, to Caroline's great delight, and I bought some Christmas decorations to add to those Weesie would bring when she met us in Barbados for her school holiday.

We had been calling Weesie once a week whenever we were in port and we tried to mail her a card or letter each day. It would be hard for her during the three weeks it would take us to cross the ocean and we wanted to keep in touch as much as possible. By this time Weesie was wishing that she had chosen to skip a year of school and travel with us, but there was no way to change her decision this late.

Johnny and John found, in their explorations ashore, a five-story marine supply house. They bought new flashlights (we never seemed to have enough!) and a comfortable chair for the navigation station that would prove to be one of the best additions to the boat. All we'd had until then was a wooden stool, so this upholstered chair with a back was real luxury.

The harbor at Las Palmas was filthy with raw sewage and oil fouling the water. For swimming we walked across town to a beach, in fact many afternoons were spent there. Most of the Europeans who frequented the beach saw no reason to wear bathing suits, and it took us a while to get accustomed to the nudity. One day John came back saying with disgust, "I sure wish the grandmothers at least, would wear some clothes!"

We were expecting a large package of mail at the American Express office in Las Palmas. It was a long ride from the waterfront, but we found the taxis to be quite inexpensive and numerous. This being our first experience with packages in foreign countries, we found that American Express only had a notice of our package's arrival and we had to go to the main post office to claim it. This seemed to be standard procedure for nearly all the countries we visited. American Express could hold letters, but the government post offices held all parcels and levied a tariff on each depending on what they contained.

One night there was a teen party at a private yacht club nearby and Caroline spent the night on deck in the hammock, falling asleep to the beat of `her kind of music'. On another night she and Hedvig went to a disco in town with Hedvig's father. They had a wonderful time and felt quite grown up.

Early one morning Johnny and John took the Jetfoil to Tenerife to buy a new Autohelm. Caroline had wanted to go but when we rowed to shore she found that she had left her shoes behind. She was sorely disappointed to miss the ride on the Jetfoil, a ferry boat powered by jet engines, which rides on a cushion of air above the waves at forty-five miles per hour.

The boys enjoyed their day on Tenerife, but reported that it was crowded and touristy so we were glad to skip it and made plans to go straight to Santa Cruz on the island of La Palma.

We left at sunrise to begin the 160 mile trip to La Palma. Finding the wind right on our nose, we motor-sailed, trying out the newly purchased Autohelm. It worked beautifully, and the steering which Johnny had tightened worked well too.

Max wouldn't eat, but since he seemed fine otherwise I attributed his lack of appetite to a minor touch of seasickness, like mine! John wasn't feeling well either. He'd had a cold for two days and when he developed a sore throat and fever, we started him on a course of penicillin.

After a twenty-eight hour run we arrived at Santa Cruz to find the harbor quite crowded and the area set aside for yachts very small. We tried anchoring bow and stern like everyone else, but we ended up having to leave the stern anchor on a buoy and move as we fouled someone else's anchor line. There were just too many boats trying to squeeze into the limited space. The Port officials allowed us and two other yachts to anchor outside that area in a place they said was outside of the large ship turning basin. They told us that a "muy grand barco" would be arriving at 2000 hours that night.

After supper John went straight to bed, but the rest of us were sitting in the cockpit when, right on time, a large cruise ship entered the harbor just as a band on the quay struck up a tune. Johnny turned on the spreader lights, illuminating our decks. We watched with interest, and then with mounting horror as the ship, growing closer, began to turn straight for us! Johnny started the engine as the ship turned two intense spotlights on us and the other two boats anchored near us. The ship came on, looming above us. Whenever the blinding spotlights flashed away from us we could see all the people lining the decks, listening to the music from shore. About 100 yards away, the ship moved into reverse, backing away from us, down the entire length of the harbor to tie up at the quay. It was a frightening experience and left all of us shaking... except John who slept undisturbed through the entire show!

La Palma is the westernmost island in the Canaries and a good place to buy last minute items like eggs, and fresh fruits and vegetables which are grown locally in great abundance. It is a lush and beautiful island and we were sorry that we were unable to see more of it, but with John sick and our long passage imminent, we were working constantly to ready Sequoiah for her second Atlantic crossing. Johnny dove to check the condition of the bottom and replace the shaft zinc, and he scrubbed the hull which was still filthy after our visits to Madeira and Las Palmas. Caroline and I did, however, take advantage of the hospitality extended to us at the Real Club Nautico, the local yacht club, which had a pool and showers.

We saw several yachts that we knew and met others, most of them getting ready for the same trip to the Caribbean. We met an eighteen year old Swedish boy named Nicholas, sailing with his father. Nicholas liked us immediately and one night he rowed all the way out where we were anchored, against a strong wind and current to pay us a visit. We were flattered by the attentions of the young. As we traveled we seemed to attract young men who were happy to sit and talk with Johnny on any subject, and then we realized that the attraction was the budding beauty in our midst and not our captain's sage words. Nicholas was no exception, and he enjoyed practicing his English while looking at our daughter. He was headed for Barbados so we expected to see him again.

Caroline spent the better part of one day hauling fuel and water in five gallon jugs to fill our tanks. This was not an easy task. In the dinghy it was necessary to motor the half mile to a little landing dock at the foot of a rocky cliff. From there the empty jugs were carried to the top and then to a nearby gas station to be filled and lugged slowly back to the cliff. The tricky part came in trying to get back down the steep rocks and into the dinghy. The jugs were very heavy and the cliff was slippery in places, making the descent a precarious business. With Johnny's help, Caroline worked hard until the tanks were full to the brim.

John was slowly improving, and although he still had a low fever, felt much better. On the morning of November 13 he and I went into Santa Cruz and found the market where we were able to buy beautiful fruits and vegetables from the local farmers. We also bought freshly laid eggs which we had to carry loose in a bag since there were no egg cartons like we have at home. Fortunately I had been saving our old ones. Loose eggs aboard might not have survived our first rough night.

We spent the whole day finishing our preparations for departure, and I kept thinking of more things that needed doing. I am especially good at that when it's time to leave. I like arrivals, but it is hard to get me excited about leaving a nice safe anchorage, even if it is a little uncomfortable, for the unknown of the open ocean. If it weren't for Johnny's determination, we probably would never have left home. I know why there are so many would-be cruisers living in marinas for years on end, dreaming of faraway places, but never quite finished with the last all-important preparations, never quite ready to untie the lines. I know because they are all like me. Half the fun for me is in the planning and packing and dreaming and just getting ready. The other half is getting there. I love landfalls. I love arriving in a new place and gradually learning my way around, learning about the people who live there and their customs, but most of all I love it when a long passage is over. The prospect of days and weeks at sea is not exciting for me. Fear of the unknown and the sure knowledge that I will not feel completely well until the anchor is once again on the bottom prevent me from wanting to leave. Usually, as the time of embarkation approaches I can conjure up all sorts of reasons for delay. There was that thunderstorm in the forecast the night we had planned to leave Charleston. We still laugh about that.

"We're leaving on a trip that will include two Atlantic crossings and you want to wait out a rainstorm?" Johnny couldn't believe it.

However, even the children had sided with me. We had been physically tired and emotionally drained after months of work and all our goodbyes, so he had agreed to wait. But on November 13, five months later, Caroline and John were ready to go too. They were tired of sightseeing and meeting new people, and were anxious to reach Barbados in plenty of time for Christmas, while I was beginning to think the Canaries would be a great place to spend the holidays.

Finally, even I was having trouble thinking of another job to be done, and at 1800 hours we raised the anchor and set sail for Barbados.

CHAPTER ELEVEN

SEQUOIAH SPEEDS

It was an ugly evening after a day of drizzling rain, but as we left Santa Cruz de La Palma a rainbow hung over the harbor and, like Noah, we took it as a good sign. The seas outside the walled entrance were rough and choppy, confused by a light northerly wind, and we rolled along slowly under main and mizzen. The wind began to rise, and by dark, still rolling heavily, we were moving fast at up to eight knots under the mizzen alone. It was a peculiar night with one line squall after another. We were running south between La Palma and the islands of Hierro and Gomera. The geographic situation of these islands can sometimes cause a wind tunnel effect... and we were feeling it! The stars were out everywhere except when each solitary black cloud passed over delivering its own particular brand of wind or rain or both. It was frustrating as the wind shifted from Northwest to Northeast, the autopilot unable to handle the large, following seas. Hand steering was necessary all night. We kept reducing sail and trying different combinations, finally settling on a storm jib and reefed mizzen.

The first three days were stormy with brief sunny interludes, and rough seas prevailed. Imperceptibly the seas grew more regular and the Northeast wind settled in at twenty to twenty-five knots.

Helen steering through rough seas the
first morning after leaving the Canaries

"Are these the Trade-winds?" we asked each other.

Trade-wind sailing is highly touted as the blue water sailor's prize. We had read much about it but, never having experienced it, weren't sure how to tell when we actually reached the Trades. There are no road signs out on the ocean and the

Northeast trades that we were hoping to find can be elusive at that time of year. After a few more days we felt sure that we had indeed found the Trade-winds. The wind vane, which had taken over the task of steering after that first night, was still in charge and Sequoiah was humming right along, averaging five and a half knots. Exactly five days after leaving the Canaries on a course of 240 degrees, we jibed and came up to a course of 270 degrees which we maintained all the way to Barbados.

The fine thing about trade-wind sailing is that it gets you where you're going...Fast! The part that no one likes to talk about is the motion produced by these `ideal' conditions. The side to side rolling motion induced by the large following seas and constant wind is enough to drive a person crazy. It might be soothing, like rocking a baby, if it were an even, rhythmic motion, but it is not. There are short rolls and there are long rolls, halting and hesitating rolls, tremulous rolls and violent rolls. Even when sound asleep and wedged into the narrowest berth on board, the one we called the `coffin', muscles were working constantly, involuntarily tightening every few seconds when yet another roll forced a change of balance. Nerve-wracking, yes, but I gradually became aware of a brighter side to this phenomenon. All this motion was creating a twenty-four hour workout and the weight I had gained tripping through the pastry shops of Europe was falling off effortlessly. Nobody else needed that kind of help, so they just ate more, but we all had good muscle tone after three weeks of the unexpected exercise.

Although I did most of the cooking I had no appetite, probably most fortunate, and just fixing the meals further reduced the appeal of food for me. I subsisted mostly on saltine crackers, fruit juices, and water, but the meals served were usually large and as varied as is possible on such a trip with no grocery stores around the corner. Fresh foods lasted surprisingly well and after three weeks we still had edible oranges, apples, potatoes, onions, and tomatoes. We craved fresh green vegetables. The canned varieties don't even resemble the fresh and were made palatable only with a judicious use of herbs.

For the first week, all of us took Antivert, our preferred antidote to seasickness, and after that I was the only one who still needed it. Poor Max became disinterested in his food when we left the Canaries and on the third day out he became quite ill. He was limp as a wet towel and could barely drag himself out of his basket. We gave him water with a medicine dropper and fed him rice and milk every couple of hours. That was his last bout with mal de mer and he recovered quickly. Within twenty four hours he was up again racing around the boat like a wild thing. When sails needed changing Max was on the foredeck chewing on sheets and hiding among the folds in the sails. When the sun went down he seemed to feel instincts passed down from ancient ancestors, becoming the hunter, stalking anything that moved. Usually John abetted this and provided him with a slow moving string or a rubber band, and they both charged around the cabin when it should have been a quiet time of relaxation before bed. It was hard for Max to wind down after an hour of this and often he would come galloping unexpectedly through our bunks, attacking toes with abandon.

Though we had been so concerned about him going overboard, Max proved to be quite cautious with an innate fear of the ocean. On rare occasions he would venture near the rail and, crouching low, stretch his neck out to stare at the expanse of moving landscape that encircled his world. After a wary appraisal he would back away and continue his antics, carefully avoiding the outer edges of the boat. He became quite adept at running and leaping all over the moving decks, but he never went forward when the weather was rough. He seemed to have good judgment or, more likely, a well-developed instinct for self-preservation.

At sea the Pelican was secured upside down amidships above the main hatch. When Max discovered it he started spending much of his day under the little dinghy, sleeping in that cool shady spot, or lying with his toes and nose hanging over the edge of the hatchway watching events in the main cabin. Often flying fish would land on deck and Max would drag them away to his hiding place where he knew we couldn't reach him. I wanted to rename the dinghy "Chez Max" but the children objected. Caroline was rebelling against the French language which she was struggling to learn, and neither child was inclined to paint a new name on the stern. At any rate the name still remains unchanged.

Max loved our canvas bucket. We kept it in the cockpit where it was within easy reach whenever we needed water to rinse the decks or take a shower. There was a long line attached to the handle that was tied to the rail before lowering it over the side and Max would curl up inside the bucket and play with the line. Max had fun with anything moveable. He was particularly fond of green beans. Whenever we were snapping the ends off he would raid the basket and take as many as he could get away with, tossing them high and pouncing on them. He was a great comedian and kept us laughing at his tricks.

Days at sea can be monotonous if nothing is done to differentiate one from another. We tried to do that by having a schedule of events taking place on certain days. Monday through Saturday were school days for Caroline and John, with Sunday a day of rest. The two of them thoughtfully offered to take my "dog watch" on Saturday nights. It was a real luxury for me to sleep all night and for them to sleep late on Sunday mornings. Friday was movie night, and we had salad and our own homemade pizza for supper, something the children always looked forward to. On Sundays we had our version of vespers. One of us might read a psalm or some

Max sitting in his favorite hideout

thing else that seemed appropriate, and Johnny's `sermons' sometimes developed into lengthy discussions. We always sang hymns; that was the favorite part, and there was much argument over which ones to choose as we all have our favorites. In the afternoons we would pull out the guitar and recorders and try to make music. We read aloud to each other before bedtime and <u>Little Dorrit</u> lasted until we reached Barbados.

166

Hurricane season officially ends November first, but on November eighteenth we heard that Hurricane Kate, packing 110 mile per hour winds, was just north of Hispaniola. A few days later it hit Florida and moved up through Georgia and South Carolina. We fervently hoped it was the last of the season especially since so many of them originate off the coast of Africa and build in strength as they sweep across the Atlantic.

Eight days out of La Palma we had covered 1,000 miles, and on that gray and drizzly afternoon we were entertained royally by Caroline. She had planned hours of fun for a gala Thousand Mile Party. While we changed into our party clothes, a dress for me and coats and ties for the gentlemen, Caroline decorated the main salon with long ropes of baggywrinkle that had never made it to the rigging. Baggywrinkle is made of short lengths of old rope that has been unraveled and tied together on a line. It makes a thick fluffy rope which is put in the rigging where the sails rub, to prevent chafe.

John, Helen and Caroline with Max, all dressed up
for a party, with baggywrinkle for decoration

The first event of the party was a treasure hunt which Caroline started off with a rhyming riddle leading us to the first hidden clue. All the clues were in verse and quite clever. We really had to use our wits to find each one. At the end we discovered some favorite candy, but we weren't allowed to sample it until after an unusual lunch featuring an original apple recipe. After that sumptuous repast Caroline taught us to play a song on the recorders which she had composed for the occasion. Finally some more games and wild dancing concluded the event and, pleasantly tired, we fell back into our routine.

Thanksgiving Day dawned wet and cloudy, the third in a row of its kind. A frontal trough engulfed us, but we were making 135-145 miles a day, so the dull weather brought no complaints. During the day we listened to Voice of America over the short-wave radio and to the Armed Forces Overseas channel with news of home, Macy's parade, and football games. It all seemed so far removed. We dressed for a formal dinner in the middle of the day, linen tablecloth and all. The only thing missing was the turkey, the one item we hadn't been able to find in the Canaries, but an English roast beef seemed perfect that day. Johnny and John spent the entire afternoon changing sails as the wind swung from East to Southeast and back...most annoying. However, the wind vane kept on steering. After a light supper we sang Thanksgiving hymns and patriotic songs and were having such fun that we started in on Christmas carols and kept going until time for bed.

The day after Thanksgiving the weather began to improve and we saw the sun again. We passed the 2,000 mile mark, celebrating with a `High Seas Happening' arranged by John and the captain. They had made a chocolate cake for the occasion, with no help from the distaff members of the crew, and it was surprisingly delicious. This was a come-as-you-are party so most of us wore bathing suits, our usual daytime attire in these latitudes. There were hand-painted party hats, and colorful posters decorated the cabin walls, the most prominent ones reading "Sequoiah Speeds" and "On To Barbados!" We sang sea chanteys and watched a movie, John's idea of the best possible afternoon.

High Seas Happening! Celebrating 2,000 blue water, non-stop miles.

Sometimes on the long night watches Johnny and I both found it difficult to stay awake. Perhaps it was just that we were more relaxed after five months of traveling or maybe it was the recurring motion of the ocean waves being steadily pushed by the Easterly trades. As far as the eye could see was water, an ocean of water, swelling, lifting, and rolling down, down only to swell, and lift, and roll endlessly on. Always constantly moving, the motion was mesmerizing, paralyzing at times.

The kitchen timer, our ordinary little wind–up baking timer that went "Ding!" when the spring ran down, became a prized possession on soporific nights. It wasn't an original idea. We know many cruisers who use them, particularly single–handers. Johnny, who has for years been plagued by insomnia, unable to sleep except under ideal conditions of total darkness and quiet, scorned the timer thinking it would be of no use to him. However, he was the first aboard Sequoiah to try it one exhausting night, thinking that although he would get no restful sleep, at least the timer would keep him awake with its ticking and the sure knowledge that if he did drift off it would jolt him awake again in minutes. Amazingly he was tired enough so that he fell asleep instantly and felt really refreshed on awakening ten minutes later. After an hour of ten minute catnaps he was so revived that he felt alert and awake for the rest of his watch, a kitchen timer convert. After his rave reviews I tried it too and got hooked on it. When my eyelids became heavy I would first try dancing with the mizzen mast to the fast beat of one of the children's tapes blaring through the headphones, or running in place while hanging on for dear life to the dodger and a shroud. I was careful to do these things only when everyone else was sleeping! When I felt too lethargic to talk myself into moving at all, I reached for the last resort and set the timer for ten minutes. Unworried sleep ensued.

Barbados is three hours behind Greenwich Mean Time so at intervals we set our clocks back an hour, spacing it out to make the hours of daylight feel normal.

The last week at sea was the longest. Everyone was feeling a touch of cabin fever. We no longer played Scrabble and chess. The motion was so rough that board games with men sliding around were hard on tempers worn thin by such close quarters.

"One thing about this trip", said Caroline, "is that I will really appreciate the small things when we get home, like a room of my own!"

Living in a small area, besides a lack of privacy, means constant cleaning, which produced daily grumbles. Nothing seemed to be worse than dishwashing duty, the children's most disliked job on board. In protest one night John plastered tape across his nose topped by a clothespin to make us aware of his opinion that dishwashing stinks! John much preferred washing the decks and would spend hours scrubbing and soaping and rinsing them with buckets of sea water, soaping himself in the process which didn't hurt a thing!

To conserve our fresh water supply we bathed in salt water and used our Sun Shower for fresh water rinsing afterwards. This worked well; and in between showers we used baby wipes to wash our faces and hands, and used powder to help make our skin feel dry in the sticky salt air environment.

Caroline and John had been reading Dougal Robertson's book, Survive the Savage Sea, about a Scottish family whose yacht was attacked by whales and sunk, forcing them onto their life raft and dinghy. They were discussing it one afternoon in the cockpit when Caroline saw some dolphins following us. She was scared because she thought they were whales so close. Several days later a whale really was following us.

There is a mysterious yet distinct feeling you have when someone is staring at you. Sitting at the wheel Caroline could feel eyes behind her. She turned with a slight shiver and looked back at the rolling ocean and the large following sea cresting above Sequoiah's stern rail. Nothing. She continued to look and finally saw the eyes. They were peering at her from a gray shape whose movements were synchronized with the wave behind us. She called the rest of us and we all looked. If we turned away for an instant, it was hard to find the shape again. Occasionally it would be lost in the continuous roll of water and then would suddenly reappear, rather like Alice's Cheshire cat. Always in the following wave and showing very little of himself, the creature continued to watch us.

After watching him for a while and searching through our books on the subject, our best guess was that we had a grosbeak whale on our trail. Grosbeaks are known to be solitary and we never saw more than just the one. They travel in those waters and are quite shy, never venturing very near boats. This one swam along in our stern wave never coming much out of the water. He appeared to be a brownish color, about twelve feet long, with a curved fin. We tried taking pictures of him and succeeded in getting very nice photos of waves! He must have been as curious about us as we were about him, for he stayed with us like that for several days. He made no noise, just looked at us, and one morning he was gone. It was a strange experience being followed by that creature with those intense, intelligent eyes, so far away from the life we knew and understood.

Water and sky surrounded us as we rolled our way ever westward. Often, friends who have never experienced off-shore sailing have asked, "Wasn't it boring, seeing the same thing day after day?" a question that had lurked in the back of my mind until I had been there myself. Traveling across the ocean in a small boat is like driving across a continent with constantly changing terrain. From one day to the next, some-times from one hour to the next, the view is never the same. The continuous motion of the water, covered with shadows and light from the changing sky, forms valleys or hills, undu-lating plains, or sometimes a lifeless liquid desert stretching as far as the eye can see. Life aboard might be boring when everything is going well and nothing happens to distinguish the days, but the passing scenery is a kaleidoscope of water and sky, never the same, one of the aspects of sailing that pro-vides endless fascination.

Whenever we began to feel cramped in our thirty-nine feet, we remembered some of the French yachts we had seen. Invariably people were packed aboard like sardines. In England we were rafted up one night with a thirty-two footer that had just crossed the Channel for a two week holiday on the Devon coast. On board there were two couples with six children between them! We couldn't figure out where they all slept. It was too cold on deck, by any standards, and they all disappeared below. Another yacht that had amazed us was the thirty-four foot boat we had seen in Horta with a man and his wife aboard, two little girls under five years old, and the wife's mother. They had made a forty-five day trip from Cape Town to Horta in time for their third daughter to be born at the good, free, Portuguese clinic there. Theirs was also the only boat we saw with an outdoor toilet. The seat was positioned over the water behind the stern of the boat, no need for flushing, and no privacy either!

One night a French yacht passed close astern on its way from the Cape Verde Islands to Martinique. We spoke to her crew several times, the only outside people we talked to for twenty-one days. Although we were well out of the normal shipping channels, there were at least six hundred yachts which crossed to the Caribbean that year and it was hard to believe we'd only seen one. We felt very small.

We were going faster and faster making 150 miles a day and more. Our last day at sea we covered 164 miles in 24 hours making it our best run ever. We could feel Sequoiah straining and hear a humming from deep inside her as she sped across the waves. That last night was clear with a low temperature of 78 degrees, and we flew along at seven knots.

Twelve year olds have excess energy, hard to expend on a 39 foot boat. John climbed the masts, did laps around the decks, and constantly played chase with Max. For the last two days of the passage Max had wedged himself in a corner of the forward berth under a rolled up sleeping bag. The motion was quite bad. When he ventured outside, he looked comical swaying on the heaving deck. He was ready to see land too.

Cabin fever had reached epidemic proportions by the time John shouted, "Land Ho!" on the morning of December 4th. Barbados appeared on the horizon as a gray shadow under the clouds. With mounting excitement we watched it grow larger and turn green as the day wore on. By late afternoon we

John sitting on the spreader, mid-Atlantic

had sailed past the southern end of the island, and turned up the west coast. At 1650 we were off the careenage at Bridgetown preparing to enter, when the captain of a tour boat directed us to call customs on Channel 12 and go to the Deep Sea Harbor to clear into the country. We rafted up to the "Jolly Roger", a pirate ship cum tourist boat, and went to the customs office. We were charged twenty-five American dollars for immigration and, having a British heritage, they took our guns for safekeeping. The process was very quick and pleasant.

The sun sinks fast at that latitude and there is no twilight. By the time we finished with customs, it was dark. We motored back to Carlisle Bay and anchored in 100 feet of water. We had covered 2,870 miles in 21 days. We all felt a sense of completion, of having finished a task, and it was good. We were totally relaxed for the first time in three weeks. No more rolling! Johnny quoted from Beowulf that night: "The sea was crossed; the voyage ended; the vessel was moored".

We had made it. Our second Atlantic crossing was completed.

CHAPTER TWELVE

CARIBBEAN CHRISTMAS

Sleeping on a still boat for the first time in three weeks was wonderful. Actually Carlisle Bay is quite open and there is usually a strong surge, but after so much rolling, everything being relative, it felt motionless to us! On our first day in port, school was cancelled. All hands were on deck after breakfast to help re-anchor, for in the light of day we found ourselves uncomfortably close to a tanker buoy and a very long way from shore. To our dismay the anchor windlass was terminally ill so Johnny hauled all the chain aboard by hand. When he had recovered somewhat, we eased in closer to shore where about twenty-five boats lay. On our first drop the anchor dragged. Everyone groaned and donned gloves. All four of us slowly pulled the chain up this time. It is a terrible, back-breaking job. The second time we fell back too close to a yacht from New Zealand. As we were preparing to haul our anchor up once more an angry man appeared on his deck shouting, "You've got the whole bloody bay! Get the hell away from me!"

We were too exhausted by this time to make any appropriate reply so we just kept pulling until we had that damned anchor up again. Fortunately, on the next try we succeeded in planting the anchor securely in a spot where we had plenty of swinging room. I know Johnny's back will remember that day forever.

Naturally, after twenty-one days at sea, away from all human contacts and the hustle and bustle of land-based activities, each of us had our own mental list of the first things we wanted to do. Before leaving the boat, Johnny dispensed what he called "crew's wages" to the children. He'd told them when we left home that whenever we reached port all hands would receive their "just due" and could spend it however they liked. Both had already spent it dozens of times in their minds. John still had some money stashed away in his drawer from previous ports, but Caroline's bank was empty and she and her new funds would soon be parted.

Mail was number one on everyone's agenda. There was a dinghy dock at the Boatyard Restaurant and we tied up there to go ashore. The dock was hazardous because the surf pounded violently against it, but most yachties took their chances with it as surfing onto the narrow beach was even more risky. We were glad to find both the American Express office and the main post office were within easy walking distance. Walking into Bridgetown the sights, smells, and sounds of civilization assaulted our senses and overwhelmed us. We perspired profusely in the oppressive city heat. Christmas music was blaring from the store fronts and seemed incongruous in the steamy weather. We craved fresh vegetables and bought lettuces and corn on the cob from street vendors at exorbitant prices which we later discovered were normal for Barbados. Located 100 miles from anywhere and much farther than that from land of any size, import duty was high. Nearly everything was imported, the exceptions, of course, being sugar and rum.

We also wanted ice cream, and after a lunch of, what else? ... Hamburgers and french fries... we all had huge ice cream cones that melted faster than we could lick. We wandered through the busy pre-holiday crowds, savoring the novel feel of civilization. Native women passed by carrying large baskets of goods on their heads, reluctant to pose for the camera. There were vendors on the corners, their carts piled high with green coconuts. They were selling coconut milk and Caroline had to try it. The barefoot native with one swipe of his machete struck the top off of a coconut, stuck in a straw and handed it to her with a grin. She was surprised by the flavor of the warm, bittersweet liquid. She had thought it would taste like the hard white meat of the fruit with which we were familiar, but this was something entirely new, and, she decided, not altogether delicious.

Bridgetown is the capital of Barbados and, with a population of about 97,000 people, is the only real city on the island. From the seventeenth century until 1966 when independence was gained, Barbados was a British possession. The British influence is everywhere: in the architecture, the lilting local accents, and even the uniforms of the policemen directing the busy traffic.

It was late afternoon when we finally returned to the boat, but there was just enough time to take Max to a veterinarian for his rabies shot and some other inoculations. Dr. Charles Vaughan was most interested in our trip, and also amazed that the customs officials had failed to inform us about the penalties for bringing animals ashore. The law reads that all animals must go through a long quarantine before being allowed ashore. Any violations result in heavy fines for the owner and death to the animal. He sent us back to the boat quickly. When I called him a week later to ask about an eye problem Max was having, he said he would come to the boat to see the cat. He arrived that evening with his daughter and son-in-law, visiting from Portugal, who wanted to have a look at Sequoiah too. After Max was examined and given some ophthalmic ointment, we had a round of drinks and a pleasant visit with these vicarious sailors. That was the only house call we have ever had from a small- animal vet!

When we called Weesie she said we should get in touch with Gordon and Gloria Dugan, parents of Hilary, a friend of hers from school who lived in Barbados. At that time Gordon was head of the economic department of the American Embassy there. We called them a few days later and thus opened a whole new world. Gloria took us in hand and showed us every square inch of the island over a period of weeks. She told us that visiting an island was wonderful but living there became boring with a monotonous lack of things to do, particularly in a cultural sense. She insisted that she had nothing better to do than chauffeur us around. After protesting only briefly, we allowed her to take charge, and we had a wonderful time.

The coral-encrusted island is twenty-one miles long and fourteen miles wide with rolling hills, the highest point just over 1,100 feet. Gloria took us up the west coast past the beautiful beaches of St. James, and through the sugar cane country across the center of the island, poinciana trees and frangipani in abundance everywhere. Outside of Bridgetown road signs are almost non-existent. The narrow roads are full of ruts and potholes, and public buses that stop without any warning. We were glad Gloria was driving! We passed through little clusters of chattel houses, wooden cottages usually owned by the inhabitants, but on rented ground, and easily moved if necessary.

We visited Harrison's Cave with its white limestone stalactites and stalagmites over 500,000 years old, and then wound our way up to the barren, rocky north coast which is rugged and wild on the windward side. The Atlantic waves crash onto the cliff walls with the relentless force of the tradewinds behind them, fetching from far across the Atlantic. The entire East coast is rough and rocky, and fascinating in a treacherous sort of way. Twice we went to the Kingsley Inn, a charming, rambling old place where we had lunch served on a comfortable porch overlooking the ocean.

Nicholas Abbey, an old plantation house, was of particular interest to us because of the Charleston ties of one of the previous owners. John Yeamans, of Yeamans Hall near Charleston, reportedly shot the owner of Nicholas Abbey in a duel and married his widow. We enjoyed talking with the current owner, Colonel Cane, who is quite knowledgeable about South Carolina history and our state's connections with Barbados. Also there was a wonderful gentleman's chair in the house that Johnny would have loved to have copied for himself.

Farley Hill Park is another lovely spot. Nothing is left but the ruins of an old plantation house on a grand scale with a magnificent view. It was easy to imagine what life must have been like when wealthy planters tried to relocate and reproduce their luxurious lifestyle on Barbados.

One more stop we really enjoyed was Welchman's Hall Gully operated by the National Trust of Barbados, where we took a fascinating walk through a lush tropical ravine. It was generously planted with native plants and trees, such as nutmeg, breadfruit, and mahogany, all labeled for easy identification. There were also many varieties of birds and monkeys everywhere.

Best of all, we enjoyed visiting the Dugan's home where they made us feel like part of their family. Johnny read the New York Times and the children watched television. One night, we had barbeque chicken on the grill. The highlight of our visits there was seeing the troupe of wild Barbados Green monkeys which lived in an overgrown wooded area next to the Dugan's garden. It was the first time we had seen monkeys up close outside the circus or a zoo cage, and we were enthralled watching the interaction of this group. It was an extended family with a large old male who dominated the fourteen others. There was one strong female and many smaller monkeys of both sexes right down to a month-old baby who was just beginning to grow hair on his body. They were shy but curious creatures, and they came into the Dugan's garden each afternoon to collect the peanuts that Gloria would place in a basket for them. Some were brave enough to grab a peanut from our hands, but would run a safe distance away to eat them. At the time we were unaware that these monkeys are thought to have been one of the main carriers of the AIDS virus into the Americas.

In between trips around the island with Gloria, the children kept up with their school work and we did manage to get some work done on the boat. Two brothers, Val and Allen Knowles, the owners of the Boatyard restaurant and bar, were a wonderful help. Besides being generous with their dock, they let us make international calls from their telephone. That sounds almost silly now, but in some of the places we traveled it could be difficult to gain access to a phone, and then often there was a stiff fee, so we were really grateful. Among the Boatyard's other services was a laundry. It was expensive, so we usually took our wet clothes back and hung them in the rigging. In the steady 20 to 40 knot winds they were dry within an hour. We were able to get our propane tanks filled at the Boatyard, and the always helpful Knowles family directed us to the best places for all the items we needed. One day Val even drove me around to find some hard-to-get boat parts.

The food at the Boatyard was good, and Caroline and John spent a large part of their "crew's wages" on hamburgers and cokes. We had dinner there several times. They offered an excellent salad bar and fresh grilled dolphin and flying fish. One night a girl from one of the cruising boats talked Allen into having a costume party, which turned out to be great fun. One of the winners was a man who came dressed as a pregnant nun with a sign saying "Bad Habit" pinned to the back of his gown. Caroline made an involved costume and appeared as a midget. John collaborated with two brothers from the yacht, Solvejg. Eric and John put on Eric's father's pajamas and came as Siamese twins with Chad leading them like a circus master. All the children who entered won flying fish dinners.

We really liked Barbados and I, particularly, didn't want to leave any time soon. However, Johnny was having a terrible time sleeping at night. In fact, even I was awakened fairly often by the noise on shore. After four days Johnny said he was ready to move on, and we would just have to see about finding Weesie a connecting flight to meet us somewhere else. Most of the island's nightclubs seemed to be located along the shore of Carlisle Bay and the volume of the music accelerated each night from about 11PM to 4AM. The cacophony created by the competing bands was unbearable. Caroline and John begged Johnny to try it a little longer, and that very day Caroline, full of determination, began searching for a remedy. She found it at a local drug store and returned triumphantly one afternoon with a box of wax earplugs. They were a perfect solution and we all used them. We bought a large supply and continued to find them useful long after Barbados was only a memory.

Yachts were arriving and leaving every day, but on a daily average there were about thirty boats in the anchorage for the three weeks we stayed in Carlisle Bay. John, the Miller boys from Solvejg, and Darren McLaughlin from the New Zealand yacht, Karaka, had fun racing dinghies in the ever-present trade-winds. An Englishman, with a Dyer Dhow like the Pelican, joined them one afternoon, but couldn't keep up. Although his tactics were more sophisticated, his size slowed him down and the children always won. The openness of the bay ensured crystal clear water and we snorkeled and swam every day, John and I diving in for a long race to shore most mornings before breakfast and school. Several times we went snorkeling on the nearby wreck of an old fishing boat, where we could watch a wide variety of fish. The boys from Minnesota were particularly fascinated, and were hoping for masks and fins for Christmas, borrowing ours in the meantime.

One night Walt Poitevin from the yacht, Ella, gave a slide show of his 1977 trip to the Bering Sea. At that time his was the first sailboat to travel there since 1917. His photography was beautiful and we still hope that someday we'll be able to see the movie he made while he was there.

Anchorages in remote places, because of their unique locations, are like very friendly international neighborhoods. Barbados is a good landfall after crossing the Atlantic, but it is 100 miles to the closest land. Anyone arriving by boat has much in common with the other yachtsmen and it is easy to meet people. The camaraderie among long distance cruisers is unlike anything else we've experienced. In Barbados we made many new friends, and there was much visiting back and forth between yachts.

During our three weeks in Carlisle Bay there were many casualties at the dinghy dock. Because of the strong surge, rubber dinghies were impaled on the rough edges of the dock and steps, and hard dinghies sometimes were overturned, ruining outboards and losing oars and lifejackets. Once I lost my footing as I disembarked and, pocketbook and camera in hand, went for a brief swim. Although I immediately washed the camera with fresh water, following the emergency cleaning directions of a professional photographer, the camera never totally recovered. Another day Caroline motored in with the Avon and as she approached the dock a sudden wave slammed her into a piling, tearing a gash in the bow. Allen and Adele Robison from Slipstream, luckily, were at the scene and towed her back. Allen leaped into the dinghy with Caroline, slapped his hand over the hole hissing with the pressure of expelled air, and told Adele to head for Sequoiah as fast as possible. They made it back to the boat before the dinghy was totally deflated and we pulled it aboard for repair. This was one of the times we were happy we had two tenders, since it took several days before we were able to secure an effective patch over the hole.

Until Weesie arrived on December 19, Caroline and John had school every morning. They took a Christmas break while Weesie was with us. Johnny and John met Weesie's plane. Naturally her luggage got lost, but it arrived the next night on the same flight with her friend Hilary Dugan, who brought it in from the airport for us. It was wonderful to have Weesie with us again, and she was glad to come to summer after the cold in Washington.

Several days before Christmas as I was baking cookies, Johnny was busy making a rope ladder to put in the shrouds. John had just finished wrapping some Christmas presents and left to deliver them to Chad and Eric. Suddenly we heard John shout in a desperate voice, "Daddy! Mother! Come quick!"

We ran outside and saw the Avon upside down. John and everything that had been in it were floating around in the waves. We both dove in. John righted the dinghy while we salvaged oars, lifejackets, Christmas presents, bailers, etc. Johnny lost his glasses in the process. When the dinghy was tied alongside Johnny started working on the outboard motor, washing it thoroughly in fresh water and then using WD 40 liberally. After half an hour he was able to get the engine started and it worked as well as ever. John was very unhappy about his wet presents and set them in the sunny cockpit to dry. The wind had been increasing since we had arrived in Barbados and most days it blew between twenty and forty knots unceasingly. The howl of the wind was simply a fact of life. John said that when he had started the engine and moved away from Sequoiah, he was sitting in the stern. A gust of wind lifted the bow of the dinghy and upended it. After that whenever one of us took the dinghy out alone we sat amidships.

December can sometimes be quite warm at home in Charleston, but not tropical. We always have visions of snow and a cheery fire burning on the hearth when Christmastime approaches. Christmas in Barbados was fun but very different for us. When the only shipment of Canadian Christmas trees arrived on the island, Gloria Dugan was one of the first to know, and she took me along to buy one. There were delighted shouts and comments from other yachts when I rowed it out in the dinghy. We were the only boat in the harbor with a real tree. Most boats we visited used artificial trees they had brought from home, or a palm branch. Some had drawn a picture of a tree, or just decorated their cabins with unusual tropical plants. Our tree was so tall we had to cut nearly a foot from the top of it to have it stand upright in the cabin. We had only a few decorations bought in the Canaries, but several friends from home had sent some beautiful ornaments, and we made more to complement those. John made long paper chains from strips of colorful wrapping paper, and Caroline wrapped up matchboxes to look like tiny presents hanging from the branches. We made popcorn chains and cookies shaped like bells, stars and trees, and hung them up along with the candy canes that Kitty and Henry Beard sent. Adele Robison made some beautiful crocheted snowflakes, and they completed our amazing tree.

Currikee, an Australian yacht, was the host for a wonderful international caroling party. There were two excellent guitar players in the anchorage and, since mine was the only other guitar around, they cajoled me into playing with them. After a few practices together we accompanied as many of the carols as we knew. It was interesting to find that some of our favorite carols are sung to other tunes in some countries, and we enjoyed listening to some that were unfamiliar, and learning about Christmas traditions in other lands.

Darren and his sister had a Christmas party one afternoon aboard Karaka for all the children in the anchorage. They exchanged small gifts, played games, and raced dinghies. Caroline and John made our traditional gingerbread men and painted them with colorful sugar frosting to give to the other children.

Early Christmas morning in Barbadoes

Christmas Day that year was like no other we had known. It was eighty-five degrees in the hot sunshine, and what the natives call the "Christmas winds" were gusting to 45 knots. Santa Claus had managed to squeeze himself down our tiny chimney to fill traditional stockings that Weesie had brought from home. After opening presents and listening to a taped Christmas service from St. Giles Cathedral in Scotland, we rowed to the Boatyard where we were able to make family phone calls. It took most of the morning trying to get through, and we all felt twinges of homesickness after hearing the familiar voices so far away.

Off and on all day people from other yachts drifted by for a drop of Christmas cheer and we reciprocated. An Englishman we didn't know rowed over and hailed us saying, "Happy Christmas! I am a baby flying fish." We weren't quite sure how to respond, but he introduced himself as Hugh DuPlessis, a single-hander from Lymington. He went on to explain that he had recently become a member of the Ocean Cruising Club and, seeing our burgee at the spreader with its flying fish emblem, wanted to come and meet us.

As our friends Allen and Adele Robison had returned to Canada for the holidays, we invited their eighteen year old English crew, Graeme Lamb, to join us for a traditional American turkey dinner. We dressed in our Christmas best, bare feet excepted, and used the beautifully embroidered linen tablecloth and napkins we had bought in Madeira for the occasion. Graeme was delightful and a great addition. As his contribution to the meal he had made his mother's recipe for English steamed pudding. We ate so much at our midday feast that we saved his special dessert and ate it with custard Christmas night instead of supper. It was a very good day, and a fine way to end our stay in Barbados.

CHAPTER THIRTEEN

Down Island Living

Boxing Day (December 26) was spent preparing Sequoiah for sea. It was sad to undress our tree and row it back to shore. After clearing customs we left Barbados at about 1700 hours headed for Union Island in the Grenadines. As soon as the sails were up we sped on our way, the wind dead astern, Sequoiah rolling like a tub. Eighteen hours later we anchored in the comparatively flat water behind the reef at Clifton, the main town on Union Island. The Christmas Winds blew for two solid weeks that year. Anchored in the calm of Clifton Harbor, we could hear the 45 knot wind singing in the rigging and look across the reef to the ocean, rough and white topped. Traveling to shore by dinghy against the wind was a trial, wet but not impossible. Clifton was depressingly poor, an ugly little town with an airstrip and a resort on the waterfront catering mainly to French tourists. Our sole reason for stopping there was to clear customs. In one of the tourist shops in the town I found some lovely pillow covers of locally dyed batik design, the only beauty I saw in that sad place.

The following morning it took us two and a half hours of motoring and beating into the wind to reach the Tobago Cays where we anchored in the lee of Petit Rameau. Only a handful of boats were there. We spent two days snorkeling on Horseshoe Reef which encircles the cays on three sides. It was very beautiful with huge fans and fabulous coral formations. The water was rough and cloudy as a result of the offending Christmas winds. We were told that it is truly spectacular in settled weather.

In the Tobago Cays I found my favorite island. Tiny Petit Bateau is a long narrow sliver of white sand lined with palms, my idea of the perfect Caribbean isle. The full moon gave the Tobagos a special glittery ambience by night and the days sparkled in the sunlight. We hated to leave, but Weesie's time was running short. Instead of going back the same way we had come which is through deep, open water, we opted for a short cut across a shallow bank. Johnny stood high above the deck on his newly finished rope ladder, and the children took positions on the bow, directing me at the helm as we threaded our way carefully through the coral-strewn south pass. In just over an hour we were back in Clifton harbor where we anchored long enough to clear out of the Grenadines. We then left on a perfectly beautiful sail to St. Vincent. Just as the sun was going down two small, brightly colored boats rowed furiously by native boys raced out to meet us and usher us into Wallilabu Bay. Each had a name hand-painted on the side. One was "Struggle On" and the other "Troy". I wish I knew the stories behind those names. When the two reached us they asked for a tow. We tossed them a stern line which they held onto with their bare hands. They instructed us where to drop the anchor, and then they took our stern line and tied it to a tree on shore. This was our first encounter with the notorious Caribbean "boat boys" and we paid them $5 EC. An Eastern Caribbean dollar is worth one half of an American dollar. With more yachts stopping at the islands each year, the boys and young men have found this to be an easy source of money. As soon as they have your boat secured they let you know immediately about all the other services they can provide: walking tours of the island - this can entail hiking through the woods or bushwhacking to the nearest volcano; garbage disposal- who knows what they do with it; jewelry sales - these items are usually necklaces and earrings hand-crafted from coral and shells; and fruit and vegetable sales. We told one boy we would buy some bananas in the morning and they disappeared into the darkness. Wallilabu was beautiful in the clear night. We could hear the surf on the shore, and crickets chirruping from the trees; the air smelled like the mountains that surrounded us.

Just after daylight a boat boy bearing bananas arrived calling, "Good morning, captain!", and pounding on the side of the hull with his bare fist to make sure we were aware of his presence. Within five minutes another boy, also carrying bananas, appeared on the scene saying we had promised to buy the fruit from him. Since we hadn't had a very good look at the boys the night before, we compromised and bought a few from each. We later found that this was an oft-repeated trick of the trade and usually resulted in more sales. It surely worked with us...at least this first time!

Weesie had to leave us on New Year's Day from Vieux Fort on the island of St. Lucia. St Lucia is twenty-seven miles long and fourteen miles wide, only slightly larger than Barbados, but vastly different. St. Lucia, like most of the Windward Islands, is very mountainous, formed by volcanic action, and with 160 inches of rain annually in the interior, the forest there is quite lush. If we had known beforehand how easily we could have found a taxi elsewhere on the island, we would never have taken Sequoiah to Vieux Fort. It was a very poor town on the southeast tip of the island and, on leaving St. Vincent, we beat into a big headwind to get there, only to find that the holding ground in the anchorage was terrible. It was situated so that wind funneled down from all angles and blew the boats around in crazy ways. No matter where we anchored we would end up eventually swinging too close to another boat. It was frustrating.

All the Caribbean islands are separate countries so it is necessary to go through customs when arriving and leaving each one. It is also proper, when traveling in foreign waters, to fly that country's courtesy flag on the starboard spreader. I love flags. In addition to the American flag flying at the stern, we flew three club burgees at the port spreader and the required national courtesy flag to starboard. By the end of our voyage we had quite a collection. In addition to flags of foreign countries, we also had a Children Aboard flag designed as the result of a contest in Cruising World magazine. Unfortunately it was so new that not many people recognized it. Also by the time we reached the Caribbean we realized that there just weren't many children as old as ours out cruising. We gave that flag to an Australian family with a young child. Hopefully by now the flag is gaining recognition because, like club flags, it is an invitation for others with a common interest to come over and introduce themselves.

Being New Year's Eve and Weesie's last night with us, we went out for dinner at the only restaurant we found. It served typical island food and lots of it. In addition to the entrees we ordered, we were also served breadfruit croquettes, fried plantain, split pea soup, fried potatoes and cole slaw. There was no way we could even think about eating it all. Our waiter was an Indian who invited us to accompany him to a bazaar the next day. By the time we were back on board most of us were too sleepy to stay awake until midnight. John and Caroline blew up lots of balloons and decorated the main cabin. They managed to keep each other up, and at the sound of the clock striking twelve they woke us with shouts of "Happy New Year!" and the sound of popping balloons. Max was scared to death and he didn't appreciate the fireworks on shore either. He climbed into the forward berth and curled up close to Johnny's head.

Weesie left first thing in the morning. Johnny had arranged to have a taxi meet them on the dock and he went to the airport with her. It was hard to say goodbye. Her visit seemed so short.

Hilary, our Indian friend, met us at midday and took us for a tour of the pitiful town and then to the New Year's Day bazaar at the local Catholic church. There were booths for food, drinks, and games set up in the small dirt yard in front of the church with a background of loud calypso music. Ours were the only white faces in the crowd and we were the only strangers, but we were welcomed with smiles by all. The people were dressed in their finest and some were dancing. We stayed only a short time, but I think it lasted well into the night.

The wind was still strong and the boat was moving around the anchor constantly. New Year's afternoon was spent drinking pina coladas on board and watching the Army-Navy game that Hertz had taped for us. At least we saw the first two quarters and the halftime show but we never found out who won because the last half wasn't on the tape! To finish off the day we, of course, had Hopping John for supper. This is an old Charleston receipt, made of steamed rice and field peas, and is said to bring good luck all year if eaten on January first.

The wind continued to rage all night. In the morning we found that the Avon, which had been tied behind Sequoiah, had capsized. Johnny worked all day on the outboard motor, but had no luck in starting it. It must have been under water for hours. Caroline carefully searched the bay with binoculars and spotted the oars caught on some rocks along the shore. It was quite rough, but when I rowed John over in the Pelican, he managed to reach them. The pump used to inflate the

Avon was lost, so we took the little boat aboard and stowed it in a locker until we could repair the still-leaking patch, buy a new pump, and find someone to work on the outboard.

We stayed at St. Lucia for two more weeks. Our next stop was at Anse des Pitons on the southwest side. This is a lovely deepwater anchorage between two mountains, Petit Piton and Gros Piton, the latter reaching just over 2,600 feet high. The only drawback is that in certain conditions the winds can scream down the mountains at up to fifty miles an hour. There is a depth of over 100 feet in the Anse until you get about forty feet from shore. We dropped a stern anchor and motored slowly towards land until the anchor caught; then the boat boys tied our bow line to a palm tree on the beach. The first thing we saw on shore was an elephant, and not a pink one! She was gray and small and her name was Boopa. She belonged to the Englishman who owned Jalousie, the banana plantation there. She roamed around loose and would carefully step over all the boat lines on the narrow strip of beach. We were intrigued by the way she cracked open coconuts by stamping on them with her huge front feet, then picking up the pieces and feeding herself neatly with her trunk. We met two other boats there with children aboard, all younger than ours, but children nonetheless, and ours were delighted to have companions to play with. John found two younger boys to go exploring with, and they disappeared into the hills for hours at a time.

We met a native boy named Laurence Nelson who took us for a hike up to see the sulfur springs at a dormant volcano, all except Caroline, who remained aboard steadfastly refusing to do her French lesson. Laurence could mimic bird calls of every description and pointed out many varieties of birds as we walked. Along the way he also pointed out coffee beans, pidgeon peas, prickly pear, grapefruit, and sour sop, all growing wild along the dirt tracks we were following. He picked guavas for us to eat and, under his direction we tried sucking on cocoa beans, which tasted surprisingly like yogurt. The narrow trails through the forest were steep and very rough and the vegetation dense, with bananas and coconut palms predominating. The sulfur springs were not very scenic; the forest was much more interesting, and the smell of rotten eggs which emanated from the steaming vapor was overpowering. On our way back to the boat, Laurence cracked open two large coconuts for us by raising them high above his head and dashing them full force onto the ground. We all tried, but none of us could duplicate his performance. We needed a hammer and wedge to crack those tough nuts.

Another day on a long afternoon walk, Johnny and I were caught in one of the sudden heavy rain showers that are part of daily life on the mountainous windward islands. We crawled under a wide-leafed shrub near the edge of the path and sat talking in relatively dry comfort. In a while, just as the weather began to improve, we heard singing and soon saw two barefoot women carrying huge bags of avocados on their heads accompanied by a man carrying limes. When they saw us one of the women, who later introduced herself as Magdalen Mathurian, bent down to get a better look and asked with a giggle, "What you doin' under there?"

They couldn't understand why we would want to sit under a bush just to avoid the rain. We went out and talked to them and they agreed to let us take their pictures; then they went on, leaving us some limes and avocados. Magdalen gave me her address and I later sent her copies of the photographs thus beginning a pen pal relationship that continued many years.

When we left Anse des Pitons we towed Pelican, our hard dinghy, behind us, our usual procedure on short trips between islands. We were going only ten miles up the coast to Marigot Bay. The wind was strong and we were close reaching under jib alone in rough water. Pelican filled with water twice before we realized that it wasn't just from spray. The centerboard box cover was loose. We decided to take Pelican aboard and that is how we discovered that I had tied the halyard improperly. To put the dinghy on board the halyard was attached to bow and stern lines. When it got caught on something at the wrong moment, Pelican nearly capsized. We lost the bailer and one bronze oarlock. With the wind beating over us and short choppy waves making the whole process unpleasant and difficult, we finally finished the job. During all these maneuvers we were pushed far offshore and had to beat back to St. Lucia, adding an extra hour to the trip. From then on we took the dinghy aboard before leaving port! We were still learning lots of things the hard way.

Marigot Bay was to have been an overnight stop, but we fell in love with the place and ended up staying a week. Marigot Bay is a beautiful, landlocked lagoon, a travel photographer's dream. My favorite story about Marigot tells that Sir Francis Drake, hotly pursued by the enemy, hid his fleet behind a spit of land in the entrance channel. Palm branches were tied in the rigging of the ships, concealing them well, and the powerful French fleet passed them by. For more than 150 years the British and French fought over St. Lucia until, in the early 1800's, the British finally won, and the island remained in British hands until independence was achieved in 1967.

Marigot Bay is where The Moorings, a yacht charter agency, keeps one of its sailboat fleets, and they own the Hurricane Hole Hotel there. Several yachts that we had seen in Barbados were there and we met others. Everything was so convenient. The use of the hotel pool was generously offered to all visiting yachtsmen; there were two restaurants right on the waterfront, and best of all, from the children's point of view, there was a free ferry taking passengers back and forth across the bay that would stop right alongside yachts when requested. This was our first experience with front door taxi service! John and Caroline enjoyed playing with three younger boys on the yacht, Lady Helen, from California, and the others they had met at the Pitons. With school and new friends, their days were full.

All of us like bananas, and they were abundant and inexpensive in the tropics. The main base of St. Lucia's economy is banana export. While at Marigot Bay an elderly native named Moses talked me into buying a whole stalk of bananas. It was so big we had to tie it to the mast just to keep it out of the way. It couldn't possibly fit down below. This one stalk (containing around a hundred bananas!) would ripen slowly from top to bottom, according to Moses. How was I to know! We ate them on our breakfast cereal, had peanut butter and banana sandwiches for lunch, and ate fruit salad for dessert after dinner. It seemed that the more bananas we ate, the more ripe ones we had left. We made banana bread and banana muffins, banana waffles and pancakes, banana chips for hors d'ouvres, banana milkshakes, and I made up a new cake recipe: Marigot Bay Fruitcake. We gave away bunch after bunch of bananas, and ate those long yellow fruits until we thought we'd never want to taste another. Max wouldn't eat any bananas, but he enjoyed watching the birds that were attracted to our rapidly ripening stalk; happily, he wasn't quick enough to catch any! Those "Days of the Bananas" seemed like weeks, and it was a long time before we bought any more.

On Saturday night we went to the jump-up (local euphemism for dance) at the Hurricane Hole Hotel. We all danced to the beat of the small steel band and enjoyed meeting a variety of people, vacationing at the hotel, chartering boats from The Moorings, or cruising as we were. That was one of our rare late nights. Most of the time we managed to get in bed early and read. Our waking hours in port were generally regulated by the rising and setting of the sun. There were electric lights on board that worked through the twelve volt system, but we preferred using the oil lamps that put no strain on the batteries. With one-inch wicks these lamps give good strong light for reading, yet softer than their electric counterparts and easy on the eyes.

Our days at Marigot Bay drifted along in a leisurely fashion, melting into one another. We still held school every morning and there were always boat jobs to be done: changing the oil, washing the clothes, topping up the water tanks; but these were almost always finished by lunchtime and then the afternoons were spent reading by the pool, hiking to a waterfall, visiting other yachts, or simply swinging in the hammock. Paradise.

The Norwegian yacht, Valkyrian, arrived on our last day at Marigot Bay, with a female cat on board. When the crew spotted Max stretched on the foredeck, they rowed over and invited him to their yacht to meet their 'she-kitty' whom they hoped might have kittens one day. Max was curious, not having seen another feline since leaving his mother, but his playful, kittenish advances were met with alarming bouts of hissing and spitting, and he was soon ready to go back home to Sequoiah.

From Marigot Bay it was a forty-three mile trip to Fort de France, the capital city of Martinique. Martinique differs from many of the other Caribbean islands in that it is neither an independent country nor a colony of another country, but a department of France, just as Hawaii is a part of the United States, with equal representation in government affairs. Stepping ashore there is like going to France itself except that the main population is black and, of course, the climate is rather different. When we had anchored in the Baie des Flammands and Johnny had breezed easily through customs, the Canadian couple from the yacht Trewartha rowed by to tell us where to find the best supermarket, the post office, and other essentials. The waterfront was filthy and reputed to be a high crime area, with many reports of stolen dinghies and motors, but the rest of the town was quite civilized, very French. We took Max to a veterinarian to have the rest of his immunizations and asked about having him neutered, but were told that he was still too young for that. None of the French islands had any regulations prohibiting animals, but, except for his medical excursions, we kept Max on board most of the time. Caroline liked to take him ashore for walks on his leash, but Max was much more comfortable within the familiar confines of the boat.

Fort de France was a large city and Caroline was delighted with the stylish shops. She and I were planning to fly to San Francisco in February for my brother's wedding, so we bought some shoes and sweaters to take along. With the restricted space on board our wardrobes were limited, and Caroline and John were at a disadvantage because they kept growing, as children will do. We had mailed our winter clothes home before leaving England and really weren't prepared for the chill of San Francisco.

After lunch on January 20 we left Martinique for the overnight sail to Iles des Saintes, a group of islands south of Guadeloupe. We raced along with the strong Trades until after midnight when we were blanketed by the island of Dominica and motored slowly for a while until the wind reached us again. The wind was so strong that we hove to for an hour and a half to wait for enough daylight to safely approach the low-lying islands. Iles des Saintes was another of our favorite stops because of the good snorkeling and beautiful beaches. Each day after completing boat chores and school, which was going very badly at that point, we packed lunch and hiked to one of the many deserted beaches to explore and swim. There were usually goats, sheep, cows, turkeys, and chickens along the roads, and there were good views from the hilltops.

The holding ground in the main anchorage off the town was not good. Once Sequoiah dragged while we were ashore and we had to re-anchor on our return. We weren't the only ones to have trouble. Solvejg was anchored with line, and I awoke one morning about 0400 to find Solvejg next to us, almost within arm's reach. About half an hour later I looked out and saw they had dragged a long way into the inlet. Johnny rowed out and went aboard, waking Steve. They came back in and anchored near us. Caroline, who was spending the night in the hammock, watched as they dragged down on us once more. About daylight they anchored yet again, but with chain this time, and didn't have to move again. Later that same day Johnny and Ernst, a Belgian friend, rowed a long way to reach a French yacht that they saw dragging out to sea. There was no one aboard, so they sailed her back in. The owner, who had been ashore, saw them, thought they were stealing his boat, and when he reached them, upbraided them angrily in French. By evening he must have realized what they had done for him, and he arrived bearing a bottle of a lethal, locally brewed coco punch for each of them. A nice gesture, but Johnny passed his on to someone with a stronger stomach!

We did quite a bit of snorkeling and one day, while out with John, Eric, and Chad, I backed into some coral, cutting myself. Strangely, I didn't feel anything, but one of the boys pointed to the blood streaming from my leg and I swam quickly to the boat, and scrubbed the wound thoroughly with soap and water and then with Betadine. It didn't look like much but I had read that coral cuts could be quite poisonous. The next day I didn't feel well and the cut looked bad, so I stayed out of the water. By the third day my foot was swollen, red and painful, with local heat, and I was running a fever. I started a round of antibiotics and soon the problem was under control, but it was months before the scars of what had started as a tiny cut were completely gone.

One day we walked up to a high promontory to visit Fort Napoleon. Several rooms there are devoted to wonderful displays depicting the hourly progression of a famous naval battle between the English and the French fought on April 12, 1782. The Battle of the Saintes was considered a major setback to the growing French influence in the Caribbean. It was interesting to me that the French would go to such trouble to erect and care for an extensive exhibit of a battle won by their enemy. We never found any such oddities on British islands.

We had no rain while we were at Iles des Saintes, but we could see showers passing over Guadeloupe just to the north of us every day. These islands are quite arid and comparatively flat, while Guadeloupe is mountainous and luxuriant. As in the other French islands, French was the primary language and the people were wonderfully friendly. French francs were the medium of exchange, as on Martinique, while the other Windward Islands used the Eastern Caribbean dollar. The French all over the world know how to bake bread and one of us was up early each morning to stand in line for baguettes and rolls fresh from the oven at the local bakery.

We moved Sequoiah to Plage de Pain du Sucre, another anchorage near a beach where we spent our last two days at Iles des Saintes. Solvejg and the Dutch yacht, Fortuin, came too and we had fun snorkeling, diving, and cooking on the beach. John and Caroline entertained Kees, the 5 year old Dutch boy, with lightsticks, those waxy chemical sticks that glow for several hours when they are bent. He was fascinated. International picnics usually produce uncommon fare and this was no exception. Our Dutch friends had never tasted potato salad or roasted marshmallows before, and we had our first taste of mussels marinated in a Dutch whiskey sauce, which we found delicious.

When we left Iles des Saintes it was a six hour sail up the coast of Guadeloupe to Deshayes Bay on the northwest side. Solvejg and Fortuin arrived shortly after we did and the boys all went into the little town for ice cream and skateboarding on the paved square. During our first night there, using only one anchor, we swung too close to another boat. Johnny had to row another anchor out in the dark as the engine refused to start. The next morning he managed to start it with a screwdriver and after that the starter button worked fine. Maybe there was a loose connection somewhere? The engine continued to be a mystery.

There was only one tiny bakery here and when we missed the first batch of bread we had to wait until 0800 for the next oven load. The school children stopped in to get baguettes to take with them for their lunch, so the bakery was a lively place in the early mornings. In this small fishing village at Deshayes Bay all the people knew everyone else. There was a funeral the day after we arrived, and it appeared that the whole town had turned out for it. Most of the stores were closed and the streets were filled with men, women, and children, all walking to the church. A hushed air of expectancy encompassed the town. We felt rather strange about having happened onto this personal and tragic event, and we went for a long walk in the opposite direction, only to end up at the cemetery, very unusual, with all the crypts above ground. It looked like a city of graves. From there we decided it was time to go back to the boat. We didn't want to meet the mourners coming up the hill.

Fortuin, Solvejg, and Sequoiah all left about the same time on January 30, but we were headed for Antigua and they for Montserrat. It was the last time we would see Solvejg, as they were hurrying homeward now and would be heading west across the Gulf of Mexico towards Houston, where they planned to sell Solvejg before going back to Minnesota.

We had a very fast seven hour sail close reaching under sunny skies. Lady Helen's dinghy met us at the entrance to English Harbour and we anchored next to them in Freeman Bay. Johnny and John cleared customs, and were warned that the cat must not go ashore under penalty of death. Since Max had never exhibited any desire to swim we felt he was safe since we were anchored far from the shore.

On Thursday nights the Antigua Yacht Club hosts a Rum Punch Party which we attended with Art and Candy, from Lady Helen, all five children in tow. It was a rainy night and the boys, who spent the evening playing outside, were drenched and filthy by the time we were ready to go back. Snuggling close to a muddy boy in a wet dinghy is a pleasure anyone but a mother could easily forego.

A charter captain recommended Mavis, a scrubbed-faced, pigtailed, native girl to do our laundry. Fortunately, by now I had learned to make two lists of everything we sent, one to include with the laundry, and one to keep myself. When the clothes were returned I found that several things were missing and three of my slipcovers had shrunk. Mavis did find the lost items but there was nothing we could do about the slipcovers. I was disgusted and wished I had done the laundry myself. It was a time consuming job with a bucket of water and a plumber's friend, but I had never succeeded in shrinking anything.

Since I still couldn't swim with my bad leg, I defrosted the freezer and did lots of cooking and cleaning. The children learned to windsurf on the cut-down rig the boys on Lady Helen had acquired. In fact they did their school work in record time in the mornings, and disappeared for long stints on the sailboard, coming back exhausted.

Antigua is one of the few places in the Caribbean which caters expressly to yachtsmen, and all kinds of supplies and parts for boats and engines can be found there. Johnny located a shop that repaired outboards, and in one day they had ours running perfectly. It was a long taxi ride to go pick it up. Our route took us through the "rain forest", a shady area where there is a bit more vegetation than anywhere else. Antigua is quite arid and suffers from drought frequently. It is also rather flatter than most of the other islands of its size.

On Sunday I discovered that the refrigeration was not doing its job. I had just replenished the fresh fruits and vegetables and filled up the freezer so I was really upset. Johnny added more freon and we hoped that would work. That afternoon we went up to Shirley Heights with the gang from Lady Helen. Shirley Heights is on a high cliff overlooking the harbor, the site of British officers' quarters in Lord Nelson's time. On the way up we stopped in at a museum located in the old enlisted men's compound. Admiral Nelson spent quite a few years in English Harbor in the late 1700's. The Dockyard there is a good example of a Georgian naval shipyard and the original buildings are being restored. Now there is a bar and restaurant at Shirley Heights and the Halcyon steel orchestra, with over twenty musicians, plays for three hours every Sunday afternoon. It was amazing the variety of sounds they could get out of what looked like old oil drums! The view of the harbor and the Caribbean Sea was spectacular. We could see Montserrat twenty-six miles away, and Redonda and Nevis out to the west; and the prismatic sunset with its calypso accompaniment made a perfect ending for the afternoon.

On Monday we found that the freon hadn't done the trick. I took all our frozen foods to the little grocery where I had shopped, and they kindly let me leave everything in their freezer until we could solve the problem. At the Dockyard we were told that the refrigeration expert was very busy and probably couldn't get to us for a few days, but we were in luck. Art knew all about refrigeration and had a set of gauges to test the system. In a fairly short time he and Johnny found a leak and fixed it by tightening a nut. I must have loosened it when I was defrosting. Art also had some refrigerant, and we were back in business.

That night Johnny and Caroline went to meet Doe and Hertz at the airport. The island is large, about 108 square miles, but the roads are dreadful and it takes a long time to go anywhere. Many of the islanders that we talked to said the politicians were to blame; that if they had continued as a colony of Great Britain instead of opting for independence, the roads, and a lot of other things as well, would be better.

After wasting time looking for a suitcase that never appeared, and riding with Doe and Hertz to their hotel, it was almost two in the morning when Johnny and Caroline returned. They were mainly disappointed because the missing luggage contained mail for us.

Despite the late night we were up early to wave goodbye to Lady Helen and go to the fuel dock to fill our tanks before moving up the coast. Max stepped off the boat at the dock, a first for him, and very much against the law there. John grabbed him and locked him below. Caroline and I retrieved our frozen foods and bought some fresh bread, and then we motored in a flat calm for an hour and a half reaching Morris Bay, on Antigua's west side, just as rain settled in for the day.

CHAPTER FOURTEEN

INTERLUDES

Morris Bay is an immense semicircle of white sand beach, the location of the Jolly Beach Resort where Doe and Hertz were staying. After eight months it was wonderful to see them, and this was a perfect place for a family reunion. Because the bay was so shallow, no more than five feet deep anywhere, we had to anchor about a quarter of a mile offshore; but, for the same reason, we had the entire bay to ourselves most of the month we were there. Luckily, conditions remained ideal, and it was calm as a millpond.

The next ten days were a fuzzy blur of family fun. We shopped, went out to eat - a nice change for the cook, toured the island, walked on the beach; the children and their grandparents rode in the hotel's paddleboats, sailed Sunfish, played shuffleboard and checkers. We talked for hours, listened to steel bands, danced, and watched movies. After a day in the capital city of St. John's, Doe wanted to ride back to the hotel on one of the local buses rather than a taxi. These buses are the main island transportation and are rather like vans but open on the sides instead of having windows. They are always crowded and, being Saturday, the main market day, they were even more so. The crowd was lively and we stood in line jostling like everyone else until we found the correct bus. There were men carrying tools, and women with babies and small children hanging onto their skirts, all laden with the day's purchases: bread, vegetables, fully feathered (but not alive) chickens in baskets, clothes, even furniture. All was squeezed on board; no one who wanted a ride was left standing. Time had no meaning and the bus began to roll only when everything and everybody were on board. We were as close as sardines in a tin, the mingling fragrances indescribable. We bumped along the pitted roads for about an hour stopping whenever someone shouted to the driver. All the natives seemed to know each other, we appeared to be the only strangers, and there was much noisy chatter along the way. We passed small villages and hilly fields. At one place a woman hung her head out of the bus and shouted to a friend sleeping in a field, making us all laugh as the man awoke with a start. Finally it was our turn to get off, and we waved goodbye to the remaining passengers as we walked down the side road toward the hotel. It had been an entertaining trip.

The "boys" went deep sea fishing, catching their share of the area's barracuda, which they left with the boat's captain at the end of the day. Caroline spent several entire days reading by the pool, hoping in vain to meet someone her own age. There was a dive shop right on the beach, and John took a SCUBA course to obtain his Junior NAUI certification. He was the only one in the class, and the instructor spent the afternoons with him studying under the palm trees. One day we took Doe and Hertz for a sail to English Harbor. It was cloudy that morning and we had a rough three hour trip with occasional rain, but the skies cleared to a soft blue by the time we dropped anchor at lunchtime. We wandered around sightseeing and doing errands after a superb lunch at the Admiral's Inn, and were back on board by mid-afternoon for a fast run back up the coast under sunny skies. Right before supper one night there was an earthquake, very brief, not violent, but it surprised us. Later we learned that there had been quite a severe quake in 1843 which ravaged the island. The natives don't like to hear the ground rumble, and neither did we!

When our time together drew to a close, Caroline jumped at the invitation to go home with her grandparents for a few weeks instead of accompanying me to San Francisco. She was beside herself with happiness, and her suitcase was packed and ready days before they left.

Life aboard Sequoiah after Caroline's departure with Doe and Hertz was unusually quiet. John continued with school in the mornings and spent the afternoons at the dive shop or out diving with his instructor. On Saturday Johnny joined them for a two tank dive on Cade's Reef. Visibility was excellent and John came back exclaiming over the fish and corals they had seen.

"It's so cool! Even seventy feet down it is so clear and the colors are so bright. You ought to try it Mother, I know you'd like it," he enthused. He had finished the practical part of the course and only had to take the written test to become certified.

When John woke up the next morning he said, "I don't feel very good. Can you get seasick at anchor?"

We knew it wasn't mal de mer because the anchorage was dead calm. We wondered if diving had affected him somehow. John had been on five dives the previous week. Perhaps the changes in pressure had been too much for his small body. We put him on a liquid diet and he spent the day quietly, reading and sitting on the beach. At bedtime John announced that he had a tummy ache, and we found that he was running a slight fever. I took out the medical books and looked up stomach pains. In one, there was a list of questions to ask the patient along with photos of just where and how to press the abdomen to elicit the responses that would be meaningful for making a diagnosis. Fearfully, I realized that John's symptoms and the tenderness in his right, lower abdomen pointed toward appendicitis. By then it was nine o'clock at night. We still weren't sure about, and definitely didn't want to believe, what we suspected; so we took the optimist's route, deciding to sleep on it and hoping everything would be better the next day.

In the morning John still had a low grade fever (99F), but he was hungry and said he felt better. Slightly reassured, we kept him on a liquid diet and he remained on board doing school work while we went to English Harbour via taxi to take care of pressing business: laundry, groceries, engine parts, and inquiries as to a good doctor. All was accomplished by midday and we went back aboard to find John curled up on his bunk studying.

"What's for lunch? I'm starved and my tummy hardly hurts anymore," John greeted us as we unloaded the dinghy.

"You have a doctor's appointment at 3:30 and he doesn't want you to eat anything before then," answered Johnny. John was furious as he was really hungry by this time.

"Maybe you can stop by the Victory for a hamburger after your appointment," added Johnny. "The ice cream is pretty good there, too, as I remember."

With John feeling better, our fears from the night before were dissipating, and the impending doctor's visit seemed superfluous. All our books said that patients with appendicitis usually had no appetite.

Leaving Johnny aboard to deal with some engine repairs, John and I made the jolting, thirty minute taxi ride over primitive roads into St. John's. It is a typical island city with dirty, crowded streets. Poverty as a way of life is obvious, though masked by upbeat island music and the gaily colored clothes of the natives. Our cab driver knew Dr. Fuller well, and entertained us on our way by describing the most intimate details of his own latest illness.

Not many people were in the doctor's office on our arrival, and we didn't have long to wait before being ushered into the inner room and introduced to the doctor. John was asked the pertinent questions, his abdomen was pressed in the appropriate places, and he tried hard not to cry when Dr. Fuller said he suspected acute appendicitis. He gave us directions to a lab on the next block where he sent us to have a white blood count done, while he tried to locate a surgeon. As we walked to the lab, John's hand squeezed mine, tears poured down his cheeks, and he verbalized his fears. He was old enough to realize that we knew nothing about the local doctors. He was afraid and did not want to go to an unfamiliar hospital with strangers to care for him.

"Mother," he sobbed, "I just can't have appendicitis in Antigua!"

He was terrified and so, despite my outward calm, was I.

When we returned from the lab, Dr. Fuller introduced us to Dr. Charles, a prominent Antiguan surgeon. John immediately announced that his pain had vanished and he was ready to go home. Ignoring his protestations of suddenly renewed good health, Dr. Charles examined him and concurred with the earlier diagnosis.

"We'll have to admit him right away," said Dr. Charles.

"I don't think so," I replied. "We'll take him back to the United States if he needs an operation. Maybe I can get a flight this afternoon."

"There's no time for that, Mrs. Warren. He needs surgery right away."

"Dr. Charles, you don't understand. Our family is full of doctors and we have never done anything like this. I mean, we don't <u>know</u> you," I said lamely, feeling desperate and close to tears myself.

"Yes, I understand your concern, but we do this type of operation regularly, and time is of the essence in this case," he said kindly.

When I learned that these doctors had been trained in Great Britain, it somehow made me feel better than if they had attended the University of the West Indies. Like every parent in distress I wanted some assurance that our son would have the best of care and that the outcome would be good.

Since Johnny had remained aboard Sequoiah to deal with the recalcitrant engine, his 6'4" frame was probably squeezed uncomfortably into the dark recesses of the bilge where he wouldn't be able to hear a call on the VHF even in the unlikely event that he had it turned on. I was in a quandary. It would take at least an hour to go get him and return, but it was unthinkable to proceed with an operation without his knowledge. Dr. Fuller solved the problem. He had to go see a patient at the Jolly Beach Hotel and he offered to bring Johnny back with him.

After his house call he found a fisherman who took him out in the bay to Sequoiah. He knocked on the hull and introduced himself, giving Johnny the spoken message that his mere presence had instantly conveyed. Johnny quickly changed and they left to meet us.

In the meantime, Dr. Charles had driven John and me to Adelin Clinic just outside St. Johns. We drove out of the town, past cows and goats, and turned into a dirt road leading through an open field to a one story building with a narrow piazza along the front. It looked like it could have been an old plantation house which had declined with the years. My heart sank as we got out of the car and John gave my hand a frightened squeeze. Everything about the place seemed slightly dilapidated. We crossed the piazza and entered a high-ceilinged room with a few chairs along the walls and a nurse sitting behind a desk. She greeted us warmly and, after a discussion with the doctor, she gave John soap and a towel, and led him down a short hall to the shower. The whole place had high ceilings and the original rooms had been sectioned off with lower partitions to create more rooms. On close inspection, I found everything, though well worn, to be spotlessly clean. After his shower, John was gently prepared for surgery by the same nurse, apparently the only one around. Another doctor appeared and introduced himself as the anesthesiologist who would put John to sleep. He explained the procedure in very simple terms and tried to ease John's fears. Dr. Charles described the operation and reassuringly answered John's questions until Dr. Fuller arrived with Johnny. As soon as the doctors had scrubbed, they took John to the operating theatre. Johnny and I waited anxiously for seventy minutes for them to reappear. Sitting there in the shabby surroundings, troubled, and thinking the worst, we were unable to comfort each other. When the doors finally opened, the two doctors came in rolling a stretcher, and personally lifted John into his bed; then they waited with us until he awakened. He wasn't turned over to unfamiliar nurses or put in a crowded recovery room, as is the case in most large hospitals. The emphasis at Adelin Clinic was on the care and comfort of the individual patient and not on the speed with which each could be dispatched. That first night I stayed with John, sleeping on a bed that was brought in and placed next to his. He was sedated, and confused and scared. Every hour or so he would cry out, "Mother, where are you?" and cling tightly to my hand until he fell again into uneasy sleep.

Children recover quickly from any ordeal. By morning John, though in pain, was no longer afraid, and was delighted when given a tiny, bright room all to himself. A gentle tropical breeze came in the two large windows, lazily blowing the ragged, red curtains. The warm sunshine and the scent of

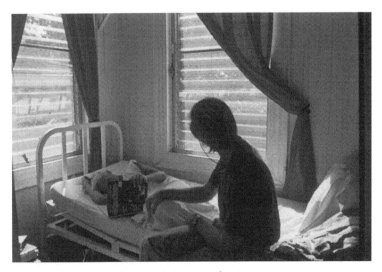

Johnny sitting with John, after his surgery at
Adelin Clinic, St. John, Antigua

dry grass on the morning air gave us a sense of well-being and
dispelled the gloom of the night before.

The day after John's operation I left for San Francisco and
the dizzying whirl of family excitement that accompanied my
brother's wedding. John was relaxed enough to let me go,
and Johnny had met a local lady who offered to drive him
back and forth to the hospital, so I was able to leave without
too much anxiety.

John was in the hospital for five days, and what an experience it was! At night there was one nurse on duty. Unlike large
American hospitals, the three or four patients at the Adelin
Clinic while John was there were allowed to sleep through
the night. The nurse checked on the patients at regular intervals without disturbing them, giving appropriate attention
to any who needed it. There was no air conditioning except
in the operating theatre (even in February it is in the 80's in
Antigua), and there were mosquito coils available to put under the beds if any flying things managed to get in through
the screens. At meal times even the food was personalized.

"What would you like for lunch today, John?" the nurse would ask, and all orders were filled if available.

Recuperating at Adelin Clinic meant walking through the field outside in the sunshine instead of antiseptic halls. It meant eating home style meals, and sleeping with fresh air blowing through the open windows. The relaxed and friendly atmosphere was worlds apart from the sterile and impersonal environment of its American counterparts. The attention John received throughout his stay was extremely personal and professional. Over the years we have spent a considerable amount of time inside hospitals with our three children. Without exception, our visit to Adelin Clinic is the best hospital experience that we have had.

After his brief stay, John moved back aboard Sequoiah where he lay in the sun studying for his written SCUBA exam, reading, and playing with Max. Now the only thing left to show for his experience is an almost imperceptible, thin line on his abdomen, and memories of the wonderful, caring people at Adelin Clinic.

We were very lucky to have been in Antigua for this emergency, but it is important to have the necessary supplies aboard for dealing with such a crisis at sea. Personally, I still think the main thing is to keep in mind all imaginable disasters. Who knows where we would be now if I'd ever stopped worrying about Sequoiah sinking!

John has always liked to write and, along with wild and rambling tales of horror and adventure, he dabbled in poetry occasionally. About this time he gave me a poem that he called "Waves".

> As the waves come dancing in,
> They toss and play
> As if they
> Were children.

> Their color is
> The sky's
> Azure blue.
>
> They race up the sand,
> Pounding the shore
> As a conqueror pounds
> His enemy.

It was interesting to read this and gain, through the eyes of a twelve year old, a new perspective on one of our most common daily sights.

After two weeks of being back in civilization I was more than ready to return to the cruising life. I had enjoyed being with my extended family, but the roar of the big city over-whelmed and depressed me. Caroline met my plane in Miami excited by news that she hoped was true.

"We can't go back to Antigua, Mommy! I showed the man my ticket and he said we had to have round trip tickets to leave the country. I told him all about the boat, but he didn't care. Come on! Hurry! We only have a half hour!"

"Caroline, you sound awfully happy about this, but we are going to leave today. I have the forms we filled out with the police before leaving Antigua, so I am sure there won't be any problem," I answered as we ran towards the Eastern Airlines desk.

However, Caroline was right. Antigua, like many other Caribbean islands, required all air passengers entering the country to have return tickets; no exceptions. This was an unforeseen problem, but one the American Express card could handle. The crazy part was that it just made everything even more complicated when we reached our destination.

We arrived in Antigua, tired after a long day of travel, and Customs officials began to question us. How long did we plan to stay in Antigua? How did we plan to leave Antigua? On hearing our answers they wanted to know how we had managed to leave the U.S without tickets home. When they found out that we did in fact have return air tickets, but still planned to leave by boat, they called in wiser heads to tackle the problem. Sometimes even a common language doesn't help!

Johnny and John met our flight and, once our mysterious travel plans were sorted out to the satisfaction of the customs officials, we made the long taxi ride back to Jolly Beach where Sequoiah still sat in solitary command of Morris Bay. After the chill and bustle of San Francisco, the warm breezy Antiguan night with the stars close overhead was solace to my whole being. Our brief interludes in hospital and America over, it felt good to be back aboard Sequoiah again.

CHAPTER FIFTEEN

ABOVE ANTIGUA

On the map above Antigua are a multitude of islands with romantic names, and all beckoned. By the time we were ready to move on it was March, and we were beginning to feel the pressure of our self-imposed deadline to be home by the end of May. So many places and so little time! Instead of overnight stands at as many ports as possible we opted for slightly longer visits to fewer islands, saving the others for future cruises.

As soon as jet lag was conquered, preparations were made for the trip to St. Barthelemy, better known as St. Barts. We sailed down to English Harbor to take on fuel and water and last minute groceries, and probably should have left that night, but sailors never leave on a Friday and we were still a bit travel weary. We missed our chance, for the weather deteriorated, with squalls rolling in from a low nearby. We moved up to the northwest coast to Deep Bay to wait it out. For three days intermittent rain and heavy winds kept blowing across with no lull in sight. John and I made one last trip into St. John's. It was a hike of about five miles along a mostly deserted road. On Antigua, all roads lead to St. John's, so we knew we would get there eventually if we aimed in the right direction. Hamburgers at the Victory Restaurant on the recently renovated Redcliffe Quay were the main attraction of the day. It was still very windy and the placemats blew off the table before our hamburgers came. We wondered how long this weather would hold us there.

Tired of waiting for clear skies, we left after supper Tuesday night under reefed sails, with the wind vane steering. We had a fast, wet, thirteen hour passage, anchoring in Gustavia harbor in time for breakfast the next morning. Gustavia is the only real town on St. Barts, a small French island, unusual in the Caribbean because 90% of the inhabitants are white. We felt as though we had stepped back across the Atlantic into a small French fishing village - fresh croissants for breakfast again! We ate the French bread, went shell collecting, enjoying the beaches and snorkeling, even taking Max ashore at the deserted Anse de Colombier for a romp on the rocks and in the bushes. He and John had a wild game of chase. Max's eyes were round as two full moons and his heart beat triple time as he explored that new environment.

From there it was a short two and a half hour sail to Philipsburg on the Dutch side of the island of Sint Maarten. This island is divided into two countries, one governed by France, and the other, Holland. Philipsburg is a very busy tourist town with hundreds of duty-free shops, much too noisy and crowded to suit us. The weather was uncooperative, making conditions in Groot Baai rough and rolly. Fortuin was there and Jess had talked with Solvejg by ham radio that day. It was good to have news of them enroute to Jamaica. Whenever we left our cruising friends we never knew when we would see or hear from them next and, every passage a new adventure, we just had to hope that they would make it safely to each destination.

We moved on to Marigot, the main town on the French side of St. Martin (each country spells the island's name differently). It was more pleasant in every respect, much cleaner and less commercial (if that's possible for a tourist-oriented town!), and we were glad we had stayed only one night at Philipsburg. The restaurants in Marigot served wonderful French food, the best we'd had since leaving Europe, and the people were delightful. Although the shopping was better on the Dutch side - Johnny had even found an up-to-date copy of the New York Times - we found the natives there surly and unwelcoming, our first experience of this attitude since arriving in the Caribbean. We were back in civilization for better or worse, and this was the first unfortunate sign of it.

The anchorage at Marigot was calm. We heard from some other sailors that usually when one anchorage was bad, the other was good, and anyone who stayed on this island for long either moved into one of the landlocked marinas, or kept moving back and forth between Marigot and Philipsburg at every change in weather.

After a short, rough sail, our next stop was at the uninhabited islands called Prickly Pear Cays. We left St. Martin early and had a whole day snorkeling and beachcombing on Prickly Pear East. It is tricky getting around the coral heads there, and we anchored off a good distance, going in to the beach by dinghy. There were hundreds of fish on the reefs and we saw enormous schools of blue tangs and parrotfish. It was an exhilarating blue-sky day and we had the perfect, white beaches all to ourselves. After an early dinner at anchor we got underway before dark, just as a windy rain squall drenched us. However, it didn't last long and we raised the jib and mizzen setting a course for the Virgin Islands, seventy-five miles away.

Johnny took watch until one in the morning and then woke me for my turn. The night was fairly clear and I could see the glow of St. Martin behind us for another hour and a half. Max kept me company as I sat in the cockpit, reading and checking our compass course at intervals with a flashlight since the compass light suddenly quit working. Around four

I got Johnny up to help me change sails and tack to avoid a ship. Later we had another gusty squall, and then it was morning and we could see lots of islands popping up in front of us. By mid-morning we were anchored off Tortola and we all went into Roadtown. It was Commonwealth Day and we found everything was closed. After clearing customs and immigration, we moved the boat to Maya Cove, a beautiful, calm pool of reef-protected water. The wind was blowing hard, but inside the reef there were no waves, an ideal anchorage.

That night and the next we all forced ourselves up at 0500 to have a once-in-a-lifetime view of Halley's Comet. Both nights were clear and the comet's long tail was bright and well defined. Weesie arrived the second night to spend her Spring Break with us and was able to see it too. What an incredible sight! It's no wonder that so many tenets of ancient religions revolve around the stars and try to explain the phenomena in the skies.

Weesie brought her winter cough and sinus infection with her. The tropical sunshine was just what she needed to get well. We sailed to St. Thomas the day after Weesie joined us and ended up staying there nearly a week. It was one of our least favorite places, much too big and commercial and crime-ridden, but we wanted to have some time with Nelson and Suzi Durant, who were there between charters on a sixty foot Morgan. They were frantically busy by day, but at night we managed to have dinner together. Nelson hired John for a day to do boat cleaning jobs, and for a while we thought we had a budding charter captain on our hands.

There are some advantages to big cities and one is the availability of services. There was an Avon dealer with a wonderful repair shop and parts department. The hole we had tried to patch in Barbados was still leaking air, and we finally had it fixed properly with an inside patch.

Unfortunately, on leaving St. Thomas we decided to tow the newly repaired dinghy. Whatever possessed us I'll never know; some people learn from past mistakes! We left the harbor with a strong, following, southeasterly wind. Within fifteen minutes the engine started overheating. Johnny busied himself trying to locate the problem. Five minutes later the dinghy attempted suicide. It rushed forward on a rolling wave and leapt up beneath Sequoiah's stern, impaling itself on the wind vane rudderpost. The weather was abominable anyway, and we knew when we were beaten. We turned around, anchored anew in the same spot we had vacated less than an hour earlier, and called Offshore Inflatables to come collect our sick dinghy again. It was just one of those days. Johnny spent the remainder of it in the engine room replacing the water pump, while the rest of us quickly disappeared into town until nightfall. Max was the only one able to get along with our engine mechanic! By the time we returned, the mechanic was gone and the captain, freshly bathed, was ready for a drink on the deck. Some British friends from the yacht, Green Dolphin, joined us and we tried to forget that we didn't want to be in St. Thomas.

March 14 was Caroline's fifteenth birthday. There were rain squalls off and on all day. Caroline and Weesie spent the entire day shopping, a favorite pastime of theirs. That night Caroline invited us to go - guess where? - the Pizza Hut for dinner, a special birthday treat, her choice of all the restaurants in St. Thomas. Afterwards we went back aboard for ice cream and cake.

To a teenager a year of solitary confinement would seem a fate worse than death, but more terrible still would be a year of constant confinement with one's parents. Parents are a breed apart, as any teenager can attest, with annoying habits and weird ideas about almost everything.

For some it may be hard to imagine how any sane human between twelve and twenty could manage to live through the unthinkable horror of a year aboard a small boat with two insufferable parents, not to mention an exceptionally active younger brother thrown in for good measure. However, Caroline is alive and well and here to prove that it can be done. At times life didn't seem worth living. At others, it was worth it only if everyone else could be made equally miserable, and then a sense of accomplishment was felt. Then there were those rare moments of complete harmony that made even the darkest hours worthwhile. Several days after her birthday, feeling emancipated in her old age, Caroline announced that she was becoming a vegetarian and taking up jogging. She then stepped out in the cockpit after a meatless supper to run in place.

When our rubber dinghy, with all its wounds repaired, was strapped on deck for safekeeping, we sailed to Caneel Bay on St. John. We anchored there for the night and went ashore for dinner with some friends from New York, Weesie's roommate and her extended family, who were vacationing there. John was unhappy because he had outgrown his long pants and blazer, so had to wear shorts with a shirt and tie. He said he felt like a baby, but later recovered his good humor and managed to have fun with the other children. After a lovely evening with the Reeses, we took Vivi (Weesie's roommate) and one of her cousins snorkeling next day on the reefs at Lovango Cay, before moving on to Francis Bay, the next stop on our circumnavigation of St. John.

Johnny was having some trouble with his back, not too surprising after his contortions in the engine room, and he spent the next several days resting while the children and I enjoyed the beaches and hiking trails nearby. John and I had a good hike one day over to Annaberg Mill, one of the five, now defunct, sugar plantations on St. John. The National

Park Service does an excellent job of maintaining the more than five thousand acres that Laurence Rockefeller donated to the government as park land.

Weesie took over as cook the last few days she was with us. It was a pleasant change for me, fun for her, and delicious meals for all of us. While Johnny's back was out, the children told him to stay in his bunk and they ran the boat by themselves, refusing any aid. John and Weesie worked the anchor, John managed the sails, and Caroline navigated, the girls taking turns at the wheel.

Our favorite spot on St. John was Salt Pond Bay, an uninhabited area where the water was exceptionally clear and we found good snorkeling on a reef in the entrance channel. We met a Park Ranger who told us about some of the nearby trails and we had some enjoyable hikes from there, one of the best being a walk to the top of Ram Head with its panoramic view of the surrounding islands planted in a vast expanse of variegated blue water.

Eventually we found ourselves returning to St. Thomas again, this time to put Weesie on a plane for school. I hugged her tight, knowing how hard the next month would be for her, as she waited to hear from colleges and prepared for her final exams. We would see her next at her graduation from Madeira on May 30th.

After a last run to the only real American grocery store we had seen in a year, we made our final exit from St. Thomas with no regrets, and pointed our bow toward Virgin Gorda. The engine was causing more and more concern as it continued to overheat and would occasionally cut off unexpectedly. With a light northeast wind we motor-sailed most of the six hour trip, and anchored off the Yacht Harbor marina finding it a bit uncomfortable with rolling swells. We cleared in with customs. The British and U.S. Virgin Islands are separate countries so yachts must clear in and out each time they leave one to enter the other, a real bother, but a necessity we were told.

The Baths, a collection of partially submerged, gigantic, granite boulders, the result of ancient volcanic action, are located on the southwestern tip of Virgin Gorda. These spectacular rock formations with pools of water among them are a popular natural attraction, but sometimes difficult to reach by boat. We anchored Sequoiah and took the dinghy to the crowded beach. We surfed in on towering breakers, soaking everything because I wasn't able to get out fast enough, and the next huge wave poured itself over us. We had great fun exploring amongst the maze of rocks with sea water rushing through the cave-like formations. We met a lady frantically hunting for her wedding ring which had been washed from her finger in the strong surf. We donned our masks and snorkels and ineffectively helped her search for the lost jewelry. The sands are in constant motion there due to the action of the water and it would have been a true miracle if she had recovered it. When it was time to go we made an exciting exit from the beach, hurling the dinghy over the crest of a huge wave, each of us hanging on for all we were worth. Those white-topped curlers pounding onto the beach were a daunting sight and we were glad to get away unscathed.

We had a super sail up to Gorda Sound tacking all the way in and anchoring behind Saba Rocks, not far from the Bitter End Yacht Club. We found the snorkeling around Gorda Sound and the outlying area to be rather disappointing as far as numbers of fish and the colors on the reefs, but in one place we saw on the sandy bottom, huge anchors and a couple of old cannons. This led, of course, to much conjecture about whose ships had met their end there. Part of Sir Francis Drake's fleet?? We discussed it over dinner at Drake's Anchorage, where we had a delicious meal, but found no one knowledgeable about the underwater treasures. As we were leaving the restaurant, the sign on the door to the showers caught my eye. It read: "Please -NO SHOWERS TODAY - We are very low on water and need it for your dinners. Think of it like your boat. You can go to the yacht harbor to fill up... we can't!" It was a grim reminder of the constant problem of many islands in "Paradise", where the sun always shines and the rainfall is low.

The next week was simply terrible. We spent one whole day readying Sequoiah for the trip up to the Bahamas. I defrosted the freezer and, in the process, unknowingly loosened some connections. Unhappily, it didn't become apparent until twenty-four hours later when we were well out to sea. Johnny, naturally, was playing with the engine, and while attacking one problem, discovered by chance that the bolts holding the alternator onto the engine had sheared off. He had to invent a new way to attach it. He and John spent an entire morning, finally managing to secure it with a wire coat hanger, of all things. There is an art to this engine maintenance business!

By mid afternoon on March 27 with a good breeze on the starboard quarter, we set sail for San Salvador, the Bahamian island where Columbus is thought to have first landed in the New World. At least historians for many years agreed that this was the place, but recent research has produced some questions leading to controversy on the subject. We had been following on the trail of Columbus ever since Madeira, but our main reason for making our landfall at San Salvador was that The Yachtsman's Guide to the Bahamas listed it as a point of entry into the country with a customs office there.

By suppertime our first night out, I noticed that frozen foods were softening and the refrigerator was barely cool. On further investigation we found a leak, which Johnny thought he could fix by spraying some refrigeration sealer on it. There were a couple of cans of the sealant on board, but no directions to tell us how to attach the spray nozzle to the pressurized can. When Johnny punctured the top of the can, the nozzle wouldn't fit and there was nothing he could do to stop the flow as sealant erupted out of the can, all over the galley, all over his hands and arms. With paper towels we tried to wipe it off his hands...and the towels stuck to him! That foamy mess stuck to everything it touched except the cold pipes in the freezer! In the end there was nothing to do but laugh - which was difficult for Johnny, whose hands were hardening up nicely in foam and paper towels. When the mess finally dried, we found that we could chip it off gradually in little pieces. There are permanent bits of evidence around the galley sink, but after a week of hard work, Johnny's hands were back to normal again, not too much the worse for wear.

After that episode, we knew we would have to eat fast as the refrigerator and freezer steadily warmed up. The seas were rough that first night and fixing dinner was a real exercise in juggling. John felt ill and went to bed without eating. We all found it difficult to sleep. This was our first long trip since landing in Barbados and it wasn't going well...except for speed. The first twenty-four hours we covered 149 miles and we continued to average over 140 miles a day for the rest of the voyage.

Easter Sunday arrived swathed in clouds. Max called loudly at 0500 to present a small flying fish he'd found on deck. Since the freezer was room temperature by this time, I reluctantly tossed most of a four week supply of meat overboard, retaining only what we could cook and eat immediately. John hung on the stern rail watching in vain for the hordes of sharks he was sure would discover this fine Easter gift. In between the torrential downpours that plagued us all day, he and Caroline dyed eggs. They sat on the floor of the cockpit and put their cups of colors in the bottom of a bucket. It was too rough to risk rainbows on the cabin ceiling! During the afternoon the cabin rang with all the Easter hymns we could remember tunes for, and, as usually happened when we started singing, we went right on through the hymnal indiscriminately enjoying all our favorites.

Early next morning Johnny woke me for my watch saying, "It's rainy and cool. You'll need foul weather gear."

I struggled into my clothes in the dark trying not to wake anyone. Staggering through the unlit cabin, I lurched as a wave caught us. Max, unseen on the floor below me, must have thought a huge yellow monster had stepped on his tail. He yelped and charged full tilt for the companionway. It was closed. He crashed into the hatch boards and fell back. He leapt up again and this time flew out through the open galley port at rocket speed. I was afraid he had shot straight overboard in his panic. Yanking the hatch cover back, I rushed clumsily after him.

"Max is gone!" I yelled to Johnny.

"What do you mean? He's not even out here. He's asleep on the floor inside." Johnny hadn't seen him come out, and the kitten wasn't anywhere in the cockpit.

"I scared him and he ran out just seconds ago," I said, beginning to cry and peering over the side at the swirling darkness. Rain was pelting down, visibility was near zero, and a cat overboard that night would have been lost immediately in the confused waves. I sobbed out loud. Max was more than just a cat. He was part of our family, a fellow adventurer, and provider of much comic relief. He just couldn't be gone. Johnny went forward to search the decks, and on his way back met an unhappy, wet cat huddled on the cabin top, afraid to go below. The yellow apparition had really frightened him. From then on, he was always afraid of our boots. After that incident I tried to remember to carry a flashlight at night so I could see Max, who often stretched out to sleep on the cool, wood floor.

Early on the morning of April Fool's Day, the trough of bad weather that we had been traveling through, finally passed behind us and the sun came out. During the afternoon we discovered the bilge had filled with water and we took turns pumping. Naturally, only one of the three bilge pumps would work. We had been motor-sailing since midnight, but turned off the engine when it overheated and the oil pressure dropped - harbingers of future problems. Johnny made brave forays into the dark recesses of the engine room and poured in what seemed like gallons of oil. During one of these ministrations John shouted, "Land Ho!" from his perch on the mizzen spreader, and described to us the long, low gem of San Salvador gleaming in the last rays of sunset. After six days at sea we were in no mood to spend another night on the ocean. With the depth sounder and lead line to guide us, we felt our way in to Cockburn Town and anchored in nine feet of water shortly before midnight. We were the only boat there. A big swell was running from the north making the anchorage uncomfortable, but we all slept well after our 771 mile trip.

We woke to a sparkling blue day and looked out on the clearest water we've seen anywhere. It was a magnificent spot. We discovered on going ashore that there were no customs or immigration offices on the island, and hadn't been for two years. For the first time ever, the current edition of The Yachtsman's Guide had failed us. However, the people we met were friendly and helpful. The local police even gave us permission to stay without clearance for a day or two, but we needed to hurry. We had planned to meet John and Harriet DuBose and their three children on April 3rd for a long weekend at Cat Island. The nearest port of entry was at Georgetown, Exuma, and this excursion would make us late. After a long refreshing swim, showers, and lunch, we turned the clock back an hour to coordinate with Eastern Standard Time. Somehow we felt like we were getting a head start when we pulled up the anchor and pointed the bow for Georgetown.

Max had been acting like a wild thing ever since our arrival at San Salvador, leaping and running around the boat at high speed, biting anyone in his path. He spent the whole morning on deck meowing at the top of his lungs, not at all his usual style. As soon as he realized we were headed out to sea again he jumped in his basket and went straight to sleep. He was about eight months old by then and we thought he was possibly approaching puberty. Could we live with another teenager on board?

We made five to six knots all afternoon and on until midnight when the wind dropped. Under a clear, starry sky, we motor-sailed slowly all night. Around 0300 I could pick out Halley's Comet, very fuzzy in the waning moonlight, my last look at that phenomenon. I was using our best pair of binoculars as I tried to identify the Conch Cay light when the mainsail jibed unexpectedly in the light, following wind. As the sheet came across, it grabbed the binoculars from my hand and tossed them unceremoniously overboard. My heart sank as I watched them disappear. If I had put the strap around my neck like I was always fussing at the children to do, then it never would have happened. I was furious with myself. It was a bad start to a bad day.

Because the engine overheated if we tried to go faster, we had been creeping along all night at three and a half knots. At 0600 just three miles from the entrance to Georgetown, Johnny was awakened by terrible grinding noises and then silence as the engine suddenly stopped. The wind was very light. John raised the big drifter, and Johnny, without any breakfast, went straight to work on the recalcitrant machine, making repairs and adding outboard oil since we had used everything else. Whatever he did, worked, and we chugged into the harbor at 0930. I stayed aboard while everyone else went ashore to clear in, make phone calls, and get a few supplies. They were back aboard and we were underway heading for Cat Island in one and a half hours, a speed record for us! Of course, they hadn't been able to make any calls; the one telephone was busy; we were back in the Bahamas. And the Bahamas Guide had been left ashore.

Luck was not with us. The wind which had been against us, or almost non-existent, all the way to Georgetown, had gone around to the Northeast and our course was 30 degrees, naturally. During the day the wind and seas picked up. We sailed hard on the wind, making long tacks, covering 75 miles in 21 hours to make good the 40 mile distance between Georgetown and Cat Island. It was a rough ride. Once when we came about, the genoa sheet caught the winch handle on the mast and tossed it overboard. This was getting ridiculous.

Late in the afternoon John DuBose called us from their plane, saying they had the Hawksnest Club in view; and we had to tell them we'd be a day late for our rendezvous. That night during my watch a huge wave came through an open port and dumped several gallons of cold water on Caroline, John, and Max. They all came awake instantly, afraid we were sinking! In the tumultuous conditions we helped the children dry their beds as well as possible. Max was silently indignant, scowling at everyone.

Just before dawn we hove to a couple of miles off the Hawk's Nest Club entrance. We could see a red and two white lights that we thought at first were from a ship, but later learned were lights on the club grounds. By 0815 we were tied up at the Hawks Nest marina, enjoying an enthusiastic welcome from the DuBose family. The next three days were spent in total relaxation, snorkeling, biking, walking on the beach, and eating the wonderful club meals, catching up on all the news from home, and savoring the company of good friends too long absent.

The days disappeared, and we waved as the DuBoses flew away in a rain shower on Sunday morning, but we had settled into the easy life at Hawks Nest and couldn't yet pull ourselves away. One morning we borrowed a van from the club and, with Bob and Kathy from the yacht, Wanderer, drove up to the Bight (the main village on the island, twenty miles away). From there we walked up to The Hermitage, situated on the highest point in the Bahamas - 204 feet! The Hermitage is just what the name implies and was built in the late thirties by Father Jerome, a Jesuit priest, when he was sixty years old. Alone, he did all the work by hand, and it is quite impressive. To get up to the top there are stone steps hewn into the hill with the Stations of the Cross carved in stone, spaced along the ascent. The Hermitage itself is also built from stone and resembles a small monastery in miniature. There are a tiny chapel, living quarters, and a bell tower. When Father Jerome died at the age of eighty he was buried in a crypt beneath the Hermitage. The place has been empty ever since, but time has not destroyed it, and visitors leave with a sense of awe.

When we finally managed to tear ourselves away from Hawks Nest on April 9, Bob and Kathy appeared on the dock at first light with hot loaves of banana and cherry bread and a fresh pineapple to send us on our way. That was a lovely surprise, one of the many delightful, unforeseen aspects of cruising.

Twelve hours later, after a good sail with the wind behind us for once, we anchored again at Georgetown, Exuma, and the next day Mother arrived to spend a week. She and Caroline stayed at the Peace and Plenty Hotel overlooking the harbor and we could wave to them on their balcony. We had a good week there, touring the island, snorkeling, sailing, etc. Johnny and John did some diving, and Johnny managed to fix the freezer and refrigerator, the engine, bilge pump, and several other nagging problems.

Max went for his very first swim at Elizabeth Island where we went for a picnic one day. As everyone else stood on the beach and called him, I rowed the dinghy slowly towards them with Max in the bow. With all the enthusiastic encouragement, he eventually jumped in and swam ashore, looking very small and rat-like in his wet fur. After a freshwater bath and a long nap in the sun, he condescended to speak to us again.

Mother and I went on a tour of Exuma with an elderly woman who had grown up on the island, and she told us about some of the customs. We tried eating the sour fruit from the tamarind tree dipped in ashes to make it sweeter. She said that was their version of candy when she was a child. Ashes were also used to brush teeth and as a remedy for indigestion (which we did not try!). Periwinkles were boiled to make a tea for high blood pressure, and some thick, fuzzy leaves were used to dry dishes.

When Mother left us after a week we sailed up to Galliot Cay, a small, uninhabited island in the Exuma chain. Trolling on the way, we caught the first fish since leaving home and had Spanish mackerel for dinner. Down-island, John had bought a Hawaiian sling but thus far had chased the elusive fish in vain. Other yachtsmen had told him about some good spear fishing places so, ever hopeful, we were still dreaming of grouper and snapper.

From Galliot it was just a short sail up the bank to our all time favorite spot in the Bahamas. Little Bell Island is at the southernmost end of the Exuma Land and Sea Park, an area protected by the Bahamas Trust. We spent five days there this time, with at least five or six other boats sharing the anchorage every night. We met Peggy Hall, the Park Warden, and Powerful, her "Bahamian Shepherd" dog, who live aboard a tugboat called Moby. Peggy, who is approaching senior citizenship, has actively taken measures to save the natural resources within her domain, instigating the passage of new protective laws, and developing programs to teach youngsters the importance of preserving their national treasures. She is a most attractive and energetic lady.

One night at Little Bell, John and Caroline camped out with four children from the Rhode Island yacht, Dawn Treader. It was a cool, windy evening and I really expected to find them back aboard shortly after dark. They proved me wrong. All the girls slept in a tent, but the two boys slept on the ground under the stars. They managed to keep a fire going long enough to cook supper and, of course, marshmallows! The next morning six sleepy campers came aboard in time for pancakes before exploring the caves at Rocky Dundas, two large, scrub-covered rocks across Conch Cut from Little Bell.

Within a short dinghy ride of the anchorage at Little Bell, there are many good places for snorkeling and diving, and beautiful, uninhabited beaches abound at every turn. Little Bell itself is a great place to walk. A path runs the length of the island, and along the way are signs identifying the various trees and shrubs.

I spent time each day feeding fish on a small reef near the anchorage. Along with the usual sergeant majors and butterfly fish that always appear for handouts, a blue angelfish ventured close enough to snatch some bread crumbs, backing away quickly after each daring foray. I was also surprised to see several eels and even a shy sting ray watching the proceedings warily from a few feet away.

One afternoon we saw a corona around the sun, a well-defined circle of rainbow colors ringing that planet, caused by the sun being covered with a thin layer of cloud. Later the colored ring was joined by two other peripheral white ones. It was quite beautiful and something none of us had seen before.

On leaving Little Bell we backtracked south to Staniel Cay where there is a delightful village with a population of seventy-three. Johnny needed to make some telephone calls. The closer we got to home the more anxious he became about returning to the real world. Although he still had ties with the law firm he had practiced with for ten years, he had always wanted to open his own office and this was beginning to seem like a good time to do just that. He wanted to call and talk to some of his law partners, to discuss his plans. The Bahamas out-island telephone system is less than desirable. At Staniel for instance, the telephone building, housing the only phone on the island, is open for two hours in the morning and again in the afternoon. Often, as on this day, the telephone doesn't work at all and Penny, the telephone operator, sits at her desk reading a book or chatting with friends, lifting the receiver every so often to listen for a dial tone. In order to call out, she has to make contact with Nassau, give them the number you want to reach, and then wait for the Nassau operator to call back when the connection is made. The procedure is quite a lesson in patience. There has been talk of a new telephone system where every house will have a phone and there will be reliable communication with the rest of the world. Maybe someday!

From Staniel we mailed our last letters home. Going to the post office at Staniel is a unique experience. After tying up the dinghy, we walked through the village to the green house on the hill and knocked on the kitchen door. The post office, a tiny wooden structure, is across the yard from the green house and is rarely open. There is a string labeled, "Pull for service" which runs from the post office to the kitchen where a bell hangs on the other end - all very efficient! It's easier just to go straight to the kitchen, where there is always a wonderful aroma emanating from the oven. Twelve loaves of bread are baked there most days, some of which are sold to visitors. After some slow, easy conversation (most of it at this time of year centering on speculation about events at the Family Island Regatta in Georgetown, where Staniel is represented by three local boats), business is transacted. Ethylin adds up the cost of each letter and the loaves of bread, and after paying her I take the letters and drop them in a slot on the post office building. The letters sit there stampless but paid for, until the mail boat comes in a week or so. Then they're taken to Nassau, moved to the main post office, stamped, and *hopefully,* put on a plane (and not a freighter!) for the rest of the way to their final destinations.

We snorkeled in Thunderball cave, where an exciting scene from the James Bond movie of the same name was filmed, and anchored at Little Major's Spot for a few days before pushing slowly northward.

A barracuda joined us, lounging under the boat enjoying the shade from the hull. The first time we had had one of these visitors we'd been frightened, but we now knew that the long silver fish with big teeth was simply curious. He might stay for days, almost still in the water, watching us come and go. If we dove and swam near him, he would back lazily away and stare with impassive eyes.

After Staniel we stopped only at uninhabited islands until reaching Nassau. We spent several days in the beautiful Pipe Creek area, a seven or eight mile strip of innumerable small cays surrounded by coral-strewn shallows. There are, however, enough deep water channels to allow a six foot draft to get into most anchorages. As in all of the Bahamas, navigation is by eyeball as there are no markers in most places and the ones in use are often unreliable. We had planned to anchor at Overyonder Cay. (Some of the names are wonderful!) On the way in with three lookouts - John on the spreaders,

Caroline on the bow, and me hanging onto the rope ladder in the rigging - we still went aground on the sand banks. While Johnny, using both sail and engine, tried to shake us loose, Caroline and I took soundings from the dinghy, but were unable to find enough water and we gave up on Overyonder Cay. We finally managed to heel the boat over and sail free right at high tide. We retraced our path and went around to Kemp Cay instead, where, in between schoolwork, varnishing, and polishing brightwork, most of our time for the next few days was spent snorkeling and exploring the shallow waterways by foot and dinghy.

From there we continued up to Warderick Wells, another of our favorite islands, where it is said a choir singing hymns can be heard on moonlit nights. Although we have been there at the right time and found the beautiful place enchanting beneath a full moon, none of us have seen any ghosts or heard the voices. Our days at Warderick Wells were idyllic. Caroline finished her Calvert School course and began helping John with his lessons. He had 60 more to go and it was beginning to look like a long summer of work at home. Serendipity, a yacht from Houston with eight year old son, Kevin, aboard had followed us from Kemp Cay and the boys had fun swimming, fishing, snorkeling, and playing cards. Up on the hill at Warderick Wells there are notes in bottles, and old driftwood boards with boat names on them. We found Deux Ami's Run Aground Award nailed up there among other names we recognized. (Deux Ami is owned by my aunt and uncle, Helen and Bob Marchman) John carved "SEQUOIAH" on a board, decorating it with copper tacks; then Kevin and I went with him to the hilltop where he nailed it up with all the other yacht signs. When Johnny and I walked the length of the island we marveled at the array of liquid color all around us, greens and blues of every hue. With a big east wind blowing, the breakers were crashing onto the Sound side, a dramatic contrast to the calm of the anchorage on the bank. We saw a tropic bird disappear into her nest and heard the babies squawking for a minute. We were very still but she didn't reappear. Max, too, enjoyed bird watching. He sat in the cockpit, tail swishing, looking at seagulls by the hour. They loved to sit on the dinghy motor, well out of cat's reach, and taunt him with their throaty laughter.

Kentucky Derby Day didn't pass unnoticed even in the out-islands. We went aboard Serendipity and watched on their television as Willie Shoemaker piloted Ferdinand to victory against 50-1 odds. In lieu of Derby Pie, Kevin's mother made a beautiful apple tart that we enjoyed for dessert.

When the day came to leave Warderick Wells, I put the engine into gear and black oil came streaming out behind. Next we heard a loud crash in the engine room and a slipping sound that continued a few seconds. The flow of oil stopped, so we motor-sailed on up the bank until the refrigeration was charged. There was a good southeast breeze and with the main and genoa up we skipped along at 4-6 knots. As soon as we were out of Park territory, John put out his fishing line adorned with a fancy contraption called a Cisco Kid to attract the fish, and soon caught a barracuda, throwing it back in disgust, his only bite of the day. Anchored at Hawksbill later in the afternoon, when John had finished his school work, he and Johnny scraped the bottom of the hull. They found hairy brown growth in patches all over. They also found the source of the morning's engine noise. The end of the dinghy painter had caught in the propeller and snapped. We had been lucky! However, the dirty oil was still a mystery and portended no good. At Hawksbill we hiked, raced dinghies, and sang, and were up early in the morning to make bread before moving on to Allan's Cay.

Allan's Cay is home to one of the few remaining colonies of iguanas in the Bahamas. These dinosaur-like lizards, some of which are three feet long, once roamed most of the Bahamian islands but have been decimated by man. They are now protected by law and once again their numbers are slowly increasing. When John had finished school we rowed the dinghy to the seemingly deserted beach to look for them. As soon as we had landed we began to hear scurrying noises and soon were surrounded by the curious creatures. They have sharp teeth and are quite bold since many people find it amusing to feed them. We only wanted to watch and found that any sudden movement would keep them at an acceptable distance. With horny skin and a long ridged crest running down the spine, they look like miniatures from prehistoric times. That night at dusk the wind dropped, and in the stillness we could hear the curious whistling of hundreds of iguana filling the air. Max was intrigued and spent the night on deck listening.

Nassau was next. It is important to leave Allan's Cay early to reach the pass between the yellow and white banks with the sun still behind you. Eyeball navigation requires good light to pick the best way between coral heads. After an early breakfast we raised the sails and said goodbye to the Exumas. John put out his fishing pole, this time with a small silver spoon as a lure. He excitedly pulled it in when he felt a tug on the line only to find his lure covered with weed. This went on all morning and by early afternoon he was getting discouraged when finally he reeled in a big yellowtail snapper. While Max watched closely, John filleted the fish, and then pulled in his line, deciding to quit while he was ahead! By 1630 hours we were tied up at the Nassau Harbour Club. John went fishing for croakers in the rain and we visited with friends on other yachts. That night we had a seafood feast. The talk turned to home. We had been away nearly a year and the excitement and tension of our return was mounting as we drew closer to the United States. We fell asleep to the unfamiliar sound of traffic on the nearby streets. It felt strange.

We spent our first day in Nassau sightseeing and shopping, and lost seven dollars in less than seven minutes at the Paradise Island Casino before finding out that children weren't allowed to play the slot machines anyway. That night Caroline and John had a pizza delivered to the boat while Johnny and I dined at the Roselawn Cafe. We hoped to leave for home as soon as Johnny completed a few small engine repairs and the wind moved out of the north. Our thoughts were on the future and life ashore.

Plans have a way of going awry and ours did. On Sunday the wind was still from the northeast but a bit lighter. Johnny started working on the engine with no success, and he had to consult a mechanic about the faulty transmission. The verdict was bad. The transmission, which weighs around 300 pounds, had to be removed from the engine. This operation took Johnny and Fritz Grant, the local expert, nearly all day. They had to rig up a system of pulleys and ropes to lift it up through the companionway into the cockpit and onto the dock. From there it was carried to a truck and taken to a workshop. After another whole day it was determined that we needed a new transmission, and that particular kind was not available in the Bahamas. Johnny spent hours on the telephone running into dead ends at every turn. We couldn't find a new transmission to fit our engine anywhere in Florida. We were almost ready to sail home without the conveniences the engine supplied, when the repair shop located some used parts that could replace the worn ones in the old transmission. All of these transactions took the better part of a week.

Nassau had been explored in intricate detail and we were tired of being there. At 1130 on our sixth day in Nassau Johnny and Fritz, the mechanic, set to work replacing the transmission in the engine and testing it. We were determined to leave no matter what. The children and I bought last minute provisions at the City Market. While we were in the store, the electricity went off and the management passed out flashlights. It was eerie shopping in the dark. We readied the boat for sea trying to stay out of the mechanic's way. When Fritz left, it took Johnny and John forty minutes to stow the huge pile of gear in the cockpit, and we left the Nassau Harbour Club at 2010. With the strong wind and tide it was tricky getting away from the dock, but we were finally on our way. We cleared out with Harbor Control by radio just as we passed the lighthouse, and the last colors of the sunset faded in the West.

CHAPTER SIXTEEN

THE CIRCLE COMPLETE

After the frenzy of leaving Nassau with the last light of the day, and putting the boat back together, Johnny was exhausted and I felt like crying. The children, however, were ecstatic. We were headed home! We sat in the cockpit silently, thinking our own thoughts.

Our year had gone by much too quickly and I wasn't ready to give up our Bohemian lifestyle. It wasn't an easier way of life, just different. At home I felt safer. I knew that we would be well fed, clothed, warm, and dry. There wasn't much chance that the house would blow down unexpectedly or move somewhere dangerous in the night. We could sleep in peace. We had friends and family nearby. On the boat it was different. We were, in many ways, isolated and had to make a real effort to get to know other people, but we learned more about each other in that year afloat than most families ever do. We grew closer as a family, yet, as individuals, I believe each of us grew more independent. Down to the youngest, there were times when each of us was faced with decisions that affected the welfare of the entire family.

We also lived by the weather, hardly a consideration at home except as an inconvenience when inclement conditions might cancel a picnic or delay a plane. On the boat, weather could make all the difference. I learned to sleep like a cat with one ear alert to any unusual sounds, instantly awake at a feel of change. Life and death could hang in the balance. The look of the sky made the decision whether to stay or go, whether to put out more chain and stay aboard or have a care-free evening ashore. Though the security of land-based life was missing, I loved the constant change and immediacy of the lifestyle aboard a cruising boat. I loved the slow pace and closeness to nature. The feeling of space and freedom of the open ocean, and deserted islands contrasted pleasingly with the camaraderie generated by newly made friends in coastal villages. Each day was different and usually brought surprises; not all were good, but life was never dull. The thought of going home brought mixed feelings. It would be nice to have baths without rationing water, and big closets, and a washing machine, and real grocery stores, and a garden, and friends and family close by. On the other hand, I would miss the night sky, almost invisible in the city, and the fresh salt air, and rocking to sleep on the waves, and the thrill of making a new landfall, and the constant companionship of my family. I felt a deep, tiring sadness as we began our last passage with coming changes pressing on my mind.

Our first night out from Nassau was a rough ride, beating into a twenty knot northerly. We passed numerous cruise ships bedecked with twinkling lights, and occasionally, from the ones upwind, we caught snatches of music on the air. In the dark, wee hours as I sat at the wheel, we took on a big wave that doused the cockpit with cold green water and dumped a bucketful onto John's bunk as well. I had on foul weather gear, but John was not dressed for the occasion. Grumbling sleepily he changed to dry clothes and moved to the forward cabin, not nearly so comfortable with its more pronounced motion.

Everyone was happy when we came around Great Stirrup Cay and fell off to a beam reach with its easier motion. Friday was sunny and hot, and we had wonderful sailing all day. Saturday, too, was clear, and when the wind abated we continued to travel at 6 - 7 knots with the added help of the engine. However, at midnight we had one of those not-so-good surprises. The oil pressure dropped and the engine stopped. We raised all sails and continued at an ever slowing pace until morning. Somehow it seems that the wind almost always goes to bed at dawn, and for nearly three hours we floated along averaging two knots, but thankfully making more than that over the ground due to the strong current of the Gulf Stream. Johnny writhed his way into the depths of the engine room, waved his magic wand, and said his incantations to bring the iron monster back to life.

Slowly Saturday turned into Sunday. It was May 18, and at three o'clock Ethel Jane Bunting was having a homecoming party for us at her house around the corner from ours in Charleston. We weren't going to make it... but we wanted to get home at least before dark. So we motor-sailed with the recently revived machine and every sail aboard was stretched to catch the tiniest hint of breeze. Two large schools of porpoise greeted us and gamboled at our bow. Excitement mounted when Johnny sighted the Charleston Light at 1715. It was hard to remain calm. We stopped keeping a strict log and Caroline packed her suitcase which she unearthed from the recesses of some obscure locker.

"I'll be ready to jump off the minute we touch land!" she cried exultantly. We were still four hours from home so I fixed our last dinner aboard Sequoiah. Nobody had much of an appetite but we managed to finish the routine and get the cabin cleaned up by the time we approached the jetties guarding the harbor entrance.

As we entered Charleston harbor we raised, along with the usual quarantine flag, the flags of all the countries we had visited during our voyage. They made a colorful addition and brought to mind Eric Hiscock, from whose books I had learned of this custom.

I called the city marina and found that our slip was being dredged. We'd have to tie up somewhere else for a few days. We had a momentary let down feeling and then heard a curiously familiar voice calling on the radio, "Sequoiah, this is Gambit."

It was Will Middleton. He had heard us talking to the marina. He and his family along with some other mutual friends were on their way out to meet us. Our spirits revived instantly. We soon saw them, silhouetted against the sunset, a crowd of friends waving from Gambit's foredeck. As we passed Fort Sumter, they came about and accompanied us into the marina where we tied up in Will's slip and Gambit rafted alongside. There were hugs, exclamations, tears of happiness, and more friends and family arrived for an impromptu party on the dock.

Johnny left briefly to check in with Customs. He called and spoke to the officer on duty who asked only three questions: Who is on board? What was your last port of call? And do you have anything to declare? Then, "Welcome home, Captain," concluded the interview. We were cleared to re-enter our native country.

The Sat Nav showed that we had covered 11,509 nautical miles. We were HOME!

When the dock party ended, we gathered a few belongings, closed and locked Sequoiah, and left the docks to find our same blue station wagon in the parking lot looking like new. The Geers had washed and waxed it to a bright shine. We piled in eagerly. This was the first time we had been in a regular car on well-paved streets in over six months, quite a novelty! Max meowed unhappily from inside his wicker basket, not knowing how long he would be confined. It was only a five minute drive home even taking the long way around the Battery to have a look, from a shore-side perspective, at the water we had so recently sailed.

Walking through our front door after a year's absence gave me a sense of déjà vu, so familiar yet somehow different. That same damp smell of old brick and plaster met us in the hall and, exclaiming that nothing had changed, we swarmed through every room. The Letson's had cleaned the entire house as it had never been done before...or since! Everything could have passed a rigid white glove test with ease. Mother had been in earlier, filled the kitchen cabinets and refrigerator with food, and made all the beds. There was a feeling of never having left. It was like coming home after a weekend sail. Except Gerta wasn't there yet, and there was an attic room full of boxes to unpack. After a year's absence we had the feeling of making a new beginning. A door was closing behind us and there was no time to look back. The future was all, and we were rushing forward to meet it.

We had arrived home on a Sunday night, and Monday brought a whirlwind that enveloped us and carried us feverishly through the first weeks. In a pensive moment, I had the sensation of being on a train with events around me whooshing by almost too fast to participate. Johnny spent his first week severing ties with Sinkler, Gibbs, and Simons, a difficult task as he felt a great kinship with those men who had been his partners for so long. He was using office space generously provided by friends, his phone was beginning to ring, and he had soon hired a secretary. He was already back in the rat race with no effort at all.

Caroline started her dishwashing job at Gaulart and Maliclet, a nearby French cafe, where she was welcomed even after telling them her age. She worked long hours, but was enchanted with the people there and seemed to thrive on it. When not at the cafe she did some babysitting. She wanted to make enough money to buy some modern furniture to replace the "dark, old fashioned junk" that she said "ruined" her room. Caroline's fan club knew, almost instinctively, the moment she touched shore. Our telephone rang constantly and there was a steady stream of male admirers lounging about the house. We were glad the owners of the cafe had agreed to take on an inexperienced fifteen year old for the summer!

John worked on his Calvert lessons each morning and disappeared with friends in the afternoons when they got out of school. He was not happy about studying all summer and we hired a tutor to help. Porter-Gaud School came to his rescue by insisting that he take their entrance examination right away. He did quite well on it and was not required to finish his Calvert course, so at the end of June he was set free to play for the remainder of summer.

Our friends sent food and flowers to welcome us back and I did almost no cooking for weeks. Eleanor brought Gerta home. She had aged a good bit but looked happy and healthy, and it was a warm reunion. She was not terribly pleased, however, to see that a cat had moved into her house. Having a tolerant nature, Gerta soon took it in stride and made friends with the interloper. Max spent the first week in his new home running. .What space there is in a house! Soon he was not content inside and spent every waking moment plotting his escape to the great outdoors.

From the first, I had trouble sleeping. Indeed, it seemed that I no longer needed sleep. During the day I felt energetic, never tired, but I couldn't seem to fall asleep until two or three in the morning, and then I was awake again at dawn. It must have been the dramatic change in our lifestyle and its accompanying excitement that brought on this summer long bout of wakefulness. My insomnia plagued the teenagers too.

After Weesie's graduation at the end of May she felt terribly grown up and could see no reason for us to set limits. I will never forget one night when a friend of Weesie's who was spending a month with us came tiptoeing through the dark front hall several hours past their curfew, and opened the door into the brightly lit kitchen where I was finishing up some project. Her face was a picture of surprise as she turned to another girl behind her saying, "Oh my God! The mother is up!" Unable to contain my laughter, it was impossible to be stern. They were the ones who were tired next day, not me.

The Spoleto Festival opening, just a week after our return, was thrilling, with Carla Wallenda walking on a wire stretched high across Broad Street from City Hall to the Post Office, without a net beneath her. We joined in the fun, getting tickets for a variety of performances from opera and ballet to jazz. Coming home was, at first, like a dreamy vacation.

When summer faded away, school began again, forcing us into more of a scheduled existence. Caroline had been accepted at Oldfields School in Baltimore, and she said she wouldn't miss us. She said she'd had enough family togetherness to last a lifetime. Weesie, however, having felt isolated from us at times while we were sailing, had elected to move home and attend the College of Charleston.

Three months after our return, with routines falling into place, I had time to put things into perspective. The children were old enough to do most things for themselves, and not having to jump into a "real job", I was having trouble adjusting to the noisy, busyness of American city life. I missed having Johnny, my best friend, around all day; that was the most difficult change I had to face, knowing that only retirement, too far in the future even to contemplate, would allow us to recapture that luxury of constant companionship. I missed the cruising life and spent more time than necessary aboard Sequoiah varnishing and polishing brightwork.

I had vowed that, on returning home, I would change some things about the way I lived. I would relax when driving the car and not let myself be intimidated by the ever-increasing volume of traffic. I would appreciate the fact that we live where fresh foods are available in abundance and enjoy the weekly trips to the grocery. I would, most of all, refuse to allow myself to be ruled by the clock. I would make time to talk with friends and never again be in a hurry. In our stress-creating society these small changes have proved to be difficult to achieve. While keeping up the brisk pace of everyday living I'm still working on them. Maybe I need another voyage to strengthen my resolve.

* * *

FIVE YEARS LATER

Five years have gone and we now separate life's events as being Before The Trip, or After The Trip. Our children are blossoming into adults. All of us have changed in countless ways, but the year aboard Sequoiah is a common bond, far stronger than any other we share, that has drawn us closer than conventional life allows. In a sense it was like stepping through Alice's looking glass. Our Wonderland was not one of imagination, but a real world of our own choosing. However, the surprises were infinite, and leaving our life on land, we were worlds away from anything we had known before. We stepped out of an insular way of life and created for ourselves a challenging substitute that left each of us with new insights about ourselves, the world in which we live and the other peoples who share our planet.

Both John and Caroline wanted to add their thoughts on returning to shore life and what the experiences of this year meant to them.

JOHN

When we left, I was your typical middle class self-centered kid who thought only of himself. By the end of the second week of the trip I had realized that there were so many people and things much more important than an eleven year old brat. When I looked out on the angry seas with no horizon in sight, I realized I was but a cell in a huge organism.

As the trip went on I matured not only physically from hard chores done every day on a working sea vessel, but also mentally. When we visited the Azores, I met many kids who were out of reach by language but we communicated with hand signals and drawings in the sand. I also made friends with adults who were on other boats. It was the first time in my life that an adult had talked to me one to one without using baby talk. Living around and talking to adults also matured me a great deal. By meeting different people and going so many places I realized that I had only gone over to Europe and back, and that there was a whole world out there filled with different people and cultures.

This trip also brought me much closer to my family. Being stuck on a thirty-nine foot boat for a whole year with three other people generally does. My sister and I fought, truthfully, about ninety per cent of the time. When I got back I swore I never wanted to see her again, but after she had gone off to school I began to miss her. Now we have found that even though we fought a lot we have a deeper love than most brothers and sisters. That also goes for my parents. Everybody says you have a sort of secret language when you're married. I was living close enough to everyone on the boat to be married to them. My family does seem to know when I'm feeling sad or happy, and I can usually tell about them. I think that bond with my family was the best thing about my trip.

After coming home and talking to my friends I realized the impact that trip had on me. My close friends and I had always seemed to be on the same wavelength but when I talked to them they were all so naive and sheltered and I realized that was the way I had been before my trip. I believe that trip was the biggest and best change I've had so far in my life.

CAROLINE

On the morning of February 14, 1985, my brother and I descended the stairs to the breakfast table with much more in store for us than a Valentine's Day card. Our parents informed us that we were going sailing for a year on Sequoiah. I was fourteen at the time and as far as I was concerned this was horrible news.

Sailing was definitely nothing new to us. (We'd been sailing ever since we could crawl) For six years prior to that bleak February, the five of us had sailed from Charleston to islands in the Bahamas during my father's three week vacations. These summer trips were pleasant, not only because I loved the little deserted islands we spent so much time anchored off of, but also because I knew that when we returned I still had two more months of summer vacation. At fourteen I was rebellious against my parents, and that (awful) morning was one of crying, temper tantrums, and vows to call the school board or inform people of this ridiculous idea of taking a child, against her will, across the Atlantic Ocean in a small boat. Beginning with this day most others for the next year were similar. Not completely aware of the extent to which I was annoying my parents, I was challenged each day to make life unbearable for them. I came close to succeeding.

There are two days I remember clearly (the worst). At these times my parents asked themselves whether the trip was a good idea after all. The truth of the matter is that it was; it was a learning experience for all of us, especially me. The impact of the environment I was put in and the people I came in contact with made extraordinary changes in my attitudes and perceptions of myself.

In June when we left Charleston, my negative attitude was still very much present but I had accepted my fate of a year away from my friends. At this point in my life education was not a notable priority; I had no desire to see other cultures, new lands, people, or - most of all - to live on a boat! Nevertheless, these experiences were my surroundings; whether I would take full advantage of them was up to me. During our first passage to Bermuda, I became restless and inspected the abundant supply of books aboard. My parents managed to fit over two hundred books on the boat, and from that day onward, I always had something interesting to read, whether it was on my daily watches or any other bit of free time I had during the course of the year.

After sixteen days on the ocean without seeing land, Sequoiah arrived in Horta, a small port on the island of Faial in the Azores. Perhaps we loved Horta so much because we had not seen land for so long, but I believe the town had something too special to express in words. The people of this town were the most genuinely friendly people I have ever met. The majority were older, and they were not wealthy; in fact the whole place was poor, but they would have given me, my family, or any other of the boats that arrived there all the help they could. The two weeks my family stayed in Horta were probably the two most provocative and beautiful weeks I have spent in my life. At the time I think we all knew that the people of Horta were special, and the place would remain with us forever. One day we went to visit a man named Othan because we had heard from a friend that this man was an amazing artist who would scrimshaw each of the boats that came into Horta for a nominal fee. His scrimshaw on whale's teeth was beautiful. Othan was a kind man and we spent all afternoon talking with him in his workshop, surrounded by whale's teeth of all sizes covering the many shelves. Othan explained the new laws regarding the killing of whales and the effect it would have on the Azores. He told me also how the natives killed the whales and were armed only with spears. They were fighting for their lives out there and it was not unusual that someone would die, for the whales were ten times the size of the boats used to catch them. When they were able to bring a whale to its death, the people of the island did not waste any part of the animal. The skin, blubber, muscle, bones, organs, – everything was used. After explaining this Othan continued to describe how other countries sent out ships five times the size of the whale itself and with weapons much more advanced than a spear, decimated the whale populations and wasted ninety percent of the whale. My brother and mother went to see Othan many more times during our stay in Horta, as he had offered to teach my brother some techniques of scrimshaw. Although I have not seen Othan since that afternoon, his words are still clear in my mind; he is one of the reasons I acquired the values I have today.

The trip as a whole, but most particularly my experience in Horta, heightened my self-awareness and gave me a chance to rethink my values and come to realizations about them. The discipline of running the boat for a certain number of hours each day gave me responsibility as did writing essays for my parents when we were traveling in Europe. Spending time in the small islands and immense cities provided me with a first-hand view of how different cultures emerge and develop. It also gave me a hunger for knowledge. I am interested in learning (about the world) and being better informed. The journey was something that at the time did not mean much to me, but as I grow, I begin to see the good in it. I thank my parents for giving me this opportunity. My awareness of the world around me was acquired by living on the water and being close to aquatic life on a daily basis. I discovered a deep respect for the ocean and its inhabitants, and an exceptional love for the land!

* * *

TWENTY-FIVE YEARS LATER

JOHNNY

Adventure is something you seek and is its own motivation. The desire to experience it is innate, but the fulfillment of it is held in check by all sorts of reasonable considerations such as danger and cost and purpose. When the desire outweighs all of those, you go. We went.

HELEN

Looking back over this memoir from the perspective of twenty-five years, the trip we took aboard Sequoiah feels like a collective dream we had together. To begin with it was Johnny's dream, but soon became my dream as well. Though it was never the dream of any of our children, they have told us that it was a positive defining time in their lives. They gained a sense of independence and self-assurance, and we developed an unusually strong family bond. It is an experience all of us cherish. Life is tenuous. I believe it is important to follow your dreams.

GALLEY NOTES

Whether ashore or afloat, we like to eat well and I enjoy experimenting in the galley. Often a new recipe has been born out of sheer desperation for something tasty when it seemed that the available ingredients were not particularly compatible. Sometimes just a few variations of an old standby can create something worth recording. Here are a few of our sailing favorites.

* * *

Shrimp Paste

> 1 lb fresh, cooked shrimp (or 1 can shrimp)
> salt and pepper
> butter
> mayonnaise or yogurt
> tabasco sauce
> lemon or lime juice

Drain and mash shrimp. Add enough butter and mayonnaise to reach desired consistency. Add remaining ingredients to taste. This is delicious at cocktail time served with crackers.

* * *

Hot Mulled Cider

This is one of our favorite cold weather drinks. It makes five drinks, so multiply according to your crowd.

1/3 Cup sugar	2 teaspoons whole cloves
3 sticks cinnamon	1 lemon, thinly sliced

1 orange, thinly sliced   1 Cup water
1 quart apple cider

Place first six ingredients in saucepan and boil for five minutes. Add apple cider and heat just to boiling. Serve in mugs, garnished with a fresh slice of lemon. To turn this into a non–alcoholic Hot Buttered Rum, use brown sugar instead of white, then add a little melted butter and rum flavoring to each mug before serving.

* * *

Silly Salad

This is good when most of the greens are gone and you still want something crunchy.

1 chopped apple   1/2 Cup peanuts
1/2 Cup raisins   1/2 Cup walnuts
1/2 Cup yogurt   1 Tablespoon honey
1 Tablespoon wheat germ

Mix all ingredients and serve on a bed of sprouts or shredded cabbage.

* * *

Cold Tomato Soup

1 can tomato soup   1 small onion, chopped
1 can celery soup   1 cucumber, peeled and chopped
1 Cup water   4 Tablespoons dried milk
1 Tablespoon parsley

Mix all ingredients together. Simmer gently for 15 minutes over low heat.

Chill and serve.

* * *

Coconut Pancakes

3/4 Cup wheat flour	1 egg, separated
1/4 Cup white flour	1 Cup coconut milk*
1/2 teaspoon baking soda	1 Tablespoon oil or melted butter
1/4 teaspoon salt	grated coconut (any amount to taste)
1 Tablespoon brown sugar	4 Tablespoons buttermilk powder

Mix dry ingredients together. Beat egg whites. In pitcher or medium size bowl beat egg yolk and coconut milk (* if there is not enough milk in the coconut, add water to make one cup.) Stir in dry ingredients. Add grated coconut and oil. Fold in beaten egg whites. Cook on hot griddle or frying pan. Use Pam or any oil to prevent sticking.

NOTE: Buttermilk powder can be found in large American grocery stores and is a wonderful staple to have aboard for cooking

* * *

Caroline's Favorite Pizza

3/4 Cup water (110-115F)	1 small can tomato paste
1/2 teaspoon salt	1 can tomatoes, chopped

1 pkg. yeast
1/2 teaspoon sugar
2 Tablespoons vegetable oil
1/4 Cup wheat germ
2 1/4 Cups flour
salt & pepper, thyme,
basil, oregano
Swiss and cheddar cheeses

1 onion, chopped
1 green pepper, chopped
1 clove garlic, minced
1 can mushrooms
1 carrot, grated
Worcestershire sauce

First make the crust. Put the warm water in a bowl and sprinkle the yeast and sugar onto it. Mix the flour, wheat germ, and salt. Next, stir the yeast to make sure it is dissolved, and then pour in the oil. Add the flour mixture a little at a time. Cover the bowl and put in a warm place while you make the sauce.

Mix the canned tomatoes (including the liquid) and the tomato paste. Add the vegetables and season to taste with thyme, basil, oregano, salt, pepper, and Worcestershire sauce. Knead the dough with floured hands until it is smooth and elastic, and spread out on a large cookie sheet. Cover with sauce, then sprinkle with lots of grated cheese. Bake at 400 for about half an hour.

* * *

Vegetable Omelet

7 eggs, separated
1 green pepper, chopped
1 onion, chopped
1 stick butter
herbs and seasonings

1 stalk celery, chopped
1 clove garlic, chopped
1 tomato, chopped
grated cheese (any kind)

Sauté vegetables in half of the butter. Whip egg whites until stiff but not dry. Beat yolks and add oregano, basil, Worcestershire sauce, celery salt, and pepper, to taste. Gently fold in whipped whites. Pour egg mixture into a hot, buttered saucepan and cook slowly, covered. As it begins to set, pour vegetables on top and add grated cheese of your choice. When done, fold in half and serve.

* * *

Jump in the Pan Grouper

Melt one stick of butter (1/4 lb.). Sauté chopped onions and minced garlic. Add fresh caught grouper fillets and cook 5 minutes on each side, or until a spatula can be inserted under them easily. Top with salt and pepper, paprika, and chives. They melt in your mouth!

* * *

Broccoli Casserole

Whenever we can get fresh vegetables while cruising, we feel very fortunate. This recipe is one we have used for years with flavorful results even when it has been necessary to substitute canned or frozen broccoli.

4 Cups chopped broccoli	1 can mushroom or celery soup
1 Cup yogurt, sour cream or mayonnaise	1 small onion, chopped
2 Cups of your favorite cheese	2 eggs, beaten
½ Cup milk	salt and pepper to taste

Cook broccoli just until tender. Add all other ingredients and mix well. Place in any greased baking pan and bake at 350 until firm. In a 9"x12" pan it takes about 1 hour.

* * *

Stroganoff Martinique

A simple offshore supper dish using ingredients easily kept aboard on a long passage.

1 can stewed steak or beef chunks	1 can Nestle cream
1 can mushrooms	1 onion, chopped
3 Tablespoons butter	2 teaspoons chives
hot paprika to taste	

Sauté onions in butter. Add mushrooms and cook until onions are translucent. Gradually stir in cream, then add juice from meat can until the desired consistency is reached. Add meat chunks and seasonings. Serve on rice or noodles.

* * *

The next two recipes are especially good when cruising in areas where crab and shrimp abound, but canned seafood may be substituted if necessary. Lobster, conch, and other "fruits de mer" are good in these recipes also.

Shrimp Charleston

1 Cup raw rice	5 slices bacon
1/4 pound butter	1 onion, chopped

3 tomatoes, chopped	1 1/2 pounds shrimp (or 3 cans)
1/2 teaspoon cayenne salt and pepper to taste	2 teaspoons Worcestershire sauce

Cook rice. In frying pan cook 2 slices bacon until crisp. Remove bacon and add butter to bacon grease. Sauté onions, tomatoes and shrimp. If using canned shrimp, add them later. Cook until shrimp are just barely pink and onions are translucent. Add shrimp and vegetables to cooked rice. Add Worcestershire sauce, salt, pepper and crumbled cooked bacon. Mix well and place in baking dish. Put the three remaining strips of bacon on top. Bake at 350 degrees for 45 minutes.

* * *

Helen's Crab and Shrimp

1 Cup celery, chopped	1 large onion, diced
1 green pepper, chopped	1 can water chestnuts, sliced
1/2 pound mushrooms (or 1 small can)	1/2 cup butter
1 pound crab meat (or 2 cans)	3 eggs, beaten
1 lb. slightly cooked shrimp (or 2 cans)	1/2 Cup milk
1 teaspoon lemon juice	2 teaspoons Worcestershire sauce
parmesan cheese	salt and pepper to taste
24 Ritz crackers, crushed or 1 Cup toasted bread crumbs	

Chop vegetables and sauté in butter. Mix seafood and crackers in large bowl and add vegetables. Beat eggs and milk and add to seafood mixture. Add lemon juice, Worcestershire sauce, salt, and pepper. Place in a lightly greased casserole dish and top with parmesan cheese. Bake at 350 degrees for 20–30 minutes

* * *

We all enjoy something sweet at the end of a meal. The following are a few of our favorite desserts.

Dog Watch Special

These are Sequoiah's favorite almond brownies. Aboard ship, nobody likes to wash dishes and this is made in one pot, the double boiler. The hot water in the bottom half can be used to wash the few utensils when you're through!

1 stick butter	1 tablespoon almond extract
4 oz baking chocolate	1 teaspoon vanilla extract
1 Cup white sugar	1 Cup sliced almonds
1 Cup brown sugar	1/2 Cup butterscotch morsels
4 eggs, beaten	1/4 teaspoon salt
1 Cup flour	

Pre-heat oven to 325 degrees. Grease 9 x 13 baking pan. Melt chocolate and butter in top of double boiler. Remove from heat, add sugar, then eggs. Mix well. Add flour, salt, butterscotch morsels, and three fourths of nuts. Add flavorings. Place in greased pan. Top with remaining nuts. Bake at 325 degrees for 30 minutes. Cool before cutting into squares. These keep well in tightly sealed container.

* * *

Marigot Bay Fruit Cake

1/2 Cup butter	1 1/2 Cups brown sugar
3/4 teaspoon baking soda	2 eggs
1/2 teaspoon salt	1 Cup mashed bananas
1/2 teaspoon baking powder	1 grated coconut
1 teaspoon vanilla	1 1/2 Cups wheat flour
1/4 Cup yogurt or buttermilk	3/4 Cups white flour

Cream butter and sugar. Beat in eggs. Add fruit. Combine dry ingredients and add alternately with milk and vanilla. Stir until smooth after each addition. Bake in two greased and floured 9" round pans at 350 for 30–35 minutes. Cool in pans for 5 minutes before removing. When completely cool, frost with Tropical Icing.

Tropical Icing

3 oz. cream cheese or butter, softened	4 teaspoons milk
1 pound sifted confectioner's sugar	2 tablespoons Cointreau
1 teaspoon lime juice	grated lime peel

Combine cheese and milk. Gradually add sugar and other ingredients until the correct consistency is obtained.

* * *

Coconut Pie

Mix all ingredients together, adding one at a time in order given.

1 1/2 Cups brown sugar
1/2 Cup flour
1/4 teaspoon salt
1 teaspoon baking powder
1 Cup milk
liquid from 1 fresh coconut
4 eggs, beaten
1/4 Cup melted butter
1 teaspoon vanilla
meat of 1 coconut, grated

Pour this into two pie pans and bake at 350 for 45 minutes or until brown.

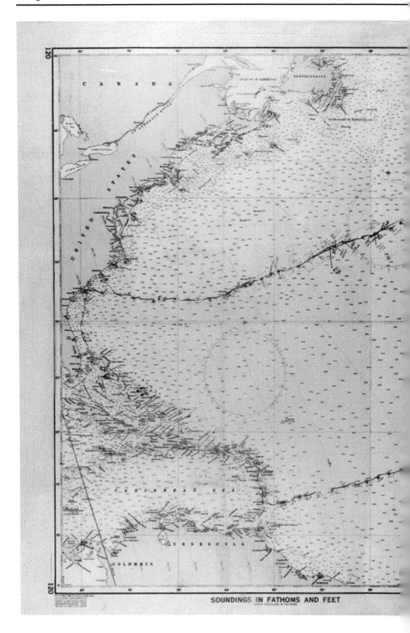

Voyage of the yacht, Sequoiah

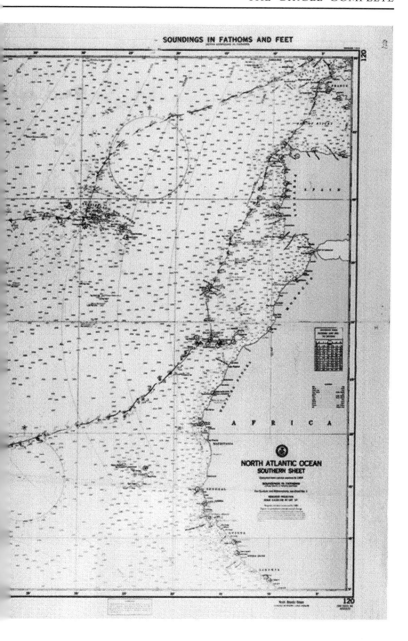

June 5, 1985 – May 18, 1986

Made in the USA
Charleston, SC
09 November 2010